T0144728

MAIMONIDES, SPINOZA and US

Other Jewish Lights Books
by Rabbi Marc D. Angel, PhD

Foundations of Sephardic Spirituality:
The Inner Life of Jews of the Ottoman Empire

MAIMONIDES, SPINOZA and US

Toward an Intellectually Vibrant Judaism

Rabbi Marc D. Angel, PhD

For People of All Faiths, All Backgrounds

JEWISH LIGHTS Publishing

Nashville, Tennessee

Maimonides, Spinoza and Us:
Toward an Intellectually Vibrant Judaism

Requests to the Publisher for permission should be addressed to Turner Publishing Company, 4507 Charlotte Avenue, Suite 100, Nashville, Tennessee, (615) 255-2665, fax (615) 255-5081, E-mail: submissions@turnerpublishing.com.

Library of Congress Cataloging-in-Publication Data
Angel, Marc.
Maimonides, Spinoza and us : toward an intellectually vibrant Judaism / Marc D. Angel.
p. cm.
Includes bibliographical references.
ISBN-13: 978-1-58023-411-5 (hardcover)
ISBN-10: 1-58023-411-9 (hardcover)
1. Philosophy, Jewish. 2. Philosophy, Medieval. 3. Judaism—History—Medieval and early modern period, 425–1789. 4. Maimonides, Moses, 1135–1204. 5. Spinoza, Benedictus de, 1632–1677. I. Title.
B755.A54 2009
296.3—dc22

2009035462

10 9 8 7 6 5 4 3
ISBN-13: 978-1-68336-184-8 (pbk)

Manufactured in the United States of America
Cover Design: Melanie Robinson

For People of All Faiths, All Backgrounds
Published by Jewish Lights Publishing
An Imprint of Turner Publishing Company
4507 Charlotte Avenue, Suite 100
Nashville, Tennessee 37209
Tel: (802) 457-4000
www.jewishlights.com

In honor of the members
of our Sunday Morning Rambam Class
at Congregation Shearith Israel, New York City

Contents

Acknowledgments

For many years, I have been teaching a Sunday morning class at Congregation Shearith Israel in New York City, in which we have studied the works of Maimonides—Rambam. Several years ago, we devoted quite a few sessions to comparing ideas in the writings of Spinoza with those of Rambam. The discussions were lively and challenging. This book is a direct outgrowth of those classes, and I thank each of the class members for sharing ideas and insights that have helped me—and all of us—think more clearly about basic issues in Judaism.

I thank the members and supporters of the Institute for Jewish Ideas and Ideals (jewishideas.org) for their friendship and encouragement. I established the Institute in October 2007, with the aim of fostering an intellectually vibrant, compassionate, and inclusive Orthodox Judaism. The teachings reflected in this book have been central to the work of the Institute.

I am grateful to Stuart M. Matlins, publisher of Jewish Lights, for his interest in this book and for his genuine commitment to Jewish ideas and ideals. I express sincere thanks to the Jewish Lights professional staff, who did a wonderful job in producing this volume: Emily Wichland, vice president of Editorial and Production; Tim Holtz, director of Production and Design; Kristi Menter, typesetter; and Melanie Robinson, who designed the book cover.

My daughter, Ronda Angel Arking, did a magnificent job editing the early drafts of this book and asking me all the right questions. I thank Randall and Hannah Miryam Belinfante for their prompt and helpful research assistance.

I express my gratitude to my wonderful wife, Gilda, and our children: Rabbi Hayyim Angel; Dr. Dan and Ronda Angel Arking; Dr. James and Elana Angel Nussbaum; and our beloved grandchildren: Jake Isaac Nussbaum, Andrew Zak Arking, Jonathan Marc Arking, Max Joseph Nussbaum, Charles Victor Nussbaum, and Jeremy Victor Arking.

I thank the Almighty, who has given me life, sustained me, and brought me to this special moment. I pray that readers will find this book helpful in deepening their understanding of Torah, Judaism, and God.

Preface

A rabbinic teaching has it that the way of Torah is a narrow path. To the right is fire and to the left is ice. A follower of Torah must be focused and balanced, so as to avoid veering off the road in either direction

To the right is fire—the fire of a religious passion that has lost control of itself. This is the fire of religious zeal that slips into extremism, fanaticism, and self-righteousness. Turning to the right entails a surrender of a person's power of reason in favor of a transcendent and mystical relationship with God. Yet, with the suspension of reason comes the possibility of chasing after false gods and superstitious beliefs.

To the left is ice—the ice of skepticism, of rationalism run amok. The warmth of Torah is lost, its inner beauty and power negated. Moving to the left entails a surrender of a person's spiritual sense in favor of a cold philosophical view of life. With the increase in ice comes the possibility of living without ever confronting and experiencing God.

We live in an age when it is increasingly difficult to walk in the path of Torah in a focused and balanced way. The intensity of fire on the right has created a religiosity characterized by extremism, obscurantism, authoritarianism. We witness a deadening conformity—in thought, behavior, even manner of dress. Thousands of people suspend their reason in order to follow the dictates of their "rebbes" or halakhic authorities. Kabbalists and pseudo-kabbalists thrive, dispensing amulets, red strings, and magical blessings.

The threats on the left are equally dangerous. The widespread secularism and agnosticism create a deep void. Sociologist Peter L. Berger has referred to the modern condition as "spiritual homelessness." To live without a sense of God's presence is to miss a vital and meaningful aspect of life.

Is it possible for us to maintain a balanced, intellectually sound view of Judaism? Is it possible to avoid veering to the anti-rationalism on the right or the super-rationalism on the left?

This book is an attempt to reclaim the narrow path of Torah. It rests on the classic traditional foundations of Judaism as a religion based on divine revelation and as a way of life governed by halakha (Jewish law). It also rests on the premise that we have the right—and responsibility—to engage in intellectual inquiry in a spirit of freedom, using our reason.

Moses Maimonides (1138–1204) is the single greatest thinker in Jewish history who stressed the role of reason and philosophy in the understanding of Torah. Although many of his teachings have become mainstream Jewish thinking, his rational outlook is largely ignored among those who have veered to the right. By revisiting the philosophical views of Maimonides, we can come to a deeper appreciation of the role of reason in Judaism. We are challenged to use our own intellectual faculties in our confrontation with God and Torah.

In rabbinic circles, Maimonides is generally known as Rambam, an acronym for his Hebrew name, Rabbi Moshe ben Maimon. In the academic community, he is generally known as Maimonides (that is, son of Maimon). In this book, I will be referring to him interchangeably both as Rambam and Maimonides.

Baruch Spinoza (1632–1677) is the single greatest thinker in Jewish history whose commitment to reason led him to abandon traditional Judaism. By evaluating his views on biblical religion, we are challenged to rethink our assumptions, to answer his critiques, and to learn from his insights. While Maimonides lays the foundation for an intellectually sound Judaism, Spinoza challenges Maimonides' views every step of the way. While I am clearly a devotee of the Maimonidean approach, I believe that Spinoza is a vital stimulus to fostering careful and independent thinking on major topics discussed by Maimonides.

To reclaim a balanced Judaism, we need the wisdom and strength of Maimonides' vision. But we also need to address the serene, perceptive views of Spinoza.

Maimonides was a medieval philosopher. Spinoza was a premodern philosopher. Both have much to teach us. Yet, much has happened in the world of philosophy and religion since their eras. Modern thinkers have moved away from metaphysics and toward such movements as logical positivism and existentialism. Advances in science, psychology, anthropology, and other fields have generated new knowledge and new ways of thinking. Since our intellectual and spiritual worlds are so different from those of Maimonides and Spinoza, we need to add a third component to this book: us. We live today in a modern (or postmodern) world, where change is a basic feature of our reality. We appreciate the value of human reason in our search for truth and meaning, but we also are very aware of its limitations. Whereas Maimonides and Spinoza both believed that there is one ultimate Truth (with a capital *T*) to which the human intellect can aspire, moderns are more likely to speak of multiple truths.

This book focuses on the teachings of Maimonides on such topics as the role of reason in religious faith, the nature of God, the authoritativeness of the Torah and rabbinic tradition, and the role of Jews and Judaism in the world. It factors in the insights and critiques of Spinoza. Chapters 8 and 9, dealing with conversion to Judaism and other issues in Jewish law, are presented through the teachings of Rambam, since Spinoza—who rejected the ongoing authority of halakha—has nothing to contribute to these topics. The discussions in this book are intended to encourage us to work through the issues using our own intelligence, our own reason, our own spiritual sense.

In citing biblical passages, I have generally used the translations found in the works of Maimonides and Spinoza as well as the Jewish Publication Society's translation of the *Tanakh* (Philadelphia: Jewish Publication Society, 1985). In keeping with the literary convention adopted by Rambam and Spinoza, I refer to God in the masculine form.

The midrash teaches that when God revealed the Torah to the Israelites at Mount Sinai, God spoke to each individual according to his or her own capacity. While all the Israelites heard the same words, each experienced them in his or her own unique way. I think this midrash is a model for how we are to study Torah today. We each have the same words—the biblical and rabbinic texts—and yet we each need to experience these words with our own individual lights.

1

FAITH IN REASON, REASON IN FAITH

Judaism is the story of the dynamic relationship between the people of Israel and God. Biblical prophets and ancient rabbinic sages presented spiritual teachings and laws that reflected the immediacy of the eternal covenant binding God and Israel together. They often wrote in dramatic and colorful language, rich in symbolism and deeper meanings. No attempt was made to offer a systematic philosophy or theology.

For many centuries, the Jewish religious sensibility was satisfied by the powerful, emotionally charged pronouncements of the prophets and sages. Poetic and mystical elements were seamlessly intertwined with laws and theological concepts.

As long as prophetic and rabbinic literature was not subjected to philosophical analysis, it maintained a certain theological fluidity, with a range of "acceptable" beliefs. Was God a powerful King sitting on a heavenly throne? Was He totally incorporeal? Did God pray? Did He change His mind? How did He reward the righteous and punish the wicked in the world to come? The biblical and classical rabbinic literature did not give precise, unequivocal, and definitive answers to these and similar questions. The goal of this literature was to inspire Jews to live righteous lives and to feel a sense of closeness to God. Each person developed a unique connection with God, based on varying levels of intellect, spiritual sensitivity, and philosophical sophistication.

Maimonides: Rabbi and Philosopher

With the emergence of Moses Maimonides (1138–1204) the religious worldview of Judaism was to undergo a cataclysmic change. Born in Cordoba, Spain, and known throughout Jewish works as Rambam, an acronym of his Hebrew name and title (Rabbi Moshe ben Maimon), he became the quintessential rabbinic advocate of philosophy and reason—for his period and for all generations to follow. Profoundly steeped in rabbinic learning as well as physics and metaphysics, Rambam was a towering intellectual figure who sought to place Judaism on a solid and systematic foundation of reason.

In his *Mishneh Torah*, Rambam provided a lucid and comprehensive code of Jewish law. He sifted through the entire corpus of rabbinic literature and put its rulings into an orderly arrangement. This had never been done before—or since. It was a monumental achievement, radically changing the study of Jewish law.

In his *Sefer haMitzvot*, Rambam took the rabbinic tradition that the Torah had 613 commandments and then listed what they were. He gave specific rules governing which commandments were to be included in the listing and which were to be excluded.

In his introduction to *Perek Helek*, Rambam listed thirteen principles of faith that all Jews were obligated to accept. Denial of any one of these principles resulted in a person's soul being excluded from the world to come. Prior to Rambam, no such precise set of dogmas had been formulated for Judaism.

Rambam presented Judaism in philosophical language in his *Guide of the Perplexed*. Believing that religion and reason ultimately led to the same Truth, he attempted to demonstrate how a faithful Jew must be steeped in Torah as well as in philosophical and scientific knowledge.

Rambam went further than simply presenting Judaism in philosophical terms. He argued that his view was the genuine and correct one and that those who thought otherwise were seriously mistaken. Indeed, those who held notions that were philosophically incorrect—for example, that God was corporeal—had no place in the world to come!

In spite of Rambam's awesome intellect and phenomenal range of knowledge, his works provoked sharp criticism in various circles. Some felt that he gave too much sway to philosophy; others felt he was overly dogmatic in his principles of faith. Traditionalists feared that his stress on philosophy and reason would lead to heresy in less gifted thinkers than he. Such individuals might reduce the Torah to philosophical allegories, engendering a decline in the observance of the Torah's commandments.

Some virulent anti-Maimonideans complained about the "heretical" nature of his works to church officials in France. This led to the 1232 public burning by Dominicans of his *Guide of the Perplexed.* This horrifying act shocked even ardent anti-Maimonideans, a number of whom realized that they had carried their opposition to a dangerous extreme. One of the leading rabbinic figures in Spain, Rabbi Yonah of Gerona, recanted his previous anti-Maimonidean position and became a zealous proponent of Rambam's work.

Anti-Maimonidean forces continued to oppose the essence of Rambam's philosophical teachings, and this opposition has continued through the centuries to our own day. What is the nature of this opposition? The argument is as follows: Jews should be faithful and pious, and they can best achieve religious fulfillment through total commitment to rabbinic tradition. Philosophy and rational thinking are not only diversions from religiosity, but a threat to it. Jews should devote themselves entirely to religious literature and defer to the opinions of rabbinic sages. Independent thinking is not to be encouraged, because it may lead beyond the boundaries of religious tradition. For many centuries, Judaism had flourished without reliance on systematic philosophy and theology; that was a good pattern, conducive to faithfulness and religious fulfillment for the elite scholars as well as for the less sophisticated masses.

Rambam was not afraid of reason, philosophy, or clear thinking. He recognized the ultimate authority of the religious tradition, but at

4 ✦ MAIMONIDES, SPINOZA AND US

the same time he believed that Judaism itself was founded on intellectually solid foundations. Judaism did not and could not conflict with reason. The revealed truths of Torah and the rationally attained truths of philosophy arrived at the identical Truth, albeit from different approaches. He thought that philosophy was indigenous to Judaism but that the Jews had lost their philosophical traditions due to centuries of persecution. He saw himself as reclaiming Judaism's original commitment to philosophy. He was not content with a Judaism devoid of systematic law, philosophy, and theology. Reason needed to be applied to the vast corpus of biblical and rabbinic literature, so as to organize the material in a rational and philosophically appropriate manner—and to interpret its "irrational" passages so that they conformed to reason.

Professor Marvin Fox, author of *Interpreting Maimonides*, describes the unique greatness of Rambam, the rabbi and philosopher: "We can learn first, and most importantly, from Maimonides an uncompromising and fearless intellectual honesty in all matters having to do with religion."[1] Dr. Fox notes that Rambam serves as a significantly interesting figure today, at a time when the "forces of closed-minded intellectual timidity" have managed to gain some prominence in certain religious Jewish circles. Rambam, while protecting the system of Jewish law, left room for individual intellectual exertion. In matters of philosophy and theology, the human mind must be given freedom "to find its own way," since freedom is essential to our very humanity.[2]

Rambam's commitment to reason has been viewed as being elitist, that is, applying to intellectuals rather than the less learned masses. In some sense, this is true. In the introduction to his *Guide of the Perplexed*, Maimonides explicitly states:

> I am the man who, when the concern pressed him and his way was straitened and he could find no other device by which to teach a demonstrated truth other than by giving satisfaction to a single virtuous man while displeasing ten thousand ignoramuses—I am he who prefers to address that single man by

himself, and I do not heed the blame of those many creatures. For I claim to liberate that virtuous one from that into which he has sunk, and I shall guide him in his perplexity until he becomes perfect and he finds rest.[3]

Rambam clearly wanted to assist intellectually sophisticated people by dealing with their philosophical questions about religion. If his philosophical expositions were only understood by the few, that was fine. Rambam was not troubled by the many "ignoramuses" who could not or would not engage in reasonable philosophical discourse.

However, Rambam was not purely an elitist. On the contrary, he was vitally concerned with the intellectual and spiritual well-being of the entire Jewish community. He developed his thirteen principles of faith so that even the simplest and least erudite Jews would be instructed in the true beliefs. Although they could not follow all the philosophical arguments proving these thirteen principles, they could at least memorize the principles themselves and thereby come to hold the correct beliefs. Moreover, in the first chapters of his *Mishneh Torah*, Rambam provided the philosophical and ethical foundations of Judaism so that all students of Jewish law (not just the philosophically trained) would become educated in these concepts. He obviously hoped that his works would inspire all Jews to engage in philosophical discussion and to use their rational faculties to deepen their understanding of Jewish tradition.

Reason and Authority

In Judaism, as in other religions, there is a strong tendency to rely on earlier authorities. After all, what can we know compared to what the biblical prophets and Talmudic sages knew? Since they were so great, we must defer to their authority.

Yet, if we are simply to defer to the authority of the ancients, what role does our own reason have in establishing truth? Are we to adopt earlier teachings uncritically, as a demonstration of faithfulness? Should we use our reason with the aim of reaching the same conclusions as they? Or should we be free to follow our own reason even when we arrive at conclusions different from those of the ancient sages? If we find the positions of the ancients to be "irrational," should we reject those positions or reinterpret them to conform to reason?

Rambam certainly believed in Truth (with a capital *T*). This Truth is derived from prophetic revelation as well as from the correct use of reason. If our particular reason arrives at conclusions that differ with Truth, then we have obviously made a mistake in our analysis. We need to start again and refine our thinking so that we arrive at Truth. Rambam disdained those who were content to espouse Truth on the basis of blind faith, without engaging in establishing the intellectual foundations of Truth. People who did not use their reason were deficient even in their faith; they were prone to superstition and were gullible to the pronouncements of charismatic (even if sometimes misguided) authority figures.

At the same time, Rambam also believed that there were things accepted as Truth that were not in fact true. Human reason was necessary as a constant and reliable agent to challenge, verify, or reject long-held "truths." Just because a great authority taught something did not ensure that it was Truth. Indeed, Truth stands on its own merit, not on the basis of the opinions of human beings.

> For when something has been demonstrated, the correctness of the matter is not increased and certainty regarding it is not strengthened by the consensus of all men of knowledge with regard to it. Nor could its correctness be diminished and certainty regarding it be weakened even if all the people on earth disagreed with it.[4]

In his *Mishneh Torah*, Rambam states that many books on astronomy and mathematics were composed by Greek sages but similar works by ancient Jewish sages of the tribe of Issachar have not come down to us. He explains that even though we know astronomy and mathematics through the agency of Greeks rather than Jews, we are not concerned about the ethnic origins of the conveyers of Truth:

Since all these rules have been established by sound and clear proofs, free from any flaw and irrefutable, we need not be concerned about the identity of their authors, whether they be Hebrew prophets or gentile sages. For when we have to do with rules and propositions that have been demonstrated by good reasons and have been verified to be true by sound and flawless proofs, we rely upon the author who has discovered them or transmitted them only because of his demonstrated proofs and verified reasoning.[5]

According to Maimonides, intelligent people need to distinguish between what is true and what is spurious. Surely, we may rely on the wisdom of the prophets and rabbinic sages, just as we rely on the advice of skilled physicians or experts in other fields. However, even when receiving advice from these authorities, we should not suspend personal judgment altogether. Rambam notes, in the introduction to his *Sefer haMitzvot*, that even the elite intellectuals of his time had a tendency to rely on authority: "They do not test the veracity of an opinion upon the merit of its own content but upon its agreement with the words of some preceding authority, without troubling to examine the preceding source itself." If this tendency is rampant among the elite, it is so much more rampant among the masses.

In his *Epistle to Yemen*, Rambam warns:

Do not consider a statement true because you find it in a book, for the prevaricator is as little restrained with his pen as with his tongue. For the untutored and uninstructed are convinced of the veracity of a statement by the mere fact that it is written; nevertheless its accuracy must be demonstrated in another manner.[6]

Just because "authorities" and "scholars" have claimed something to be true does not make it true. Rambam, in his *Letter on Astrology*, remarks that "fools have composed thousands of books of nothingness and emptiness."[7] Men "great in years but not in wisdom" wasted much time studying these worthless books and came to think of themselves as experts. They taught nonsense to the public, imagining that they were conveying truth. Unsuspecting people believed these "experts" because they seemed to be erudite and convincing.

Rambam explains that we should only accept something as reliably true if it belongs to one of three categories: (1) It is proved clearly by human reasoning such as arithmetic, geometry, and astronomy; (2) it is perceived with certainty through one of the five senses; (3) it is received from the prophets or the righteous. In considering whether or not something is true, we must determine through which category we have derived its truthfulness. If we cannot verify something through one of these three categories, we cannot accept it as being true.

A dilemma arises. Rambam categorically rejects the validity of astrology, considering it a foolish superstition rather than a bona fide science. Yet, the Talmud and midrashim record the opinions of righteous sages who themselves seemed to ascribe veracity to astrology! Thus, by Rambam's own standards of determining truth, shouldn't we believe in astrology, since we have received this belief from the righteous? Rambam resolves this seeming problem:

> It is not proper to abandon matters of reason that have already been verified by proofs, shake loose of them, and depend on the words of a single one of the sages from whom possibly the matter was hidden. Or there may be an allusion in those words; or they may have been said with a view to the times and the business before him. You surely know how many of the verses of the holy Torah are not to be taken literally. Since it is known through proofs of reason that it is impossible for the thing to be literally so, the Targum [Aramaic translator of the Torah] rendered it in a form that reason will abide. A man should never cast his reason behind him, for the eyes are set in front, not in back.[8]

According to Rambam, once we have verified the truth of something on the basis of reason, we should not accept the literal meaning of texts that contradict this verified truth. If a sage has made a statement that violates a proven truth, then either (1) he was mistaken; (2) he was speaking in allegorical or poetic language, not to be taken literally; or (3) he was speaking within the context of his time and place. If the Torah itself—which is Truth—records something that contradicts verified truth, then the Torah must be interpreted to conform to this established truth. It is axiomatic that the Torah of truth cannot teach something that violates rational truth.

It appears, then, that Rambam's primary source of Truth was reason—science, mathematics, and philosophy. The Bible and rabbinic sages, although sources of Truth, were themselves subject to the dictates of reason. This position is what frightened (and still frightens) the anti-Maimonideans. Reliance on human reason can undermine the authority of the Bible and the sages. Perhaps Rambam was such a great thinker that he could reconcile reason with the classic religious texts; but few, if any, were so intellectually gifted. If people thought they had the right to interpret Torah and rabbinic tradition based on their own reason, then the firm foundations of religion would weaken—even collapse. Subjective interpretations would take the place of faithfulness and trust in rabbinic authority. The anti-Maimonideans argued that it is better to insist on the absolute authority of the biblical and rabbinic traditions than to allow people to subject sacred texts to their own reason. Humans cannot be trusted to use reason wisely or correctly. Blind faith in the literal truth of the Bible and Talmud is far better—and safer—as a means of ensuring a proper religious life.

Rambam was obviously aware of this line of argument—but he rejected it outright. With all the risks of allowing people to use their reason, it was essential to put religion on a philosophically sound basis. It was religiously and intellectually wrong to foster a fundamentalist, obscurantist, literalist view of religion that ascribed irrational teachings to the Bible and our sages. If it is dangerous to rely on reason, it is even more dangerous to violate reason.

Rambam had little patience with those pietists who promoted the opinion that faithful Jews must accept the words of our sages literally. In his introduction to *Perek Helek*, Rambam describes different approaches to understanding the statements of the sages. The majority group, according to Rambam, accepts the words of our sages literally, without imagining any deeper meanings. By taking everything literally, even when the words of the sages violated reason, this group actually casts aspersions on our sages. Reasonable people will come to believe that the sages were intellectually unsound and therefore come to reject their words altogether. This literalist group, though in the majority, is misguided—and dangerous.

> The members of this group are poor in knowledge. One can only regret their folly. Their very effort to honor and to exalt the sages in accordance with their own meager understanding actually humiliates them. As God lives, this group destroys the glory of the Torah and extinguishes its light, for they make the Torah of God say the opposite of what is intended.[9]

Rambam also applied this attitude to those who interpreted the Bible literally, even when the words of the Bible contradicted reason. The classic example of this is the Bible's use of anthropomorphisms and anthropopathisms. Since reason has verified that God does not have physical or emotional attributes, then all biblical passages that ascribe such qualities to God must be taken symbolically—not literally. Those who take these passages literally are not only in error, but they forfeit their place in the world to come!

Rambam was confident that he—and other philosophically trained people—could study the Bible and rabbinic literature wisely, knowing when a text was to be understood literally and when it had to be understood symbolically. Those who were not philosophically trained needed to follow the guidance of those who were.

Reason and Revelation

Rambam believed that Truth (with a capital *T*) rests on the foundations of reason and revelation. In his description of Abraham, Rambam makes clear that our forefather first arrived at Truth through the agency of reason. Rabbinic tradition offers two opinions as to when Abraham discovered God. One view is that Abraham was only three years old at the time. This opinion underscores the miraculous quality of Abraham's faith. He was incredibly precocious and/or received divine assistance in achieving faith in One God. The other rabbinic view is that Abraham was forty years old when he discovered God. This opinion supports a non-miraculous road to faith. Abraham, by dint of his reason, discovered the Truth at a mature age, when his reason was fully developed.

Rambam cites both opinions in relating the story of Abraham in his *Mishneh Torah*: "As soon as this mighty champion [Abraham] was weaned, he began to think by day and by night, though still an infant, wondering how it was possible that this sphere should keep moving continually if there was no one to guide it." Yes, Abraham was a precocious lad who pondered deep theological issues. Yet, although he grappled with these questions for many years, "Abraham was forty years old when he acknowledged his Creator." Only after having reached the age of forty was he able to attain true faith in One God, and only then did he begin teaching this Truth to the entire world and drawing many thousands to join him.

God appeared to Abraham after Abraham had already discovered Him by means of reason. The revelation, thus, was a confirmation of the validity of Abraham's reasoning. Abraham passed on the Truth to Isaac, who passed it on to Jacob, who passed it on to his children, whose progeny almost lost it during their long servitude in Egypt.

> But owing to God's love for us, and because He kept his solemn promise to Abraham our father, He appointed Moses to be the teacher of all the prophets and sent him to us. When Moses had begun to function as prophet, the Lord chose Israel as His heritage and adorned them with precepts, showing them the way of worshipping Him, and how to treat idolatry and those who stray after it.[10]

With the revelation at Mount Sinai, God allowed the Israelites to experience His presence. Through the Torah and later prophetic works, God provided direct messages to the Israelites and all humanity. If revelation provided Truth from God to humanity, reason aspired to Truth from humanity to God.

In Rambam's view, the Bible, being God's own word, obviously expresses Truth. Philosophical speculations that transcend the boundaries of biblical teaching are necessarily false. Yet, reason is needed to determine exactly what biblical Truth is. The Bible cannot be read correctly from a literalist viewpoint; nor can its teachings ever violate verified reason. Thus, Truth is attained only through a rigorous commitment both to revelation and to reason.

By insisting on balancing the claims of revelation and reason, Rambam set the agenda for Jewish philosophy in the ensuing centuries. Although various thinkers approached the issue differently, no one could entirely avoid the confrontation of the two sources of Truth. But then, in the seventeenth century, a philosopher arose who challenged the foundations of Rambam's philosophical enterprise—and indeed the foundations of biblical religion altogether.

Spinoza: Religion and Reason

Baruch Spinoza (1632–77) was born in Amsterdam. His father, Michael, had been born in Portugal to a family of crypto-Jews. In the 1590s, when Michael was still a child, his family fled Portugal and returned to Judaism in Amsterdam, a major center for the return of conversos (Jews who had been converted forcibly in the Iberian Peninsula). By the time Baruch was born, Amsterdam had a vibrant and flourishing Jewish community.

Michael Spinoza was active in his synagogue and saw to it that his children received a proper Jewish education. Baruch attended the Jewish schools and apparently was an excellent student. As he grew older, his intellectual horizons expanded beyond the curriculum of the community's schools. In 1650, he studied Latin, natural sciences, and philosophy with radical Dutch thinker Dr. Franciscus van den Enden of Bremen. He read the works of Descartes.

As Spinoza became more involved in philosophical studies, he came to value human reason as the sole means of determining Truth.

He questioned the authority of the Bible and of rabbinic teachings. He challenged the lessons of his rabbis and teachers. Although by nature a quiet and noncontentious person, his intellectual integrity did not allow him to back down from holding "heretical" opinions. When his father died in 1654, Baruch felt less restraint in defying communal religious norms. As a result, his ties to the traditional Jewish fold became more tenuous. In 1655, he was publicly accused of heresy in the synagogue. Unrepentant, he continued to pursue philosophical studies and to espouse ideas that were viewed as undermining religion. In 1656, he was officially excommunicated from Amsterdam's Jewish community, and he went on to live in relative solitude in various locations in Holland for the rest of his short life.[11]

Spinoza was a true "outsider." He was born a Jew in a Christian society that had disdain for Jews; he was rejected by his own Jewish community; he was quiet and of modest means, without political, social, or academic insider status. He published relatively little during the course of his lifetime. Yet, this "outsider" became one of the luminaries of Western philosophy. Professor Jonathan Israel has noted that no one else during the century of 1650–1750 even "remotely rivaled Spinoza's notoriety as the chief challenger of the fundamentals of revealed religion, received ideas, tradition, morality, and what was everywhere regarded … as divinely constituted political authority."[12] That Spinoza was to have such a major impact on the intellectual life of his time—and on future generations—is a testament not only to his genius, but to his willingness to challenge accepted beliefs in a cogent manner.

Like Rambam, Spinoza placed a premium on human reason. Also like Rambam, he sought to attain Truth through systematic analysis. In his *Ethics*, most notably, he presented his philosophical arguments in the form of mathematical axioms and corollaries, as though to indicate that his statements were as true and irrefutable as mathematically proven truths. However, unlike Rambam, Spinoza relied solely on reason in his quest for Truth; he felt unbound by the teachings of revelation as embodied in the Bible.

The gist of Spinoza's approach is spelled out in a 1665 letter he wrote to Willem van Blyenbergh, who had sought a correspondence with the philosopher. Initially, Spinoza expressed pleasure at hearing from an individual who claimed to be devoted to truth and who wanted to engage in philosophical discourse. But after receiving van Blyenbergh's second letter, Spinoza realized that his correspondent insisted on the truth of the Bible and believed that reason always had to be made to conform to biblical teachings. Spinoza informed him that he did not wish to continue the correspondence, since it would not be mutually instructive:

> For I see that no proof, however firmly established according to the rules of logic, has any validity with you unless it agrees with the explanation which you, or other theologians of your acquaintance, assign to Holy Scripture. However, if it is your conviction that God speaks more clearly and effectually through Holy Scripture than through the light of the natural understanding which he has also granted us … you have good reason to adapt your understanding to the opinions which you ascribe to Holy Scripture…. For my part, I plainly and unam-biguously avow that I do not understand Holy Scripture, although I have devoted quite a number of years to its study. And since I am conscious that when an indisputable proof is presented to me, I find it impossible to entertain thoughts that cast doubt upon it, I entirely acquiesce in what my intellect shows me without any suspicion that I am deceived therein, or that Holy Scripture, without my even examining it, can contra-dict it. For truth is not at odds with truth….[13]

Spinoza believed in one Truth; Truth was attained through the efforts of human reason; Truth proved by reason had to be accepted. Although he agreed that the Bible contains wisdom, he felt that it is not a clear and definitive text of philosophy. In Spinoza's view, if reason establishes something as true, then any contrary views in the Bible (and/or the opinions of its "authoritative" interpreters) must be rejected. To argue that reason must conform to the teachings of the Bible is absurd because (1) God gave us reason with which to determine truth; and (2) the Bible is not literally the word of God and there-fore has no power to offset the findings of reason. Rambam would agree with Spinoza that truth is not at odds with truth and that the Bible and reason must arrive at the same ultimate truths. Rambam, however, believed that the Bible is the word of God and although it must be interpreted in light of reason, its authority is binding.

Spinoza viewed the Bible as a human document, filled with errors and superstitious beliefs. Although the Bible certainly had its value, it could not be cited as a proof against the findings of reason. Moreover, people who cited the Bible were often really citing interpretations of the Bible by human religious authorities—and who is to say that these authorities understood the Bible correctly?

In defending reason as the arbiter of Truth, Spinoza challenged those who relied on the Bible (or at least their understanding of it) instead of reason:

> I am astonished that anyone should wish to subject reason, the greatest of gifts and a light from on high, to the dead letter which may have been corrupted by human malice; that it should be thought no crime to speak with contempt of mind, the true handwriting of God's Word, calling it corrupt, blind, and lost, while it is considered the greatest of crimes to say the same of the letter, which is merely the reflection and image of God's Word. Men think it pious to trust nothing to reason and their own judgment, and impious to doubt the faith of those who have transmitted to us the sacred books. Such conduct is not piety, but mere folly.[14]

Spinoza mocked those individuals who turned their backs on reason and who preferred to live with a piety that was based on ignorance. He was particularly critical of those governments or other communal bod-ies that limited freedom of inquiry and that insisted that anyone who deviated from the "accepted" faith was to be persecuted as a heretic. In his view, using force to suppress free thought was an affront to rea-son—and was ultimately destructive to humanity.

No, the object of government is not to change men from rational beings into beasts or puppets, but to enable them to develop
their minds and bodies in security, and to employ their reason
unshackled…. In fact, the true aim of government is liberty.[15]

One of Spinoza's major problems with the Bible was not the Bible itself,
but the religious functionaries who claimed to be the sole and absolute
interpreters of the Bible. One can well imagine the child Spinoza questioning the teachings of his rabbis—and being told in no uncertain
terms that he did not have the right to dissent from the "accepted"
interpretations. Although Spinoza may have been critical of the rabbis,
his later critique was aimed even more especially at the Christian cler-
ical hierarchy who believed themselves the only authoritative interpreters of Scripture. The rabbis, after all, had no power outside their
own small community. The Christian clergy, in contrast, had vast
power over their societies, including governments and universities.
The rabbis could excommunicate Spinoza from the synagogue, but the
Christian clergy could vilify Spinoza throughout Europe on every rung
of the social and intellectual ladder.

Spinoza's disgust with the official spokesmen of religion was pal-
pable: "How hurtful to religion and the state is the concession to ministers of religion of any power of issuing decrees or transacting the
business of government."[16] Spinoza believed that ministers of religion
should only give answers to questions duly put to them and stay out
of government affairs, that is, there must be a separation of church and
state. If the clergy abused governmental powers to quash dissenting
opinions, then the government itself became the agent of suppression.
"The most tyrannical governments are those which make crimes of
opinions, for everyone has an inalienable right over his thoughts…."[17]

Spinoza insisted "that in a free state every man may think what he
likes, and say what he thinks."[18]

What greater misfortune for a state can be conceived than that
honourable men should be sent like criminals into exile,
because they hold diverse opinions which they cannot dis-

guise? What, I say, can be more hurtful than that men who have committed no crime or wickedness should, simply because they are enlightened, be treated as enemies and put to death?... He that knows himself to be upright does not fear the death of a criminal, and shrinks from no punishment.... He holds that death in a good cause is no punishment, but an honour, and that death for freedom is glory.[19]

Spinoza's impassioned defense of freedom of thought and freedom of speech directly challenged the authoritarian policies of the chief institutions of Christian Europe. His views were particularly offensive to church leaders, who, like the anti-Maimonideans, did not want the public to rely on reason but to obey the dictates of the religious teachers. Allowing free thought and free speech inevitably would lead to false ideas, heresy, and a diminution in loyalty to religious institutions and leaders.

Love of truth, in the view of Spinoza, entailed sincere and respectful consideration of reasonable arguments. Genuine seekers of truth were not contentious or egocentric, but rather were gentle, amiable, eager to learn from others, and humble. Spinoza felt that religious schisms often originated not in a search for truth "but rather in an inordinate desire for supremacy." Further, he suggested that "the real disturbers of the peace are those who, in a free state, seek to curtail the liberty of judgment which they are unable to tyrannize over."[20]

Although he advocated freedom of thought and speech, Spinoza nevertheless believed that there was one Truth and that it was attained through reason. Spinoza realized that the masses might never attain Truth, but he granted them the right to express their opinions anyway. Rambam, too, believed in one Truth, but he felt that the masses needed to be given the fundamental truths (that is, the thirteen principles of faith) so that they would not veer off into heresy and idolatry.

Both Rambam and Spinoza, in different ways, expressed dissatisfaction with the "authoritative" interpretations of Scripture that violated reason. Perhaps if Spinoza had had a Bible teacher like Rambam, he would not have left the synagogue! On the other hand, Spinoza was well aware of Rambam's work and chose to defy Jewish religious tradition anyway.

Prophets and Philosophers

Interestingly, both philosophers envisioned the ideal seeker of Truth in similar terms. For Rambam, human perfection is reached by apprehending God in as clear a manner as possible. "The way of life of such an individual, after he has achieved this apprehension, will always have in view loving-kindness, righteousness, and judgment, through assimilation to His actions, may He be exalted…."[21] Such a person will be serene and filled with inner joy. For Spinoza, the ideal person will love God (apprehended through reason) and will be in control of his mind and emotions. The wise man "is scarcely at all disturbed in spirit, but, being conscious of himself and of God and of things by a certain eternal necessity, never ceases to be, but always possesses true acquiescence of his spirit."[22]

Nevertheless, an unbridgeable gap separates Rambam and Spinoza in their understanding of the "ideal" human being. Rambam sees the prophet as the highest example of humanity, and Moses as the highest example of prophets.[23] The prophet is not only endowed with great intellect and power of reason, but is also uniquely pious and devoted to God and Torah. Prophecy is a gift from God, raising the already brilliant philosopher to a higher level of closeness with God. Different prophets reached different degrees of prophecy, with Moses having reached the most intimate knowledge of God that is possible for humans.

Rambam pointed out in the introduction to his *Guide of the Perplexed* that human beings are simply not able to reach a full understanding of the ultimate mysteries. He used the image of lightning to describe how different intellects attain aspects of Truth. Humans are in a dark night; when lightning flashes, they get a sudden glimpse of the reality around them. Moses was on such a lofty spiritual and intellectual level that it was as though the lightning flashed constantly for him and the night became as day. Lesser prophets received lesser numbers and lesser degrees of lightning flashes, so they perceived far less than Moses but far more than others who were not blessed with these great flashes of insight. Some human beings experience the lightning at greater or shorter time intervals. Others only attain illumination indirectly, from reflections of the lightning on shiny objects. And yet others remain in darkness and never see light.

For Spinoza, the ideal human being is a philosopher, not a prophet. Indeed, Spinoza's reading of the Bible led him to the conclusion that the prophets were not necessarily outstanding thinkers, but rather were highly emotional visionaries. Some of them were relatively simple shepherds, with no biblical evidence pointing to their intellectual abilities.

Spinoza's philosophy did not have room for a God who could communicate with humans, including prophets. God was the ideal Truth to which the human intellect needed to direct itself. This intellectual love of God was for its own sake, without the possibility of God talking with or rewarding the philosopher. In his *Ethics* (part 5, propositions 15 and 16), he teaches that "he who clearly and distinctly understands himself and his emotions loves God, and loves Him better the better he understands himself and his emotions. This love of God above everything else ought to occupy the mind."[24]

Both Rambam and Spinoza extolled the virtue of reason, yet for Spinoza, reason was all that humanity had in its quest to understand/ love God. The philosopher, who was devoted to rational analysis, was the one most able to fulfill human potential. Spinoza's idea of God is precisely that: an idea—a philosophical construct.

Rambam, though, recognized that God was not merely an "idea" but a "being." The ultimate truth of revelation is that God can and does communicate with humans. Although Rambam's understanding of God is quite intellectualized, it has room for a God with whom human beings can and do have a genuine, ongoing relationship.

Shaping Our Intellectual and Religious Worldviews

Rambam and Spinoza have both made important contributions to the development of Western intellectual life. We moderns who delve into their teachings must appreciate how much we have learned from them.

Both Rambam and Spinoza faced fierce opposition; yet neither flinched from his commitment to Truth, and neither bowed to the prevailing "establishment." The quest for Truth entails reliance on reason, and not believing everything we read or hear from "scholars" and "authorities." Surely, we can learn from others; but this learning must be sifted through our own minds, analyzed critically, and accepted only after our reason justifies acceptance.

Rambam applied the tools of reason not just to philosophical speculation, but also to the study of biblical and rabbinic literature. He believed that the teachings of the Bible and the rabbis must necessarily be in harmony with the dictates of reason and that if these teachings appear to contradict reason, then they must be reinterpreted or reevaluated. Rambam laid the foundation for religious life that fosters the use of reason. He acknowledged that there are limits to what the human mind can apprehend and there are revealed truths that cannot be cast aside even if our reason does not understand them fully. In his *Guide*, Rambam makes clear that while human reason can understand many things, there are things that "it is not capable of apprehending in any way or through any cause; the gates of apprehension are shut before it…. Man's intellect indubitably has a limit at which it stops."[25] Granting the limits of human understanding, Rambam advocated pushing our reason to its limits as we confront the texts and teachings of our divinely revealed religion. Rambam endowed the philosophical religionist with great dignity.

Spinoza, even as a "heretic," has helped shape the religious worldview of moderns. He was an early and vital voice on behalf of freedom of thought and freedom of expression. He argued cogently and convincingly that governments need to protect these rights. Today, we take these rights for granted in free societies.

The whole world is not free, however. Even in free societies, there are groups who strive to suppress dissenting views through censorship and censure. Some religious leaders function as cult leaders, demanding total allegiance from their followers and denying their followers the right to think for themselves. Authoritarianism is alive and flourishing in many societies. Spinoza's calm, strong voice continues to be a source of inspiration to those who seek to live in freedom.

Although Rambam and Spinoza have contributed mightily to our religious and intellectual worldviews, much has happened in the centuries since their deaths. On the one hand, metaphysics—so central to Rambam's thinking—has been severely challenged by modern philosophers. Many have denied the possibility of attaining knowledge of things that are beyond the limits of scientific verification: if it cannot be tested, it cannot be proved; if it cannot be proved, it cannot be known to be true. According to this way of thinking, concepts such as God, revelation, and prophecy are not comprehensible.

The efficacy of reason, so central to Spinoza's system, has also come under attack. The "uncertainty principle" has demonstrated that even in the world of pure science there are things the human mind cannot understand through reasoning. The great physicist Richard Feynman has commented that quantum mechanics "describes nature as absurd from the point of view of common sense. And it fully agrees with experiment. So I hope you can accept nature as She is—absurd."[26]

Moreover, thinkers have increasingly come to realize that reason is limited in scope and is also fallible. Not only does reason lack the ability to comprehend the "truths" of mysticism and spiritual intuition, but it also varies from person to person; that is, people who consider themselves to be perfectly reasonable still come to different conclusions on numerous matters. Many moderns have concluded that there is not one Truth—as both Rambam and Spinoza believed—but numerous "truths" arrived at by different thinkers and these "truths" do not always coincide with each other.

As thinking people in search of God, we deepen our understanding by studying the ideas of Rambam and Spinoza. We also, however, need to process these ideas through our own minds, in light of our own reason, and in light of developments in human thought over the past centuries.

2

THE NATURE OF GOD, THE GOD OF NATURE

> The Lord is my shepherd, I shall not lack. He makes me
> to lie down in green pastures; He leads me gently beside
> the still waters. He refreshes my soul. He guides me in the
> paths of righteousness for His name's sake.
>
> (Psalms 23:1–3)

The beautiful and powerful words from Psalm 23:1–3 reflect a warm, intimate relationship between God and human beings. God is a shepherd who looks after us, who guides us and keeps us on the proper course. The psalm goes further: A person who puts full trust in God need fear no evil, not even death. God will reward the faithful abundantly and offer protection from enemies; the greatest good is to dwell in the house of the Lord for length of days.

This psalm has provided spiritual solace to billions of people for three thousand years. Its pastoral imagery conveys tranquility, beauty, and the eternal rhythms of nature that transcend any particular threats or calamities. God is kind and watchful, caring and protective. "Though I walk through the valley of the shadow of death, I will fear no evil; for You are with me" (Psalm 23:4).

The psalm is true to the biblical perception of God as an all-powerful Being who is involved in the lives of humans. Postbiblical Jewish tradition has fostered this view of God, as manifested in the prayer book, the Talmud and midrashim, Kabbalah, and works of Jewish theology and thought. The *Zohar* includes a passage that has become part of synagogue liturgy in many congregations, recited when the doors of the ark are opened before the Torah scroll is brought to the reader's desk:

> May it be Your will to prolong our life in goodness, and may I also be accounted among the righteous, that You may show me love and in Your keeping hold me and mine with all Your people Israel. You are He who provides food for all and sustains all. You are He who rules over all.... I am the servant of the Holy One, blessed be He, before whom and before whose glorious Torah I bow myself at all times. Not in man do I trust, nor do I rely on angels; but only in the God of the heavens who is the God of truth, whose Torah is truth and whose prophets are truth, and who abounds in doing goodness and truth. In Him alone do I trust, and to His glory and glorious name I utter praises.[1]

According to this passage, God is approachable. He listens to our prayers and can answer them positively. He has given us a Torah by which we can guide our lives according to His words. Whereas human beings are mortal and unreliable, God is immortal, perfect, and absolutely trustworthy.

This is the classic Jewish religious understanding of God. Yet this view is quite different from that of secular philosophy, which sees God in impersonal terms—as a Prime Mover. According to this view, God is, in a sense, a scientific principle or a logical necessity—not a loving divine Being who actually interacts with humans in a personal way.

Rambam's God

Rambam was profoundly steeped in biblical and rabbinic tradition—but he was also a devotee of Greek philosophy. How did he reconcile the two very different notions of God that characterize these two viewpoints?

In the opening passages of his *Mishneh Torah*, Rambam draws on the language of philosophy:

> The foundation of all foundations and the pillar of all sciences is to know that there is a First Being who brought every existing thing into existence. All existing things, whether celestial, terrestrial, or belonging to an intermediate class, exist only through His true existence. If it could be supposed that He did not exist, it would follow that nothing else could possibly exist. If, though, it were supposed that all other beings were nonexistent, He alone would still exist.[2]

Aristotle, or Spinoza for that matter, would have had no problem with this description of God. But Rambam then adds, "For all things are in need of Him; but He, blessed be He, is not in need of any one of them."[3] In pointing out God's uniqueness and transcendence, Rambam adds words that neither Aristotle nor Spinoza could have used: "blessed be He." The "secular" philosophers recognized that God was the First Being, had a unique essence, and was totally independent of material things. However, Rambam went a step further, stating that this First Being was not merely a philosophical/scientific principle, but was a Being who was to be blessed, to whom humans had an emotional (not merely intellectual) attachment.

If the God of the philosophers is infinitely remote, the God of the Bible and rabbinic tradition is infinitely near. How did Rambam bridge the gap between the abstract distant God of the philosophers and the approachable, hovering God of his religious heritage?

First, let us try to understand Rambam the philosopher. His reason led him to conclude that God is "without matter and is simple to the utmost degree of simplicity, whose existence is necessary, who has no cause and to whom no notion attaches that is superadded to His essence, which is perfect."[4] God is unlike any of His creations and "has nothing in common with them in any respect."[5] God is so utterly and infinitely different from His creations, we have no way of understanding His essence.

> Glory then to Him who is such that when the intellects contemplate His essence, their apprehension turns into incapacity; and when they contemplate the proceeding of His actions from His will, their knowledge turns into ignorance; and when the tongues aspire to magnify Him by means of attributive qualifications, all eloquence turns into weariness and incapacity![6]

According to Rambam, since God is the ultimate perfection, He is not describable by human words. Anything we say about Him is inadequate and incomplete. We can only say with some certainty what God is not: He is not a multiplicity; He is not material; He is not divisible; He is not bound to time or space. This process of negation—describing what God is not—does not, however, give us knowledge of the true reality of God. Indeed, we must recognize that God "cannot be apprehended by the intellects, and that none but He Himself can apprehend what He is."[7]

In Rambam's view, if the Bible and our prayer book ascribe positive attributes to God, this is because "the Torah speaks in the language of human beings" (Talmud, *Yevamot* 71a; *Bava Metzia* 31b). Biblical language (and the language of liturgy, which emulates the Bible) does not pretend to be philosophical. On the contrary, it is poetic and figurative and must not be taken as a refutation of the philosophical truth that God cannot be described with positive attributes. Rambam cites the Talmudic passage (*Berakhot* 33b) in which Rabbi Haninah chastises a person who was praising God with many adjectives. Rabbi Haninah asked him, "Have you finished all the praises of your Master? We are only allowed to use those adjectives that have been sanctioned by Moses in the Torah, and the Men of the Great Assembly who formulated our prayers." Even these adjectives are granted to us only by the authority of the Torah itself; we would not have had the right to utter such praises on our own.

Rambam was highly critical of poets and preachers who took literally the Torah's descriptions of God's positive attributes: "The utterances of some of them constitute an absolute denial of faith, while other utterances contain such rubbish and such perverse imaginings as to make men laugh when they hear them … and to make them weep when they consider that these utterances are applied to God, may He be magnified and glorified."[8]

Rambam maintained the philosophical truth that God is infinitely beyond our understanding and that attributing to God positive qualities is rationally untenable, since any adjective we ascribe to Him necessarily limits Him. Yet Moses and the Men of the Great Assembly did in fact sanction the recital of descriptive, positive attributes of God, terms such as the Great, the Mighty and Awesome, the Compassionate and Gracious. Rambam assumed that these descriptions of God are figurative and poetic, not literal. The Torah, in speaking the language of humans, recognized that we need to have some emotive language that can help us feel God's presence. It would be impossible to expect people to pray to a "personal" God if we could only recite philosophical axioms of what God is not.

Rambam required us to make a "leap of faith." Although we are supposed to understand intellectually that God is absolutely unknowable, we are also expected to understand emotionally that God is present—and even cares about us. Rambam did not spell out exactly how we are to accomplish this leap of faith; apparently it is the result of an internal process of philosophical and spiritual contemplation.

How can we pray to something we cannot understand, that is infinitely beyond our capacity to understand? In *Maimonides: A Guide for Today's Perplexed*, Dr. Kenneth Seeskin offers this analysis:

> Maimonides' solution is to direct our attention away from God as He is in Himself to the consequences or effects that flow from Him. The crucial point is this: Although the divine nature can never admit plurality, and therefore cannot be the subject of a normal subject/predicate statement, there is no reason why God cannot have a plurality of effects.[9]

Rambam makes this point in his *Guide* by offering a comparison to fire. Although fire has different effects on different things (for example, it melts wax, hardens clay, darkens sugar, lightens various chemicals), it would be nonsensical to suggest that fire itself is identical with its effects. By analogy, God is One but has multiple effects. Thus, Rambam concludes that "the diverse actions proceed from one simple essence in which no multiplicity is posited and to which no notion is super-added."[10] When our sacred texts describe God, they refer not to His essence but to His effects. No human being, not even Moses, could understand God's essence—but we do have access to God by experiencing and contemplating the effects of His essence. This would include, for example, moral qualities we attribute to Him, such as compassion, justice, and faithfulness.

We can have no clear idea how God produces the effects that flow from Him. Nonetheless, since we do have ideas relating to the effects, we may praise God based on our perception of the effects. We may develop that spiritual mental framework that experiences the emanations from God's essence and that draws us to praise God and feel near to Him.

Spinoza's God

In his *Ethics*, Spinoza offers propositions and demonstrations to prove that God exists and is absolutely infinite and consummately perfect. Proposition 14 in chapter 1 states: "Besides God no substance can be nor can be conceived." Proposition 15 states: "Whatever is, is in God, and nothing can either be or be conceived without God."

Proposition 17 teaches: "God acts from the laws of His own nature only and is compelled by no one."

For Spinoza, neither intellect nor will pertain to God. Since God is infinitely perfect, everything that exists could not have existed in any other way; otherwise we would presume that God had to "make choices" and could have had other options. But if God is infinitely perfect, His manifestations could only be as they are, and no other options (obviously imperfect since they were not "chosen") actually existed.

Spinoza offered an analogy to a triangle: By its very nature, it must have three sides whose angles equal 180 degrees. There are no other options; that's just how triangles are. Likewise, God, by His very nature of perfection, cannot be or do otherwise than what He is, and therefore everything that is, is as it has to be based on God's nature.

Thus, God is not "free," in that He has no choices. His perfect existence leaves no room for intellectual or emotional decision making. Perhaps this can be understood better by analogy with nature. Nature exists; nature operates by certain determined laws. Nature does not make decisions, does not express emotions, and does not act with free will. Nature just is. God can be understood as Nature (with a capital N)—a vastly perfect, impersonal Being that includes everything that exists and that necessarily operates based on its own essence.

This understanding of God has obvious implications for humanity and for religion. According to Spinoza's reasoning, God cannot "change" Himself by doing miracles or interceding in human events; He is not to be prayed to; He does not communicate by means of prophecy or divine revelation to human beings; He does not give commandments. God is immutable, and all His attributes are immutable. "The existence of God and His essence are one and the same thing."[11]

Spinoza's God stands in stark contrast to the idea of God held by devotees of biblical religion, who conceive of God as having freedom, will, and other attributes common to humanity. To one of his critics, Spinoza wrote:

> Further, when you say that you do not see what sort of God I have if I deny in him the actions of seeing, hearing, attending, willing, etc., and that he possesses those faculties in an eminent degree, I suspect that you believe there is no greater perfection than can be explicated by the aforementioned attributes. I am not surprised, for I believe that a triangle, if it could speak, would likewise say that God is eminently triangular, and a circle that God's nature is eminently circular. In this way, each would ascribe to God its own attributes, assuming itself to be like God and regarding all else as ill-formed.[12]

Spinoza believed that reason inevitably led to an understanding of God that transcended the popular descriptions of God among religionists. He thought that the contemplation of this perfect God leads to serenity, wisdom, happiness, and the intellectual love of God. For humans to worship or glorify any other conception of God is to engage in folly and superstition.

Rambam: Beyond Reason to Revelation

On a purely philosophical level, Rambam had basic points of agreement with Spinoza. For Rambam, too, God does not have physical or emotional attributes. God's essence, since God is absolute perfection, is not subject to change.

Rambam, though, did not limit his understanding of God to the realm of pure philosophy. He recognized that reason alone cannot lead to a full understanding of the infinite and eternal God. In contemplating God, we need to factor in two other components: human experience and religious tradition.

Noting the biblical commandments to love and to revere God; Rambam describes how a person might achieve these goals,

> When a person contemplates His great and wondrous works and creatures and from them obtains a glimpse of His wisdom which is incomparable and infinite, he will straightway love Him, praise Him, glorify Him, and long with an exceeding longing to know His great Name…. And when he ponders these matters, he will recoil frightened and realize that he is a small creature, lowly and obscure, endowed with slight and slender intelligence, standing in the presence of Him who is perfect in knowledge.[13]

Contemplation of nature—the manifestation of God's wisdom and power—will lead to the love of God, to the desire to come closer to God. Quite aside from our reason, we feel overpowered emotionally by contemplation of the infinite greatness of God. Loving God is actually the result of transcending our own limitations, of feeling an internal unity with the great One of the universe. This love is attained through philosophical speculation that moves us to a direct spiritual experience of God.

Likewise, the fear of God stems from our sense of smallness in the presence of God's infinity. Who are we that God should notice us, that our lives should have any real ultimate meaning? Staring at the skies on a starry night reminds us of our cosmic insignificance; we shrink with fear and awe at the recognition of God's unlimited power. This fear of God—like the love of God—is the result not merely of intellectual perception, but of spiritual experience.

Whereas Spinoza limited the human relationship with God to the intellectual realm, Rambam recognized that human beings have the capacity to relate to God in powerful, transcendent experiences linked to our minds and our hearts. Whereas Spinoza gave no credence to "truths" outside the domain of rational demonstration, Rambam asserted that transcendent experiences can indeed be rooted in objective truth; they are not (at their best) merely self-delusional wish fulfillments.

Rambam did not doubt his—and so many others'—direct feeling of contact with God when contemplating nature. The love and awe were so genuine, it was not possible to explain them away as fanciful fictions. Spinoza, who may also have experienced these feelings, transmuted them into an intellectual—rather than emotional/spiritual—perception of God.

Rambam's view was predicated on the truth of biblical and rabbinic tradition. The Torah's account of God's revelation to the hundreds of thousands of Israelites at Mount Sinai describes a unique historical event. The entire nation witnessed God's presence, and this event changed the history of the world forever after. For Rambam, the revelation was an undeniable historical fact that cannot be disproved by philosophical speculation.

Although Rambam was a rationalistic philosopher, he understood that not all truth was attainable through the efforts of human reason. We must carry reason to its limits but then turn to the biblical tradition of revelation to draw ourselves closer to Truth.

An example of Rambam's approach is found in his discussion of the origins of the universe. He asks: Is matter eternal, as Aristotle posited, or was it created by God from nothing? If Rambam had been convinced through philosophy that indeed the universe is eternal, he would have reinterpreted biblical passages that implied that God created it ex nihilo.[14]

> However, no necessity could impel us to do this unless this opinion [of the eternity of the universe] were demonstrated. In view of the fact that it has not been demonstrated, we shall not favor this opinion, nor shall we at all heed that other opinion, but rather shall take the texts according to their external sense and shall say: the Law has given us knowledge of a matter the grasp of which is not within our power, and the miracle attests to the correctness of our claims.[15]

Just as we cannot fathom why God created the world, we cannot expect to fathom how and why He performs miracles, exercises providence, and communicates through revelation and prophecy. Our belief in God's creation of the world (rather than the unproved proposition that the world is eternal) allows us to understand that God does not work by necessity. The belief in God as Creator serves as a foundation for the belief in God as an active, unrestricted Being.

Rambam offers a parable to illustrate the inadequacy of human reason to deal with realities that existed prior to creation. Assume that a male child was born and that his mother died shortly thereafter. This child was raised by his father (or other men) on an isolated island and never saw a woman or a female of any other animal species. After he grew up, he asked: "How did we come to exist, and in what way were we generated?"

> Thereupon the man to whom the question was put replied, "Every individual among us was generated in the belly of an individual belonging like us to our species, an individual who is female and has such and such a form. Every individual

among us was—being small in body—within the belly, was moved and fed there, and grew up little by little—being alive—until it reached such and such limit in size. Thereupon an opening was opened up for him in the lower part of the body, from which he issued and came forth."[16]

Upon hearing this, the orphaned child would be incredulous. Was it really possible for a human being to live in the enclosed belly of a woman for an extended period of time, without breathing, eating, drinking, or producing excrements? His experience indicated that it was not possible for a living being to survive under such conditions. His reason and his observations "proved" that "it is in no respect possible that man should be generated in that manner."

Likewise, argued Rambam, Aristotle's "proofs" for the eternity of the universe were based on observations made after the universe already existed. Just as the orphaned child could not understand the truth of his actual creation (since he could only evaluate things based on his observations after already being created), so Aristotle cannot understand the truth of the creation of the universe, since he is operating only with information available after the creation. The followers of Moses, though, have the biblical tradition of God's creation of the universe and are therefore able to avoid the philosophical errors of Aristotle.

The Lord Is My Shepherd

Neither Rambam nor Spinoza believed that God was really our Shepherd in any literal sense. Poets used such phrases about God, but these phrases were not based on reason or rational proof.

For Spinoza, such phrases were empty of philosophical content and did not reflect true reality. God is a Being who is as He is, who does not change, who does not intervene in human affairs. When Spinoza read Psalm 23, he might have found it to be beautiful from a literary point of view, but he would have found it devoid of philosophical truth.

For Rambam, Psalm 23 did not intend to make a philosophical statement. As poetry, it appeals to our emotion rather than to our reason. God is not literally a Shepherd; and yet, humans may perceive Him as such—a caring, providential Being. When Rambam chanted Psalm 23, I suspect that he did so with a religious sentiment and that he felt God's closeness.

Rambam the philosopher rejected anthropomorphic and anthropopathic descriptions of God—but Rambam the rabbi understood that the Bible "spoke in the language of humans." Applying human attributes to God was a way of helping us feel closer to God on an emotional, spiritual level. We know intellectually that God is not a Shepherd, but we feel intuitively that He watches over us, just as a shepherd watches over the flock. Whereas Spinoza gave no credence to "truth" derived from revelation or emotional experience, Rambam—though highly rationalistic—understood that there were "truths" attainable beyond the reach of human reason.

Spinoza's rationalism shared elements with that of the Rambam; however, it could not move beyond the constraints of human reason. Since religion transcends reason through revelation and through personal experience, it was not verifiable to Spinoza. Conversely, from a religious viewpoint, Spinoza's philosophy is deficient, even sterile.

Rambam's rationalism is humbler than Spinoza's in that it recognizes the limits of reason. For Rambam, we are obligated to use our reason to the maximum; we then enter an area of meta-reason. This area of meta-reason exists between the boundaries of reason on one side and prophecy on the other. We know that this area of meta-reason is true because we have an authoritative tradition of revelation and because we personally experience it to be true. In this area of meta-reason, most do not attain prophecy; nevertheless, we do receive some level of awareness that we are in the presence of God.

Meta-Reason and Our Spiritual Life

Think of experiences in your life when you lost your sense of ego, when you transcended yourself and felt part of something greater.

Such experiences, which occur to everyone, strike us suddenly, spontaneously. We cannot calculate and prepare ourselves for them. They simply happen to us. And yet, our own level of receptivity will influence how often or how deeply we feel these experiences.[17]

An illustration of this kind of experience is falling in love. Popular language reflects the power of love to overcome us, and we speak of "falling" in love rather than of directing ourselves into it. The notion of being lovesick is reflected in the Song of Songs in the Bible. Love is meta-rational, not a product of reason.

Other experiences also fall into this category. Sometimes we are particularly moved by music. The music takes hold of us; our hearts leap, our minds drift into it. For those few moments, we experience an ineffable ecstasy. We might have a similar transcendent experience when we observe the awesome beauty and grandeur of snow-covered mountains; or a star-filled sky at midnight; or the steady churning of ocean waves. For an instant, we abandon the concepts of subject and object but rather feel part of the totality of the experience. We feel a real and profound unity between ourselves and the world. These feelings may also occur during prayer or sacred meditation.

The fulfillment of spiritual life is the feeling of being in God's presence. At those special moments, we experience a sense of having transcended the self. But this religious experience, like falling in love and the other experiences mentioned before, happens as a moment of grace. There is no path that automatically leads to this experience of God. The role of religious observance and meditation is to provide us with spiritual receptivity, so that we will be ready for the experience when it does come.

The Torah teaches a seemingly paradoxical lesson: "And you shall love the Lord your God with all your heart, with all your soul, and with all your might" (Deuteronomy 6:5). This verse is generally taken to be a positive commandment to love God. However, love cannot be commanded! All we can do is prepare ourselves to love, and hope that we will indeed love.

This verse in Deuteronomy might be understood not so much as a commandment to love God, but as a statement of the consequences

of living a spiritually sensitive life. If you observe God's commandments, study the Torah, teach the Torah to your children, then it will
transpire that "you will love the Lord your God with all your heart,
with all your soul, and with all your might." The result of one's religious preparation and sensitivity will be the blessing of actual love of
God with the totality of your being—heart, soul, might.

Kabbalists developed various techniques to increase a person's
receptivity to God's spirit. Rabbi Eliezer Azikri (sixteenth-century
Safed), for example, suggested that "one day a week, a person should
distance himself from others and be alone with himself and his Master;
he should attach his thoughts to Him as though he is already standing
before Him on the day of judgment. He should speak to God, blessed
be He, with soft words as a slave speaks to his master and a son to his
father."[18] In another passage, Rabbi Azikri writes that when the pious
ones were in solitude, they removed from their minds all matters of
this world and attached their thoughts to the Master of the universe.
He recommended that solitude be practiced once a week or at least
once a month.[19]

Jewish mystical thinking has understood that religious observances and meditation serve as the ground from which love of God
springs. By creating a thoughtful mood, they help us become receptive
to a deep, loving relationship with God.

Since Jewish tradition mandates three daily prayer services, these
are built-in opportunities to feel the presence of God. However, the
very routine of these daily prayers can lead to the mechanical recitation
without the appropriate spiritual framework. Rambam explained the
requirement of praying with *kavanah*, proper intention:

> Any prayer that lacks proper intention [*kavanah*] is not prayer.
> If one prayed without proper intention, he must repeat the
> prayer with proper intention. If one's mind is confused and his
> heart troubled, it is forbidden to pray until he returns to a calm
> state. What is proper intention? One should clear his heart
> from all [extraneous] thoughts and see himself as though he
> stands before the Divine Presence. Therefore, one should sit

down a bit before prayers, in order to focus his heart, and then pray with calmness and supplications. One should not treat prayer as one who carries a burden, who casts it down and goes on his way.[20]

Rabbi Yosef Karo, in his *Shulhan Arukh* (Code of Jewish Law), draws on Rambam's description of prayer. He reminds us that

one who prays must concentrate his heart on the meaning of the words which are uttered from his lips. He should imagine that the Divine Presence is with him. He should remove all thoughts that trouble him until his thought and concentration are pure in his prayer.... And thus did the pious and saintly people: They meditated and concentrated on their prayers until they reached the level of transcending physicality and elevating the power of the mind until they reached near the level of prophecy.[21]

Prayer on this spiritual level is not easy to attain on a regular basis, yet it can be experienced—and has been experienced—by many individuals, at least on some special occasions.

From our own experiences of transcendence and feeling the proximity of the Divine Presence, we can extrapolate feelings of love and reverence for God. We don't need to prove God's existence; we *feel* His presence and *know* He is there. This is not an example of self-delusion, since this is the universal experience of humanity in all civilizations and at all times. Human beings have longed for a relationship with the Ultimate, the Transcendent One. Sometimes they worshipped stars or idols; sometimes they worshipped many gods; and sometimes they have achieved recognition of the One God. When the Torah teaches that Adam was created in the image of God, I believe this means that each human being has an innate drive to come close to God. God's "image" within us propels us to yearn for contact with God Himself.

Although we attempt to verify the truths of meta-reason by means of religious tradition and personal experience, these truths—by definition—cannot be attained by human reason. This puts us in the domain of subjectivity and volatility. Different people will deal with the realm of meta-reason in different ways. Some, like Rambam, will still stay rooted in philosophical rationalism. Reason will serve as a necessary corrective to mystical excesses. Others, though, may get lost in kabbalistic or superstitious musings and justify their spiritual excesses as being in the legitimate domain of meta-reason. Once validity is granted to meta-reason, we will have to deal with self-proclaimed prophets and spiritualists who claim to have found the genuine truth. Such individuals may become untamed by reason and can be self-righteous—and even dangerous.

By relying solely on human reason, Spinoza avoided the pitfalls of meta-reason. He could envision a purely rational humanity, devoted to the intellectual love of God. Such a vision precludes granting legitimacy to those who pass beyond the domain of reason. At the same time, such a vision limits human knowledge to the domain of reason—something we intuitively and experientially know to be false. Human beings are endowed not only with reason, but also with a deep and abiding spirituality that transcends reason. This aspect cannot be ignored.

Rambam the philosopher saw the highest good as intellectual contemplation of God. The more our mind is connected to God, the more we enjoy God's providence. But how does prayer fit into this picture? Does God need our praises? Is it plausible to expect God to "change His mind" based on our supplications? It would seem that "the God of the philosophers" is above and beyond the category of prayer.

Rambam the rabbi knew that daily prayer is a positive obligation and that our liturgy is filled with praises of God, words of thanksgiving, and petitions for our mundane needs. The Bible and Talmud include many examples of pious people at prayer and of God listening to the prayers.

Some scholars suggest that Rambam "really" believed in the philosophical God but made room for prayer as a concession to the masses of people who felt the need for worship. Others suggest that Rambam "really" believed in religious prayer and that he offered his philosophical explanations merely as a sop to intellectually inclined students who were perplexed and dissatisfied with traditional religious notions of prayer.

Professor Marvin Fox offers what I think to be the correct understanding of Rambam's position on prayer, a means of maintaining both the popular and the philosophical ideas of worship in a single system:

> It is my contention that … Maimonides has no choice but to maintain simultaneously conventional and philosophical ideas of prayer. These ideas, and practices, are not, as many suppose, intended to be mutually exclusive. They are intended to exist side by side within a single system of thought, maintaining a delicate and difficult balance. They are conceptions that live together in severe dialectical tension…. Maimonides is saying that our human condition leaves us no option but to live in the precarious situation in which we affirm and pursue in practice both a philosophically sophisticated conception of divine worship and a popular conventional pattern of prayer.[22]

Why do we need to posit this dialectical understanding of prayer? Why not simply adhere to the philosophical view that perfect contemplation of God is enough and that we do not need to engage in—nor is there reason to engage in—personal prayer? Dr. Fox answers: because we are not perfect! "Prayer is a basic and irrepressible expression of the human spirit…. Human beings, even philosophic ones, are not perfect disembodied intellects."[23] Even the greatest philosophers need to find a means of expressing their feelings toward the Divine. Words are surely inadequate—but they are the only means we have available to us as human beings. "Our human condition makes it necessary for us not only to pray, but to believe sincerely in the significance and meaningfulness of prayer. These are necessary beliefs … in the significant and admirable sense that no religious person can do without them, however sophisticated he or she may be."[24]

Rambam could substantiate this view by pointing to the example of Moses, the greatest prophet, who came closest to a direct relationship with God. For Rambam, Moses was the quintessential philosopher, who achieved not only the highest possible intellectual love of God, but also the closest possible personal experience of God. The Torah describes Moses as praying! Even for Moses, the abstract contemplation of God was not enough to satisfy his mind and spirit. Prayers of praise, thanksgiving, and petition were invoked by Moses as a valid and necessary human expression of connection with the Almighty.

Both Rambam and Spinoza—through their insistence on rationality—provide important correctives to unbridled religious emotionalism. Whereas Spinoza overstates humanity's power of reason, Rambam offers a realistic framework for religious experience. He stresses the philosophical approach to God but also recognizes the role of tradition and personal experience in allowing us to transcend the limits of reason.

When there is a genuine contradiction between a religious precept and philosophical truth, Rambam attempted to reconcile the contradiction by adhering to reason. But when there is a divergence—not contradiction—between a religious commandment and a philosophically demonstrated principle, Rambam strove to balance the two. In the words of Professor Fox, "To know how to keep them in balance and to live with the tension is precisely what is required of the religious man who seeks and discovers philosophical truth. We should never forget that it is to just such a person that Maimonides addressed his great work."[25]

This is an important point to keep in mind, not only in relation to Rambam's views on prayer, but also to his general approach to dealing with balancing the claims of religion with intellectual integrity.

3

TORAH FROM HEAVEN

The Torah (Five Books of Moses) serves as the bedrock of Judaism. Traditional Jewish belief maintains that the Torah was revealed to Moses by God, that it is literally the word of God. As such, it is a record of what God wants us to know and observe in order to live our lives properly, according to His will. While the Torah is the foundation of the revealed religion of Israel, later texts were also deemed to have been written with divine inspiration, albeit on a lower spiritual level than the Torah itself. The holy texts were canonized by our ancient rabbis and came to form the Hebrew Bible, known by the Hebrew acronym *Tanakh—Torah, Nevi'im* (Prophets), *Ketuvim* (Writings).

The Mishnah (*Sanhedrin*, beginning of chapter 10) records that a person who does not believe that the Torah is from Heaven (*Torah min haShamayim*) has no place in the world to come. At the same time, rabbinical literature includes various opinions as to what exactly "Torah from Heaven" means. One view is that God dictated the entire Torah to Moses from beginning to end; Moses was essentially a dutiful scribe who accurately recorded each of God's words letter by letter. Another view is that God transmitted the first four books to Moses, but Moses himself—with his prophetic inspiration—was the author of Deuteronomy.[1] Other opinions suggest that Joshua wrote the last few verses of the Torah that report Moses's death;[2] that King David deleted parts of the Torah and put them in the book of Psalms instead;[3] that we do not have a letter-perfect text of the original Torah.[4] In *Breaking the Tablets*, Professor David Weiss Halivni argues that the original Torah text has been "maculated," subjected to various errors in transmission; our task is to attempt to restore the Torah text to its pristine form.[5]

The Talmud (*Gittin* 60a) records two views on the composition of the Torah: (1) Moses received the entire Torah at one time; (2) Moses received the Torah in segments (*Torah megilah megilah nitnah*). The Talmud also records different views on the nature of the Oral Law that Moses received together with the Written Torah. The Oral Torah includes laws and interpretations that clarify the teachings of the Written Torah. The school of Rabbi Akiva believed that Moses received every detail of the Oral Torah, whereas the school of Rabbi Yishmael argued that Moses received general principles of interpretation.[6]

Significantly, the Torah itself provides no direct information as to how or when it was composed. It does not spell out the nature of the Oral Torah. These central religious teachings—themselves subjects of differing views among our sages—have come down to us via traditional transmission from generation to generation. The bottom line of traditional Jewish belief is that the Torah is divinely revealed, that it is accompanied by an authoritative Oral Torah, and that it provides teachings and commandments that are binding on us.

Rambam: The Literal and Nonliteral Word of God

Although he certainly was aware of the different rabbinic views on the nature of the Torah, Rambam sought to provide one authoritative formulation of Jewish belief. He also provided a philosophical methodology for studying the text of the Torah, as well as an approach for understanding and fulfilling the Torah's commandments.

In his listing of the thirteen basic principles of Jewish faith, he writes:

The eighth fundamental principle is that the Torah is from Heaven, that we must believe that the entire Torah that we have today is the Torah that was given to Moses, and that it is of divine origin in its entirety. It was given to Moses by God. The manner in which it was given to him we call, by analogy, speech. The only one who knows the nature of this process of communication was Moses, the one to whom it was given. However, he can be compared metaphorically to a scribe taking dictation, writing down all the events that took place, the stories, and the commandments…. Menasseh was considered by our sages as one who denied God, a heretic worse than any others, only because he thought that the Torah contained a husk and a core, and that the narratives and stories were of no value, being Moses's own statements. This is an example of one who says "the Torah is not from Heaven." … Every letter in the Torah contains wondrous knowledge, as is appreciated by one to whom God has granted understanding. The scope of its wisdom is beyond grasp…. Similarly, the interpretation of the Torah transmitted by tradition also stems from God. The manner in which we make a sukkah, *lulav*, shofar, tzitzit, tefillin, etc., is exactly as God told Moses, who communicated it to us. He was merely a messenger carrying out a mission, which he performed faithfully.[7]

Rambam chose the rabbinic view that God dictated the Torah to Moses, word for word. In his *Mishneh Torah*, he lists three categories of people who are considered as deniers of Torah: (1) those who say that even one verse or one word of Torah is not from God or that Moses composed any of the Torah on his own; (2) those who deny the Oral Torah; and (3) those who say that God replaced or nullified any of the Torah's commandments.[8]

The obvious problem with Rambam's formulation is that great Talmudic sages did indeed believe that parts of the Torah were written by Moses on his own, or that Joshua wrote the last few verses of the Torah, or that the Torah text that we have is not identical letter-by-letter to the Torah text that Moses had. Were these sages really to be considered as deniers of Torah and as heretics?

Dr. Marc Shapiro has suggested that Rambam felt it necessary "for the masses to affirm what, in reality, was not true, namely, that the text of the Torah in their hands was entirely free from any textual corruptions, even to the last detail."[9] This was in response to the Muslim accusations that the Jews had falsified the biblical texts. Although the Muslim claim was absurd, Rambam apparently did not wish to open discussion on the integrity of the biblical text. Such a discussion could prove confusing to the masses of Jews who were not steeped in biblical and rabbinic lore. Rambam argued for the letter-perfect Torah text as a means of bolstering Jewish faith among the masses of Jews.

Dr. Shapiro's plausible explanation seems to imply that Rambam himself knew better! Although he wanted the masses to believe in the perfect transmission of the biblical text from God to Moses and from Moses to us, Rambam really understood that things were not quite so simple. Yet, since Rambam was emphatic in his actual writings, it might also be possible that he believed what he wrote on these topics and that he had considered the various rabbinic traditions and concluded that the ones he recorded were the most correct.

Given that the Torah text is "from Heaven," the next question is: How are we to approach the text? Is each letter filled with divine wisdom and mysteries, as suggested by the school of Rabbi Akiva? Or is the Torah a "literary" document that must be read with literary skills, as implied by the school of Rabbi Yishmael's statement that "the Torah speaks in the language of human beings"?

It seems that Rambam used both approaches. On one level, he believed that a divine document contained profound wisdom and mysteries in each letter. But on another level, he believed that God composed the Torah in language that would be appealing and understandable to humans. This meant that God used literary techniques such as verbal repetitions, poetic expressions, and symbolic language so that not every letter should be interpreted for hidden meanings. Rambam seemed comfortable holding both positions, since he felt that he knew when to apply each method to each text.

Rambam was certain that the Torah was from Heaven, based on the age-old teachings of Jewish tradition. Moreover, he believed a thorough study of Torah revealed its "divine" nature, its transcendent wisdom, its superhuman insight, its endless profundity. No matter how many scholars have pored over the Torah for so many centuries, the study of Torah continually yields new insights and interpretations. It proves its relevance to each generation, regardless of historical context. In Rambam's view, no merely human document could do this; the Torah could only have been composed with divine inspiration.

Critics, though, could point to aspects of the Torah that do not necessarily reflect divine authorship or inspiration. Among them are (1) the Torah's use of anthropomorphisms and anthropopathisms, contradictory to the philosophical truth that God has neither physical nor emotional attributes; (2) the Torah's inclusion of narratives that appear to be simple folk stories rather than reflections of divine wisdom; and (3) the Torah's recording of commandments, especially ritual commandments, that seem to have no particular significance other than to demand blind obedience. The Rambam responds to each of these critiques.

The first book of Rambam's *Guide of the Perplexed* demonstrates that the Torah often uses language in a symbolic, metaphorical way. Anthropomorphisms and anthropopathisms are not to be taken literally but are to be understood as literary devices designed to appeal to the average reader. Indeed, Rambam went so far as to argue that those who take these phrases literally are guilty of heresy in that they deny God's purely spiritual nature. Such individuals have no place in the world to come, and their sin is akin to idolatry.[10]

According to Rambam, when the Bible speaks of God's mercy, anger, or other emotions, it is using metaphorical language. It poetically ascribes these qualities to God, analogizing from how human beings experience things. For example, God's mercy on us is compared to the mercy that a father shows to his children:

> It is not that He, may He be exalted, is affected and has compassion. But an action similar to that which proceeds from a

father in respect to his child and that is attached to compassion, pity, and an absolute passion, proceeds from Him, may He be exalted, in reference to His holy ones, not because of a passion or a change.... For He, may He be exalted, brings into existence and governs beings that have no claim upon Him with respect to being brought into existence and being governed. For this reason, He is called gracious.[11]

As to the biblical narratives, Rambam insisted that they are not superfluous folktales or genealogical records, but are essential repositories of divine wisdom. Since they are included in the text of the Torah, they necessarily have profound significance and must not be treated casually. Rambam described these passages as belonging to the "mysteries of the Torah" and reminded us, "Know that all the stories that you will find mentioned in the Torah occur there for a necessary utility for the Law; either they give a correct notion of an opinion that is a pillar of the Law, or they rectify some action so that mutual wrongdoing and aggression should not occur between men."[12]

As for the commandments, Rambam devoted much of the third book of his *Guide of the Perplexed* (chapters 25–49) to demonstrating the rational basis of the mitzvot, including the seemingly ritual ones. For him, the commandments necessarily reflect the deepest wisdom, since they emanate from God Himself. God would not (and could not) command us to do things that lack inner meaning and rational coherence. Although the Torah includes *mishpatim*, easily understood commandments, it also includes *hukkim*, commandments that seem to defy obvious explanation. Still, even the *hukkim*, such as the laws pertaining to ritual purity and the prohibition of weaving wool and linen together, are not frivolous irrational commandments; they too are rooted in divine wisdom, and we can strive to understand their underlying significance. This is not to say that we can fully attain God's intent—but we can come closer to it through intellectual endeavor.

For Rambam, the Torah aims at two things: the welfare of the soul and the welfare of the body. The commandments help us in our goal to achieve spiritual perfection, as well as in our need to live healthy lives in a cooperative and just society. Rambam went to great lengths to offer explanations of the Torah's commandments, demonstrating their rational basis. Even if a person were to find any of his particular explanations unsatisfactory, Rambam felt that his method was correct and should be emulated by all wise people. If we start with the assumption that God commanded the Torah's mitzvot, we necessarily should seek the divine wisdom that is encapsulated in each commandment.

Rambam approached the Bible as a philosopher. He was confident that the Torah was a divinely revealed document that reflected absolute Truth, and that the truths of Torah and the truths of philosophy were ultimately one Truth—and could be reconciled and harmonized. He read and interpreted the Torah through his philosophical lens, and he thus was able to deal with the Torah's theological principles, narratives, and commandments.

Spinoza: A Timeless and Temporal Human Document

Spinoza studied the Bible carefully, as one who did not believe in its divine origins. He scorned those who took the Bible's words as literal expressions of a perfect God and had disdain for those theologians who propounded dogmas and philosophical axioms that they claimed were implicit in the Bible.

In a sense, Spinoza's attitude corresponds to that of Rambam. Both stressed that "truth is not at odds with truth," that the truth of reason and the truth of the Bible must be identical. Both thinkers believed that if reason proved a certain truth, then that truth had to be accepted. However, Rambam and Spinoza differed on how to apply this principle. Rambam believed the Bible to be an expression of divine Truth. If reason proved something to be true and the Bible's words seemed to contradict this truth, Rambam felt justified—even compelled—to reinterpret the biblical words to conform to reason. In this way, truth was not at odds with truth. Spinoza, though, had a different view of the Bible. He did not see it as a Heaven-given infallible work and did not feel that he had to defend its statements or views. If reason proved something and the Bible violated this proven fact, then the Bible was simply wrong. Whereas Rambam sought to harmonize and reconcile reason with the Bible, Spinoza felt no such compulsion. Reason was always right; the Bible, being the imperfect creation of imperfect human beings, contained many things that did not correspond to the truths of reason.

Spinoza was critical of Rambam's approach. Rambam, after all, claimed to follow reason and went to great lengths to interpret the Bible to conform to reason. Spinoza found Rambam's interpretations to be strained, not true to the biblical text.[13] He believed that the authors of the Bible spoke in figurative, poetic language; they spoke truth as best they understood it, albeit without philosophical sophistication. In Spinoza's view, the Bible is a fine, wonderful book, but it cannot be taken as the source of ultimate Truth. Only reason can be the source of ultimate Truth. Rambam, in his loyalty to the belief in the divine authorship of the Bible, was compelled to engage in interpretive gymnastics to keep reason and the Bible in harmony. Spinoza found this effort unsatisfactory, and untrue to the real meaning of the Bible.

For Spinoza, the Bible is "particularly adapted to the needs of the common people, continually speaks in merely human fashion, for the common people are incapable of understanding higher things."[14] The biblical authors depicted God in human form—full of emotions as well as physical qualities. Whereas Rambam believed that these descriptions were merely figurative and that the Torah really knows the truth that God is beyond these qualities, Spinoza thought that the biblical authors were speaking as simple, philosophically unsophisticated people. They envisioned God as a glorified human being and did not entertain the philosophical notions that Maimonides espoused about the incorporeal nature of God. Spinoza insisted that the text of the Bible must be understood solely on its own merits, without the imposition of external philosophical notions on the simple meaning of the Bible's words. "We cannot wrest the meaning of texts to suit the dictates of our reason, or our preconceived opinions. The whole knowledge of the Bible must be sought solely from itself."[15]

Spinoza argued that the Bible's essential goal is to teach righteousness and proper conduct. To reach these ends, it speaks of rewards for the upright and punishment for the wicked; it ascribes emotions of happiness and anger to God; it avoids philosophical language. It speaks "in merely human terms according to accepted beliefs of the multitude; for its aim is not to teach philosophy, nor to make men learned, but to make them obedient."[16]

According to Spinoza, simply stated, the basic teaching of the Bible is "to love God above all things, and one's neighbour as one's self."[17] The particular words of the Bible are only reflections of this ultimate truth. Even if the Bible's words contain philosophical errors, even if they are halting and inadequate, they point to the love of God and of one's fellow human being. That is no small accomplishment. The Bible does not present, and does not try to offer, high speculative thought. A person cannot learn any of God's eternal attributes from Holy Scripture.[18]

For Spinoza, the many ritual commandments of the Torah were meant for the Israelites of ancient times, as a means of uniting them into a political state. The mitzvot, according to this way of thinking, were of temporal value and did not reflect divine law or ultimate Truth. The ceremonial laws were specifically for the Hebrews—and had no relevance to the rest of humanity, and no ongoing role for the Hebrews themselves once their political sovereignty in ancient Israel came to an end. The ceremonial laws "had nothing to do with blessedness and virtue, but had reference only to the election of the Hebrews, that is, to their temporal bodily happiness and the tranquility of their kingdom, and that therefore they were only valid while that kingdom lasted."[19]

Flexing Our Intellect

For traditional Jews, the Torah (and the rest of the Bible) reflects the will of God. It is divinely revealed Truth. Rambam described the revelation as God's dictation of the Torah to Moses. By this account, every letter of the Torah is of cosmic significance because it emanated directly and literally from God. We have seen earlier, though, that other great and pious Jewish thinkers did not understand the revelation in the same way as Rambam's formulation. Authoritative rabbinic literature entertains opinions that indicate that Moses had a personal role in the authorship of the Torah (and was not merely a scribe taking dictation from God); that the Torah was composed in segments, not all at once; that Joshua wrote the last few lines of the Torah; and that we don't have an absolutely accurate text of the original Torah as given to Moses. Although we might believe that the Torah is a divinely revealed document, we do not know for sure what this means nor how exactly God revealed His words to Moses and our other prophets.

Moreover, we might well question Rambam's insistence that the Torah encompasses a clearly definable set of philosophical dogmas. Indeed, in *Must a Jew Believe Anything?*, Professor Menachem Kellner argues that Rambam's dogmatizing was not only a deviation from classic Jewish thinking, but also the introduction of serious problems regarding who is and who is not a true believer.[20] Since pre-Maimonidean Judaism did not insist on particular formulations of dogmas, it was relatively unconcerned with heresy hunting. Rambam, though, listed principles of faith that were specific; anyone who deviated from these beliefs had no place in the world to come. Thus, believers could separate themselves from nonbelievers, and even persecute heretics, with some degree of self-righteousness.

Rambam's attempt to harmonize the Torah's teachings with Aristotelian philosophy rings false—and unnecessary—to modern readers. Although his efforts were heroic and relevant to the intellectual and spiritual conditions of his time, they seem dated and somewhat irrelevant to us. With Rambam, we can believe that the Torah teaches Truth and that its teachings are not in conflict with rationally proven truth—but we may be more skeptical about what is a "rationally proven truth"; various philosophical and scientific "truths" of one generation have been later shown to be flawed or incorrect by subsequent generations. Instead of pinning the truth of Torah to some particular philosophical or scientific "truths," we need the intellectual flexibility to deal with these "truths" in a nondogmatic manner.

The lasting lesson of Rambam's approach to the Bible is not his particular reconciliations between Torah and philosophy, but his methodology. Rambam has taught us that the Torah must be read intelligently and reasonably, without ascribing literal truth to each word or phrase. We need to have the literary and philosophical tact to know when the Bible is to be taken literally and when it is to be understood in a metaphorical, symbolic manner. This obviously is not an exact science, and different readers may come to different ways of understanding each text. Human reason is vital to a proper reading of the Bible, and we are obligated not to suspect our rational faculties when contemplating the texts and truths of Holy Scripture.

Spinoza's approach, while discounting supernatural revelation of the Bible, has much to teach even the traditionally religious student of Bible. For Spinoza, the Bible—even if it is not a divinely revealed work—is a powerful record of the strivings of the Israelites toward the Divine. The Bible's essence is the teaching of righteousness: love of God and of one's fellow human being.

The great nineteenth-century English writer Matthew Arnold drew on the teachings of Spinoza in regard to the Bible. In underscoring the Bible's significance, he wrote:

> And as long as the world lasts, all who want to make progress in righteousness will come to Israel for inspiration, as to the people who have had the sense for righteousness most glowing and strongest; and in hearing and reading the words Israel has uttered for us, carers for conduct will find a flow and a force they could find nowhere else.[21]

We bring our own preconceived notions to the biblical text. If we start with the assumption that it is a divinely revealed document, we find infinite wisdom and power in its words. We struggle to understand each word, each narrative, each law. The deeper we probe, the closer we come to the divine will, and hence to ultimate Truth. Those of a kabbalistic bent find hidden mysteries and coded messages in the Bible. Those of a philosophical bent find profound philosophical insights. Readers who assume, however, that the Bible is simply a collection of tales and statutes of ancient Israelites will not search for—and therefore rarely find—the deep layers of meaning in the text. The Bible, in this case, carries no more significance or Truth than do other writings of ancient peoples.

Since the Bible has proved its spiritual and literary profundity for the past thousands of years, it behooves us to read it carefully and thoughtfully. It should not be studied as a storybook or as an example of ancient folklore and traditions. Rather, it should be studied as a source of wisdom to guide us in our lives today. To take issue with Matthew Arnold's analysis, the Bible is neither mere literature, nor mere dogma; it is a profound record of the spiritual relationship between its characters and God. A sensitive reader will enter the text and feel the personal relationship with the Almighty.

4

DIVINE PROVIDENCE

The Hebrew Bible and classical rabbinic literature take it for granted that God plays a direct and active role in human affairs. Divine providence is an unquestioned truth. God rewards people for their good deeds and punishes them for their sins, sometimes in this world and sometimes in the world to come. He performs miracles. He communicates with human beings through prophecy.

Although providence, reward-and-punishment, miracles, and prophecy are all general principles of faith, we do not—and cannot—know exactly how they operate. These matters are in the realm of God; we can only understand these concepts in a vague, impressionistic manner.

The Grades of Providence

Some rabbinic sages taught that God's active providence extends to everything in the universe. Nothing happens anywhere except with God's knowledge and concurrence. Rambam offered a more nuanced view:

> But I believe that providence is consequent upon the intellect and attached to it. For providence can only come from an intelligent being, from One who is an intellect perfect with a

supreme perfection, than which there is no higher. Accordingly,
everyone with whom something of this overflow is united, will
be reached by providence to the extent to which he is reached
by the intellect.[1]

For Rambam, providence is an "overflow" from the perfect divine intellect, and it attaches itself to the intellect of human beings. God also
keeps an eye on nonhuman forms of life as well as the inanimate
world, but His active providence relates to human beings according to
their individual intellects. Providence is graded: On the highest level,
it relates to humans with the most developed intellects. It then diminishes in relation to humans with lesser intellects, then diminishes further in relation to animal and plant life, and then descends to the
lowest grade in relation to inanimate objects. Rambam does not believe
that "this particular leaf has fallen because of a providence watching
over it; nor that this spider has devoured this fly because God has now
decreed and willed something concerning individuals."[2]

Rambam thought that God created the world and implanted scientific principles to maintain its operation. The sages taught that
"everything follows its natural course."[3] When they said that humans
rise and sit down in accordance with the will of God, "their meaning
was that, when man was first created, his nature was so determined
that rising up and sitting down were to be optional to him; but they
did not mean that God wills at any special moment that man should
or should not get up."[4] In a general sense, we may understand all natural phenomena as expressing the will of God, since they conform to
the laws of nature, which God created. It is incorrect, though, to view
God as actively involved in willing each and every phenomenon in the
universe.

When it comes to providential concern for human beings,
Rambam asserts:

If a man's thought is free from distraction, if he apprehends
Him, may He be exalted, in the right way and rejoices in what
he apprehends, that individual can never be afflicted with evil

of any kind. For he is with God and God is with him. When, however, he abandons Him, may He be exalted, and is thus separated from God and God separated from him, he becomes in consequence of this a target for every evil that may happen to befall him. For the thing that necessarily brings about providence and deliverance from the sea of chance consists in that intellectual overflow.[5]

If a human being's intellect is deeply and thoroughly attached to God, then the person participates in God's intellect and is thus subject to God's providence.

However, few human beings can attain such a lofty level—and virtually none can maintain such a level constantly. Thus, says Rambam, human beings become subject to the vagaries of nature as they become "disconnected" from the intimacy of their relationship with God.

The issue of divine providence affects the way we interpret events in our lives. If we contract an illness or suffer a setback, does this indicate a divine punishment for a sin? Or should a negative phenomenon simply be viewed as a sign that we have strayed from total connection with God's intellect and are now subject to the laws of nature? Indeed, this latter option seems to be the most likely. It is quite evident that people contract illnesses or suffer setbacks regardless of their moral and intellectual stature. When disease spreads, it does not distinguish between the righteous and the wicked; so why should one assume that a person's affliction is anything other than a "normal" aspect of natural law?

In his *Mishneh Torah*, Rambam notes that it is a positive Torah commandment to cry out at a time of suffering for the community. Trumpets are sounded, prayers are uttered, and repentance is called for. If people say that the sufferings are merely a fact of nature, chance occurrences that do not warrant crying out to God for help, this is a mean-spirited and cruel way of thinking. Such a view does not lead people to repent or to come closer to God. If they persist in seeing these things as natural happenings, then God will distance Himself from them and leave them to the workings of nature. He will withhold His providential care from them.[6]

Yet, when Rambam discusses the individual's response to suffering later in that same chapter, he writes:

> Just as the community should fast because of distress, so too each individual should fast over his distress. How is this done? If one has a sick person or someone lost in the wilderness or locked in prison—he should fast on behalf of [the victim] and pray for [divine] compassion over him.[7]

In this passage, unlike the passage dealing with communal distress, Rambam does not suggest that the suffering was the result of sin or that repentance was called for. Rabbi Haim David Halevy, in noting this difference in Rambam's language, has suggested that communal suffering should be seen as a divine chastisement; but individual suffering could well be the result of normally operating natural laws—not punishment for sin.

> If we know for certain the cause of the accident that happened to a person, we have no need specifically to seek [explanations by searching for] decrees and punishments. It is quite likely that [the setback] was the result of chance or of carelessness.... But when the cause of the accident is not clear enough, and there is no certainty that it was the result of human error, then it is possible that it did come as a punishment....[8]

In his *Guide*, Rambam explains providence as being contingent on one's intellectual attachment to God. When this attachment is deficient (or temporarily has lapsed), then a person is subject to the laws of nature. This can correspond with Rambam's description in the *Mishneh Torah* of how an individual should react to suffering. He should not necessarily jump to the conclusion that his discomfort is a direct and immediate punishment for some particular sin; rather, it might simply be the result of chance, carelessness, or the diminution of divine providence due to the quite normal deficiency in one's intellectual attachment to the Almighty.

In the case of a public disaster, though, Rambam states that the community should consider the real possibility that the misfortune was brought on by communal sin. They should not brush it off as being the result of chance or natural causes. Still, even in the case of public disasters, Rambam does not suggest that anyone can make a definite, unequivocal correlation between a particular sin and its "punishment." Rather, he suggests that it is in the community's interest to interpret the disaster as a sign of divine displeasure (whether or not it is in fact a punishment) and to engage in prayer, fasting, and repentance. These are valuable ways for a community to cope with tragedy, regardless of its cause.

Rambam would scorn those "religious" spokesmen who confidently blame individuals and communities for specific sins for which they are being punished. How do they know the ultimate causes? Who gave them access to God's inscrutable will? How dare they be so arrogant as to speak with certainty about matters that only God can know? Although calling for prayer, fasting, and repentance is always in order, no one (unless granted the gift of prophecy) has the right or authority to characterize any tragedy as a divine punishment for a particular sin.

While Rambam lists among his thirteen principles of faith that God rewards the righteous and punishes the wicked, we do not know what rewards and punishments are meted out in this world and which are reserved for the world to come. In fact, we cannot even know with certainty what things in this world are in the category of rewards and which are in the category of punishments. Sometimes good things happen—that ultimately turn out to our disadvantage. Sometimes bad things happen—that ultimately redound to our benefit. Sometimes we may receive reward in this world—which is then subtracted from the far greater reward we would have had in the world to come. Sometimes we may receive punishment in this world—which will spare us from suffering worse punishment in the next world. In short, this is an area of discussion that is entirely beyond human ken. This is in the province of God—and is best left there.

The ideal religious person serves God with no ulterior motive of receiving reward or avoiding punishment, but rather from pure love of God. The Bible and rabbinic literature refer to rewards and punishments as a means of influencing the unsophisticated masses. By analogy, a child is given candies and toys as rewards for various achievements. As the child matures, though, he or she comes to realize the intrinsic value of these achievements and does not need to be "bribed" with treats. The performance of the right thing is its own reward. Likewise, people of simple faith must be promised rewards (and threatened with punishments); the hope is that they will ultimately mature spiritually so that they will not need these external incentives, but will obey the Torah for its own sake.[9]

The ideal religious person affirms God's providence but does not attempt to provide authoritative explanations of how God's providence operates. When bad things happen to individuals or communities, it is proper to pray, fast, and, repent, but it is wrong—and highly presumptuous—to state that the tragedy is a direct punishment for a specific sin.

Grappling with Free Will

If human beings are rewarded or punished for their actions, this presupposes that they have the free will to decide how to act. If their actions were in fact predetermined, then they could not have done anything other than what they did. They could not be held morally responsible for things done entirely out of their personal control.

Rambam understood that free will is a foundational principle of religious faith. Without free will, human beings are merely programmed robots who are worthy of neither reward nor punishment. In the *Mishneh Torah*, Rambam states:

> Free will is bestowed on every human being. If a person desires to turn toward the good way and be righteous, he has the power to do so. If a person wishes to turn toward the evil way and be wicked, he is at liberty to do so.... Man, of himself and

by the exercise of his own intelligence and reason, knows what is good and what is evil....[10]

However, a philosophical problem arises: If God is all-knowing, then He already knows what a person will "choose" to do. Since His knowledge is infallible, a person really has no free choice; whatever he or she "chooses" has already been known, that is, determined, by a perfectly omniscient God. Rambam dismisses this argument curtly, saying that we should pay no attention to "the fools of the nations of the world" who believe in predestination. Rather, we know that God does not predetermine our choices and that we have free will to be as righteous or as wicked as we choose. How do we know this? Rambam does not offer philosophical proofs. Rather, he notes that God's wisdom is far beyond anything we can comprehend. Since the Bible, which is inspired by God, informs us that we have free will, then indeed we do have free will. If we cannot solve the philosophical problem of how we can have free will if God knows everything, that is the result of our inability to understand God's knowledge and God's ways.[11]

Striving for Prophecy

For Rambam, the greatest human achievement is to reach the level of becoming a prophet. Prophecy is attained only by a select few individuals who have reached the highest level of intellectual and spiritual perfection. Even if a person has climbed to the highest levels, this does not guarantee that he or she will receive prophecy. God may intervene to prevent the person from gaining prophecy. "For we believe that it may happen that one who is fit for prophecy and prepared for it should not become a prophet, namely, on account of the divine will. To my mind this is like all the miracles and takes the same course as they."[12]

Rambam stresses the need for each individual to strive for the highest possible degree of intellectual excellence. Although they may not be graced with the miraculous gift of prophecy, they will nonetheless come closer to God and be more subject to His providence. In his introduction to the *Shemonah Perakim*, he writes:

Know that to live according to this standard is to arrive at a
very high degree of perfection, which, in consequence of the
difficulty of attainment, only a few, after long and continuous
perseverance on the paths of virtue, have succeeded in reaching. If there be found a man who has accomplished this—that
is one who exerts all the faculties of his soul, and directs them
toward the sole ideal of comprehending God, using all his
powers of mind and body, be they great or small, for the attainment of that which leads directly or indirectly to virtue—I
would place him in a rank not lower than that of the prophets.
Such a man, before he does a single act or deed, considers and
reflects whether or not it will bring him to that goal, and if it
will, then, and then only, does he do it.

Miracles and Faith

The Bible describes numerous miracles performed by God. These miracles seem to defy the laws of nature. If God established eternal laws
of science, is He bound to let these laws function unobstructed? If so,
how can He perform miracles that violate His own scientific laws? Or,
did God create scientific laws but reserve for Himself the right to
change the rules as needed?

Rambam's general approach is to view natural laws as the will of
God that operate in a fixed, eternal way. Nonetheless, God does have
the power to perform miracles, although He does so very rarely. When
biblical or rabbinic literature speaks of God's miracles, these references
can often be understood as events that have a natural explanation or
that were figurative, hyperbolic descriptions of unusual (although natural) events. People who are ignorant of the laws of nature may
describe a phenomenon as miraculous when, in fact, it is actually a
normal manifestation of nature's laws.

Rambam makes his point very clearly:

They [the ignorant] like nothing better and, in their silliness,
enjoy nothing more than to set the Torah and reason at oppo-

site ends, and to move everything far from the explicable. So
they claim it to be a miracle, and they shrink from identifying
it as a natural incident, whether it is something that happened
in the past and is recorded, or something predicted to happen
in the future. But I try to reconcile the Torah and reason, and
wherever possible consider all things as of the natural order.
Only when something is explicitly identified as a miracle, and
reinterpretation of it cannot be accommodated, only then I feel
forced to grant that it is a miracle.[13]

Sometimes, biblical miracles were performed through natural phenomena, but the miraculous aspect is that these phenomena happened at exactly the right time and place. Sometimes the miracle
was a natural phenomenon, for example, the plague of locusts in
Egypt, that manifested itself to an unusual degree. There were also
miracles that were essentially natural phenomena but extended for
a remarkable duration. If the Bible speaks of miracles that defy the
laws of nature (such as Aaron's rod turning into a snake), such miracles did not endure, but were ephemeral events for a particular
reason.

In the *Guide*, Rambam notes that our sages themselves believed
that miracles were also, in a certain respect, part of nature. "They say
that when God created that which exists and stamped upon it the
existing natures, He put into these natures that all the miracles that
occurred would be produced in them at the time when they
occurred."[14] In other words, God implanted these miracles into nature
from the very outset of creation; these "miraculous" phenomena were
really intrinsic to nature and would manifest themselves on a timed-
release basis at some later date.

In downplaying the supernatural quality of biblical miracles,
Rambam attempted to keep religion on as rational a basis as possible.
Miracles, for the most part, did not violate natural law but functioned
within these laws, albeit in unusual ways. Rambam objected to the
simplistic view that God performed miracles in order to impress people with His power or to prove the veracity of His providence. Rambam

also repudiated those who, in their ignorance, were quick to define unusual natural phenomena as being miracles.

For Rambam, Judaism's faith is not based on miracles. The people of Israel did not follow Moses because of the miracles he performed. Faith based on transient miracles is flimsy; the believer in such miracles may ultimately suspect that they were not miracles at all, but only the result of magic or illusion. Indeed, the Bible records various miracles after which those who witnessed them still continued to sin and to act rebelliously. The miracles obviously did not convince them of anything.

On what, then, is the faith of Israel based? Rambam explains, "And how did [the Israelites] come to have faith in him [Moses]? At the revelation at Mount Sinai, where our own eyes saw and our own ears heard the fire and the thunders and the flames. Moses went into the cloud and the voice [of God] spoke to him—and we heard…."[15] True faith for the Israelites emerged from their own personal experience—not from miracles.

For those of us who live in later generations, faith is supported by the biblical account of the revelation at Mount Sinai. We trust the biblical and prophetic tradition that records the eyewitness report of the revelation by hundreds of thousands of our ancestors. But beyond faith supported by this ancient tradition, we each find our own faith in God based on our intellectual perception of Him in our own lives. We do not merely "inherit" faith in God, but must each find our own way to Him through our reason, emotion, and experience.

Spinoza: Debunking Free Will in Favor of Nature

For Spinoza, there is no particular value in the discussion of providence, free will, reward and punishment, prophecy, and miracles. Since God is bound to His own nature, He cannot act in any other way than He does act, that is, through the laws of nature. God is not free to intercede with or change natural law. He does not give rewards or punishments, does not communicate with human beings through prophecy, and does not (and cannot) do miracles.

Dr. Jonathan Israel has written that "no other element of Spinoza's philosophy provoked as much consternation and outrage in his own time as his sweeping denial of miracles and the supernatural."[16] Spinoza believed that attributing everything to the active will of God was "the sanctuary for ignorance."[17] He writes: "I have taken miracles and ignorance as equivalents because those who endeavor to establish the existence of God and religion from miracles are seeking to prove the obscure through the more obscure, of which they are quite ignorant."[18]

Spinoza argued that God does not act from freedom of the will and that things could not have been produced by God except in the way they have been produced.[19] Since God is perfect, everything reflects that perfection and could not be other than it is.

Human beings feel themselves to be free, yet their freedom actually consists in their acting according to their natures. Spinoza offers an example of a stone that was impelled with a fixed quantity of force. It will necessarily continue to move until the force of the impulsion has ceased. So is every single thing "necessarily determined by an external cause to exist and to act in a fixed and determinate way."[20] Let us posit that the impelled stone thinks that it continues in motion through its own free will. We know that this is not true. So it is with human freedom that "men are conscious of their desire and unaware of the causes by which they are determined."[21] A baby thinks that it freely desires milk; an angry child thinks that it freely seeks revenge; a frightened crowd thinks that it freely chooses to flee danger. In fact, though, this is "imaginary human freedom,"[22] just as an impelled stone thinks it is freely choosing to move.

Spinoza's critics argued that if human beings indeed lacked free will, they could thereby escape taking personal responsibility for evil deeds. They could act without restraint and simply claim to be acting according to their fixed natures. The structure of morality would collapse.

To this, Spinoza responded that human beings should be righteous for the sake of righteousness, not because they fear punishment. "For my own part I refrain, or try to refrain, from such [evil] behavior because it is directly opposed to my particular nature, and would cause me to stray from the love and knowledge of God."[23] In his *Ethics*, Spinoza asserts that "blessedness is not the reward of virtue, but is virtue itself; nor do we delight in blessedness because we restrain our lusts, but, on the contrary, because we delight in it, therefore are we able to restrain them."[24]

On the one hand, Spinoza thought that human freedom was, in a sense, illusory—that humans necessarily acted according to their natures. Each human being—like everything else in the natural world—has a "conatus," an inner drive toward self-fulfillment that has been planted within. "The endeavor [conatus] wherewith each thing endeavors to persist in its own being is nothing more than the actual essence of the thing itself."[25]

On the other hand, Spinoza seems to have left some room for free will, in that humans have the power to delight in blessedness and restrain their lusts. However we untangle the strands of his writings on human freedom, the bottom line is that Spinoza rejected the classical religious view of a God who metes out rewards and punishments for freely chosen actions of human beings.

Which Will It Be?

If we cling to the domain of rational philosophy, Spinoza's arguments are cogent. The "God of the philosophers," as espoused by Spinoza, is not a glorified human being, but an impersonal, vast power that operates according to its own eternal nature. Although Rambam was attracted to the "God of the philosophers," he could not fully accept the consequences of this concept, since the experience of revelation teaches that God does interact with humanity and does have the power to intercede in nature. Rambam, thus, reached a complex position. He affirmed prophecy and miracles—but limited these phenomena to extremely rare cases. Spinoza saw no need to take this compromise position but carried reason to its logical conclusion: the God of the philosophers is fixed and determined, neutral and without an active will that can "change" the natural world. For him, humans act due to the causes that impel them to act.

Spinoza's argument, though, can be turned against him. How can he be so sure that the original causes can be comprehended by human reason? Isn't that just as much a leap of faith as believing that a "personal" God set things into motion and can exert an active will? For example, his view of God entails the belief that the laws of nature are fixed and immutable. But how can one prove this? Since the human mind cannot encompass billions of years of existence, how can it be sure that the laws of nature today always operated in the past in the same manner or that they will always operate in this manner forever? This is an assumption, based on the belief that our reason is reliable, even infallible; but this itself is circular reasoning, since we cannot prove in the first place that our reason is reliable!

Rambam's recognition of the limitations of reason is just as important to his religious philosophy as his recognition of the importance of reason. His willingness to rely on faith in the biblical and rabbinic tradition need not be seen as a "compromise" with reason, but as an open-eyed admission of the limits of reason. Since divine revelation is a fact of history, thought Rambam, there was little point in locking ourselves into the straightjacket of reason. We need to draw on the truths of revelation as a complement to the truths of philosophy.

Spinoza's view of God, humanity, and the universe rests on the perfect ability of reason to comprehend Truth. If his axioms are accepted and we follow them to their logical conclusions, the result is a God who lacks free will, who does not (and cannot) intercede with nature and humanity, who does not "command," and to whom it is pointless to pray. Although Spinoza seems to leave a bit of room for human free will, his overall view is that human life is essentially predetermined and could be no different from what it is.

Good and Evil

Religious thinkers have long been troubled by the problem of "good and evil." If God is perfect and good, why does the world contain so much evil—suffering, disease, natural catastrophes? Why is there no seeming correlation between righteous people and rewards; wicked people and punishments?

Spinoza's answer was this: Things are as they are and could be no other way. There is no point in speaking of "good" or "evil." We simply must do our best to cope with neutral reality and not expect rewards or punishments to be linked causally to our behavior patterns.

Rambam, unwilling to attribute evil to God, noted that many of the "evils" we experience are caused by fellow human beings and cannot be blamed on God. Even in the domain of "natural evil," Rambam suggested that God does not create evil directly; rather, evil should be understood as an absence of good.

> All His acts, may He be exalted, are an absolute good; for He only produces being and all being is a good. On the other hand, all the evils are privations…. Even the existence of this inferior matter, whose manner of being it is to be a concomitant of privation entailing death and all evils, all this is also good in view of the perpetuity of generations and the permanence of being through succession.[26]

The prophet Isaiah was not reluctant to attribute evil to God. He stated candidly that God "forms light and creates darkness; He makes peace and creates evil" (Isaiah 45:7). By comprehending the universe as a unity, containing light and darkness, good and evil—all created by God—Isaiah puts the issue of good and evil into a different framework. He does not attempt to eliminate the double bind engendered by holding the two seemingly irreconcilable positions that God is perfect and good and that evil exists. Rather, he sees these "opposites" not as being in opposition to each other, but as part of a grand natural balance and harmony. Whatever "evils" we perceive in nature are only evils in our eyes, but not objectively so. Disintegration and death are part of nature and are positive "goods" when viewed in the long scheme of things. Life and death, growth and decay, light and darkness—all are part of a divinely ordained balance.[27]

The Bible states that God saw the world He created and declared it to be very good. Commenting on Genesis 1:31, Rabbi Moses ben

Nahman (Nahmanides) relates an ancient Jewish notion that God was pleased that "the order was very properly arranged since the evil is needed for the preservation of the good, just as it is said 'to everything there is a season, and a time to every purpose under the heaven' [Ecclesiastes 3:1]." That is, evil is a necessary feature of the universe.

If we study the natural world, we find many things that appear cruel. We find mutations and defects. These things are not mistakes but are somehow necessary for the balance of nature as a whole. For example, lions eat zebras. To the zebra being torn apart by the lion, this system does not necessarily seem fair. Yet lions must eat zebras as part of the natural order of things. If, out of compassion, we decided to protect zebras from lions, lions would die of starvation, and zebras would multiply to a level that would endanger their own survival. Nature has its own wisdom, its own set of checks and balances. The universe contains peace and harmony, but also eruptions and disharmony. Both dimensions are part of the same reality and are part of God's creation. They should be understood as mutually dependent phenomena.

Nature acts in a neutral fashion. When earthquakes or other natural disasters strike, all are equally subject to the consequences, with no distinction made between good and bad people.

The above discussion leads to the following conclusions: (1) God has created the universe with all its features; (2) natural phenomena are not intrinsically good or evil—we use these adjectives based on our own experience of the natural phenomena; (3) the natural world that God created is neutral, making no distinctions based on the righteousness or wickedness of people; and (4) God can defy the laws of nature in a miraculous way but does so very seldomly, and we do not have a right to expect miracles on our behalf.

The Talmud (*Hagigah* 14b) tells of four rabbis who entered the *pardes*, the realm of metaphysical speculation. One of the problems that apparently troubled them was how an all-perfect and good God could allow evil to occur. This pursuit of God's mysterious ways led to serious consequences. One of the rabbis died. One lost his mind. One—Elisha ben Avuyah—became a heretic, having concluded that "there is no justice, there is no Judge." He could not reconcile the double bind, so he decided that there was no satisfactory resolution. Rabbi Akiva, though, entered the *pardes* in peace and left it in peace. Confronted by the same problem that plagued his three colleagues, Rabbi Akiva came to realize that the problem itself was based on mistaken assumptions. Like Isaiah, Rabbi Akiva saw the universe as a harmonious unity, in which God has balanced various qualities that we call good and evil, light and darkness. Evil and good are not mutually exclusive opposites, but exist in a necessary relationship with each other. If there were no darkness, light would have no meaning. If there were no evil, good would have no meaning.

It is impossible for human beings to have a comprehensive view of the universe, since we are finite and intellectually limited. Only God, who is beyond time and space, can encompass the mystical unity of the universe. The scientist Lewis Thomas offered an interesting observation:

> The individual parts played by other instrumentalists—crickets or earthworms, for instance—may not have the sound of music by themselves, but we hear them out of context. If we could listen to them all at once, fully orchestrated in their immense ensemble, we might become aware of the counterpoint, the balance of tones and timbres and harmonics, the sonorities. The recorded songs of the humpback whale, filled with tensions and resolutions, ambiguities and illusions, incomplete, can be listened to as a part of music, like an isolated section in an orchestra. If we had better hearing, and could discern the descants of seabirds, the rhythmical tympani of schools of mollusks, or even the distant harmonics of midges hanging over meadows in the sun, the combined sound might lift us off our feet.[28]

What we perceive in tiny fragments, God encompasses in toto. This is an awesome and humbling thought.

Both Rambam and Spinoza recognized that much of the evil in our world is not due to natural disasters, but to human cruelty. Rambam himself suffered from the fanatical Muslim invaders of Spain who forcibly converted non-Muslims or caused them to flee the country, as did Rambam's own family. Spinoza's family and community included many who were persecuted by the Spanish and Portuguese Inquisitions, many who were tortured and robbed by a fanatically self-righteous church. Neither philosopher was unaware of the hatred, violence, and greed that characterize so many human beings. Both believed that it was within human power to live righteous and compassionate lives. Both thought that blessedness was a consequence of virtue.

It is remarkable that these two thinkers—both of whom suffered directly from the cruelty of fellow human beings—did not give up on humanity. Rather, they developed philosophies that rested on the assumption that human beings could achieve righteousness and blessedness through lives of intellectual and spiritual strivings.

This fundamental optimism of both Rambam and Spinoza seems particularly relevant in our modern era. The twentieth century witnessed two world wars, the Holocaust of European Jewry, and numerous smaller wars and violent revolutions. It would be easy enough for an objective observer to declare humanity to be morally bankrupt, without possibility of redemption. In today's world, we seem condemned to a never-ending cycle of hatred and warfare. We have access to more destructive weapons than ever existed in the past. Nuclear technology is falling into the hands of dangerous regimes and possibly even of terrorist groups. Chemical and biological warfare loom on the horizon.

Given humanity's terrible record, it is possible to sink into a helpless depression and to lose faith in the ability of human beings to change the status quo. Rambam and Spinoza, though, call on each of us to strive for a meditative, spiritual, and blessed life. In spite of all the evils that exist in our world, we each have the power to perfect ourselves. In this personal striving, we are able to find personal blessedness and meaning. As more human beings attain intellectual love of God, humanity as a whole moves closer to its own perfection.

5

THE ORAL TORAH AND RABBINIC TRADITION

On a basic philosophical level, Rambam and Spinoza share much common ground. They diverge significantly, though, when it comes to the truth of biblical revelation and rabbinic tradition. Whereas Spinoza did not recognize a source of Truth other than reason, Rambam believed that revelation (the Bible) is also a valid source of Truth. Spinoza did not accept the "Oral Torah," the rabbinic tradition of understanding and applying the teachings of Scripture, whereas Rambam laid great stress on the authenticity of the rabbinic tradition.

In his introduction to the *Mishneh Torah*, Rambam writes that all the commandments of the Torah were given to Moses at Sinai, together with their interpretations. Moses made written copies of the Torah for each of the Israelite tribes, as well as one master copy, which was placed in the holy ark; however, the Oral Torah was not put into writing. Rather, Moses explained it to Joshua and the elders and all the people of Israel. Rambam underscores the accuracy of the transmission of the Oral Torah: Moses taught it to his court of seventy elders. Elazar, Pinehas, and Joshua received the tradition directly from Moses. Joshua transmitted the Oral Torah to many elders, and they in turn transmitted it—generation after generation—to the prophets and sages who followed. Rambam lists the authoritative sages who were the receivers and transmitters of the Oral Torah.

Rambam spells out the process of transmission in his introduction to his commentary on the Mishnah. Each commandment that Moses received from God at Sinai was accompanied by its oral interpretation. Moses taught each commandment, together with its interpretation, to Aaron, Elazar, and Itamar, the seventy elders, and then to the entire congregation. Everyone heard the explanation four different times, and then people studied and reviewed what they had learned. They kept personal notes on what they had heard. If people were uncertain about a law or its interpretation, they asked Moses, who clarified it for them. After Moses died, Joshua—who had learned directly from Moses for many years—became the ultimate authority for explaining the commandments according to the oral tradition.

The Oral Torah was preserved with great care, so that its teachings were clear and undisputed. If a controversy did arise, it was immediately addressed by the authoritative body of elders, and they resolved the problem right away by majority vote.

Rambam lists five categories of Oral Torah. The first category, about which there never arose any controversies, consists of explanations of words and laws that might also have been derived through the use of hermeneutic principles. For example, when the Torah states "an eye for an eye" (Deuteronomy 19:21), this was unanimously understood to mean that the one who caused damage had to pay financial compensation for the eye—not that his own eye was to be taken out. Also, when the Torah refers to the "fruit of a beautiful tree" (Leviticus 23:40) that was to be taken on the Sukkot festival, it was always understood to refer to an *etrog* (citron) and not any other fruit. When the Torah states that "her hand shall be cut off" (Deuteronomy 25:12), this was always understood to mean that she had to pay damages, not that her hand was actually cut off. These are all examples of received interpretations about which no doubt ever arose as to the intent of Scripture, since we have an oral tradition going back to Moses as to how these verses are to be understood. If a sage pronounced a law and said that he had received it as a tradition going back to Moses, then no one had the right to dispute it.

The second category of Oral Torah consists of those laws that are called *halakha leMoshe miSinai*, laws that Moses received orally at Mount Sinai—and that could not have been discovered by means of hermeneutical principles. Examples of this are that tefillin must be black, that a person must eat the volume of an egg in order to be obligated by Torah to recite Grace after Meals, and that there can be no interpositions that would prevent the water of the ritual bath to reach all parts of the body. These laws cannot be contested by anyone but are accepted entirely on their status as laws going back to Moses. We could not have figured out these laws on our own through the use of reason and traditional principles of interpretation.

These first two categories presume that when Moses received the Written Torah, he had to know what the words meant and how they were to be applied. It was necessary for God to give him many details beyond the literal text of the Torah, to enable him to teach the Israelites how to implement the Torah's commandments. This Oral Torah was transmitted with perfect fidelity and was maintained intact throughout all the generations.

The third category consists of laws that were derived by our sages through their power of reason and interpretation. Although rooted in a careful reading of the biblical text, these derived laws were sometimes disputed among the sages. Different scholars came to different conclusions based on their own reasoning and analysis. When there was a difference of opinion, the sages would make a definitive ruling based on majority opinion.

In the *Mishneh Torah*, Rambam writes:

> The Great Court in Jerusalem is the essence of the Oral Torah. They are the pillars of instruction from whom statutes and judgments issue forth for the entire people of Israel.... Whoever believes in Moses and in his Torah is obligated to make all of his religious acts dependent on [this court] and to rely on them.[1]

This category is far and away the largest segment of the Oral Torah. It is not based on specific information given to Moses by God. Rather, it is derived through the human wisdom of rabbis who interpreted Scripture according to traditional hermeneutical principles. The Torah itself instructs us to follow the teachings of the sages of each generation, thus giving divine sanction to the workings of this category of Oral Torah.

The fourth category of Oral Torah includes the laws established by the prophets and sages of each generation in order to safeguard the Torah. These decrees were put into place to keep the public away from transgressing Torah laws. For example, the Torah forbids eating, cooking, or benefiting from meat and milk together; the sages went a step further and forbade fowl with milk. If the public were allowed to eat fowl and milk, they might draw the erroneous conclusion that they could also eat meat and milk; they would not necessarily understand why they should differentiate between meat and fowl. Thus, by forbidding fowl and milk, the rabbis were preventing people from possibly transgressing the Torah law forbidding meat and milk. (Yet, not all rabbis agreed with this ordinance. Rabbi Yose haGelili permitted fowl and milk, and the people of his town followed his ruling [Talmud, *Shabbat* 130a].) Once a prophetic or rabbinic decree was accepted throughout the Jewish people (as the prohibition against fowl and milk ultimately was), then it was binding on all Jews as part of the Oral Torah.

The fifth category includes ordinances that the sages instituted for the better functioning of society. It also includes customs that the sages established to enhance religious life. The Torah granted the sages of each generation the right and responsibility to implement usages that improved the communal, commercial, and ritual life of the community.

Rambam ascribes formal authority to the *Tannaim* and *Amoraim* (sages of the Talmud), not because they were intrinsically superior to sages of later generations, but because they were the ones whose opinions form the basis of the Talmud. In matters of Jewish law, latter-day rabbis had to defer to the rabbis whose words were recorded in the Talmud. In non-halakhic matters, such as science, medicine, and homiletical insights, the Talmudic sages enjoy prestige, but not binding authority.[2]

With the dispersion of Jews throughout the world, the Talmud became the de facto focus of halakhic inquiry and authority. Throughout the generations—and to our own day—halakha is determined through an analysis of Talmudic texts. Numerous commentaries and halakhic codes have been composed by rabbis, but all derive their ultimate status from their fidelity to Talmudic sources.

Without a central Great Court to legislate and interpret Torah law for the entire Jewish people, rabbinic authorities emerged in all eras and wherever Jewish communities flourished. Consequently, halakha—even though based on the Talmud—became subject to multiple interpretations and applications. Halakhic rulings varied depending on time and place and the prevailing intellectual currents. Rambam attempted to create a unified basis of halakha for world Jewry by composing his monumental code of Jewish law, the *Mishneh Torah*. However, this work almost immediately became subject to glosses and commentaries; with the passage of time, other codes of law also entered into the halakhic canon. The result has been a tremendous diversification within the halakhic tradition, albeit within boundaries justified by Talmudic interpretations.

Since the rabbinic tradition became so large and diverse, the notion of an authoritative Oral Torah became more complicated to defend. How could one argue for an unbroken tradition dating back to Moses if there were differences of opinion on almost every aspect of Jewish law? The general answer was provided by Rambam himself. A certain number of laws, upon which there has never been any controversy, definitely date back to the original Oral Torah given to Moses at Mount Sinai. However, the bulk of halakha should be understood not as an absolutely fixed body of laws, but as a process based on ancient principles of interpretation given to Moses at Sinai. Indeed, Rambam makes it clear that each Great Court could review—and overturn—decisions of previous Great Courts under certain circumstances.[3]

Just as the Great Court in Jerusalem was the basic agency of the Oral Law, so the leading sages of subsequent generations filled this role for their communities. When we also add the various local ordinances and customs that emerged over the centuries, the category of Oral Torah is vast.

Challenging the Oral Torah

As we have seen, the authority of the Oral Torah rests on the authority of the sages of each generation, going back to Moses. For Rambam, as for normative Jewish tradition, the Oral Torah is divinely sanctioned and is an intrinsic element in Judaism.

At the same time, the validity and authority of the Oral Torah have been contested throughout Jewish history. In antiquity, the Sadducees insisted on following the laws as recorded in the Torah but did not accept the Oral Torah as taught by the rabbis. This position was in contrast to the Pharisees, who vigorously upheld the authority of the Oral Torah and viewed the rabbinic tradition as essential for understanding and applying the laws of the Written Torah. Following the destruction of the Second Temple by the Romans in 70 CE, the rabbinic leadership in Israel and the Diaspora saw themselves as heirs of the Pharisaic tradition. The Sadducees faded from history. With the redaction of the Talmud, mostly accomplished by the sixth century CE, the traditions of the Pharisees continued to shape Judaism through the modern period.

However, the Pharisaic view of the Oral Torah did not go unchallenged. Beginning in eighth-century Babylonia, the Karaite sect stressed the divine nature of the Written Torah but rejected the rabbinic/Talmudic tradition. Saadyah Gaon (882–942), the leading rabbinic sage of his time, wrote polemical works aimed against the Karaite views. Rambam, whose community in Egypt included a Karaite minority, was a strong opponent of Karaism and the foremost advocate of rabbinic tradition. Yet, although intellectually opposed to the Karaites, he called for a compassionate concern for those raised in the Karaite community. Even though they held false beliefs, they were children and grandchildren of people who pushed them into these beliefs. "Therefore," Rambam argued, "it is fitting to bring them back in repentance and to draw them closer with words of peace until they return to the bastion of the Torah."[4]

Saadyah Gaon, Rambam, and other medieval rabbis confronted the Karaite challenges, but the Karaites were not the last group to question the authority of the Oral Law. A significant opposition emerged in the sixteenth and seventeenth centuries among Iberian crypto-Jews who were returning to Judaism in Amsterdam and other centers of Western Sephardic life.

The Converso Phenomenon

In 1391, anti-Jewish riots erupted throughout Spain. Many Jews were murdered; many accepted Catholicism under duress in order to save their lives; many fled Spain to reestablish themselves in safer lands. Of those who converted to Christianity, a significant group maintained their Jewishness in secret, as crypto-Jews. These people, known as conversos or New Christians, still had access to and ongoing relations with the existing Jewish communities in Spain.

In 1492, the Jews of Spain were given the choice of converting to Catholicism or being expelled. The fanatical Catholic rulers decided to purge their kingdom of Jews, so that the Jews would be unable to influence the New Christians. In 1497, open Jewish life came to an abrupt end in Portugal, where Jews again were compelled to convert under duress. While many thousands of Iberian Jews sought new homes in the Ottoman Empire, North Africa, and Europe, many remained in Spain and Portugal as New Christians—including those who practiced Judaism in secret.

During the sixteenth and seventeenth centuries, thousands of conversos found ways of fleeing Spain and Portugal in order to reclaim their identities as Jews. Important centers of ex-conversos developed in Amsterdam and other western European cities such as Hamburg, Venice, Livorno, Paris, Bordeaux, Bayonne, and London. During the seventeenth century, communities were established in the New World, including Curacao, Suriname, New Amsterdam/New York, and other cities and towns in the Americas.

The first generation of conversos had direct knowledge of Judaism, as they had lived openly as Jews prior to their forced conversions. But the subsequent generations were born and raised as Christians and had never experienced Jewish life openly. It is a phenomenon of the first significance that Jewish identity was able to survive for centuries under such adverse conditions.

The returning conversos, especially those who had been raised as Christians and had lived their entire lives as crypto-Jews, faced serious spiritual challenges upon reclaiming their Judaic roots.[5] While in Spain and Portugal, their knowledge of Judaism derived from family traditions, the Bible, and descriptions of Jewish practices that were publicized by the Inquisition. They were almost totally ignorant of the vast rabbinic tradition and did not know of a divinely authorized Oral Torah.

Because the returning conversos had a Bible-based understanding of Judaism, they needed to be taught the lessons of the Oral Torah. Books in basic Judaism were published in Spanish and Portuguese. The ex-conversos had to learn how Judaism was actually observed, which entailed coming to grips with the ancient, authoritative rabbinic traditions encapsulated in the Talmud and rabbinic literature.

For the most part, it seems that the returnees were amenable to accepting the teachings of Judaism as presented to them by their rabbis. They adopted the beliefs and observances that characterized Jewish religious life and became part of traditional Jewish communal life. Still, there were those who developed a skeptical approach to the Oral Torah and even to the Bible itself. Although Baruch Spinoza was the most famous heretic, he had been preceded by Uriel da Costa (1585–1640), who had also been excommunicated by the Amsterdam Jewish leaders, and who ultimately committed suicide. Da Costa and others were not ready to accept rabbinic authority uncritically.

That there was intellectual ferment within the ex-converso communities goes beyond the cases of da Costa and Spinoza. During the seventeenth century, a volume of uncertain authorship known as *Kol Sakhal* promoted heretical views held by some members of these communities.[6]

The major focus of the *Kol Sakhal* was to discredit the Oral Torah. This book presented what its author considered to be a rational approach to the principles of religion. It challenged the authenticity of the Oral Torah and the dominance of rabbinic authority. It offered a bitter critique of normative Jewish laws and practices.

This criticism could not go unanswered by the rabbinic leadership of the time. Rabbi Imanuel Aboab wrote a volume, *Nomologia* (published 1629–30), in which he argued forcefully for the authenticity of the Oral Torah. He demonstrated that the Bible could not be understood properly without an authoritative tradition of interpretation. He offered a description of the origin and chain of tradition of the Oral Torah, explaining the nature of the Talmud and subsequent rabbinic literature.[7]

Spinoza grew up in a place and at a time when spiritual life was in flux. Although the majority of Amsterdam's ex-converso community adopted traditional beliefs and observances, there were certainly pockets of doubters and outright deniers. The inquisitive mind of the young Spinoza was obviously attracted to the discussions surrounding the authenticity of the Bible and the Oral Torah. His rabbis were unable to answer his questions to his satisfaction. He became disaffected from Jewish religious tradition as taught by his teachers; the rest is history. After his being excommunicated from the Jewish community in 1656, Spinoza continued his life—seemingly unperturbed—and devoted himself to his philosophical pursuits.

In writing his *Theologico-Political Treatise*, Spinoza applied his philosophical rationalism to an analysis of the Bible, and he is viewed by many as the father of modern biblical criticism. If Spinoza debunked the divine authority of the Bible itself, it was not a big step to deny divine influence on the Oral Torah. He believed that the rabbinic tradition was entirely man-made and, while containing some valuable qualities, was full of rationalization, intellectual errors, and plain nonsense. In Spinoza's view, the Talmud and codes of Jewish law served the function of maintaining an orderly society and were concerned with obedience rather than Truth.

Spinoza's aversion to the Oral Torah may have been exacerbated by his own bad experiences with his rabbis and teachers. If these very fallible human beings were supposed to be the links in the chain of oral tradition, then that chain could not be very strong. Indeed, Spinoza's anti-clericalism was applied not only to the rabbis, but perhaps even more forcefully to the Christian clergy, whom he viewed as authoritarian, autocratic, and opposed to free intellectual inquiry.

Spinoza argued that scriptural interpretation was the prerogative of every intelligent reader and not the sole province of the rabbis or Christian theologians.

> For as the highest power of Scriptural interpretation belongs to every man, the rule for such interpretation should be nothing but the natural light of reason which is common to all—not any supernatural light nor any external authority; moreover, such a rule ought not to be so difficult that it only can be applied by very skillful philosophers, but should be adapted to the natural and ordinary faculties and capacity of mankind.[8]

Spinoza recognized that an understanding of the Hebrew words in the Bible ultimately depended on the traditions maintained by the Jews. Nonetheless, one could question the rabbis' vocalizations of words or their division of words into sentences, as well as the rabbinic account of how the traditional interpretations of Scriptures were transmitted from generation to generation.[9]

The Authority of the Oral Torah

The Talmud (*Shabbat* 31a) tells a story of a person who was interested in converting to Judaism. He came to the sage Shammai and asked, "How many Torahs do you have?" Shammai answered, "We have two, the Written Torah and the Oral Torah." The would-be proselyte responded, "I believe you concerning the Written Torah, but I don't believe you concerning the Oral Torah. Convert me on condition that you teach me the Written Torah." Shammai unceremoniously sent this person away. The would-be convert then went to the sage Hillel and made the same request that he be taught only the Written Torah, not the Oral Torah. Hillel accepted him as a student. The first day Hillel taught him *aleph, bet, gimel, dalet* (the first four letters of the Hebrew alphabet). The next day, Hillel taught him the opposite (that is, he called the *aleph* a *bet*, and the *bet* an *aleph*). The student said, "But yesterday you taught me otherwise!" Hillel responded, "Don't you see that you must rely on me [even for the simple matter of the names and shapes of the letters]? You must also rely on me when it comes to the Oral Torah."

This story touches upon the centrality of the Oral Torah in Jewish tradition. Ultimately, our entire understanding of the Bible depends on the traditional transmission from antiquity. How would we know even the simple translation of the Hebrew words without a traditional lexicon passed down from generation to generation? If we believe the rabbis have transmitted the Written Torah along with the linguistic tools to understand it, shouldn't we also trust them to have transmitted the Oral Torah, which is the means to interpret Scriptures? Rambam, reflecting the normative rabbinic view, saw the Written Torah and Oral Torah as an integrated unit. He believed it is simply incorrect to read the Written Torah without comprehending the words through the lens of the Oral Torah. The Written Torah often contains ambiguous words and incomplete renditions of laws. According to Rambam, it would have been impossible for Moses to have taught the Written Torah to the Israelites unless he had received from God an authoritative way of translating and interpreting the text.

Spinoza denied that God gave the Torah to Moses; he argued that the Torah was written at a much later date. But let us imagine for a moment that the Written Torah dated from the period of Ezra, as is suggested by Spinoza. Let us imagine that there had been no authoritative Written or Oral Torah before that time. The Torah says in three places that it is forbidden to cook a kid in the milk of its mother. What could this prohibition imply other than its literal meaning? The Oral Torah explains that this law is repeated three times in order to teach us three separate prohibitions: we are not allowed to cook meat and milk together, nor eat meat and milk together, nor benefit in any way from meat and milk that had been cooked together. These laws of the Oral Torah are far-reaching and have dramatic impact on people's eating habits. How are we to imagine Ezra (or any group of rabbis) introducing this interpretation of Scriptures in such a way that the Jewish public found it so textually compelling that they immediately changed their eating patterns? After all, the people of Israel had been a nation going back at least a thousand years prior to Ezra. It would have been highly unlikely that Ezra could come on the scene and introduce a new "Torah" along with his own interpretations and legal rulings. Why would the people have accepted the rules relating to meat and milk if this practice had not already been part of their pattern of life? Surely, the text itself could not give authority for such rules. It is far more plausible to argue that the Israelites received the Torah in the days of Moses and that Moses received an oral interpretation from God explaining how the verses should be understood and applied. The ancient rabbinic texts take it for granted that these verses relate to the prohibition of mixing meat and milk for cooking, eating, or deriving benefit therefrom. Since this tradition is so ancient and so universally accepted (in spite of its not being the literal meaning of the Torah text), this indicates that it is part of the Oral Torah.

Indeed, Rambam's first two categories of the Oral Torah include laws that could not have been logically derived from a plain reading of the Torah text. Following this line of thinking, these laws—all of which were accepted without dispute—must have originated from the very beginning of the Torah religion. It would have been quite unlikely that anyone could have come along at a later period and imposed these laws on the Jewish public. Why would the Jews have adopted such interpretations issued at so late a date in Jewish history?

Rambam studied the Torah and rabbinic literature as a believer, an insider. Thus, he saw the plausibility of the Oral Torah and made the case for its historical authenticity. Spinoza studied the Torah and rabbinic literature as a skeptic, an outsider. Thus, he dismissed the claim that the Torah is from Heaven and cast aside the notion of an authoritative Oral Torah.

Modern traditionalists can see the rationale of Rambam's claims for the first two categories of the Oral Torah, that is, those that clearly go back to the original giving of the Written Torah, since they provide otherwise unknowable information about how to understand the texts and fulfill the commandments. Even Spinoza acknowledged the necessity of ancient oral traditions that explained the meaning of words and phrases in the Bible, although he thought the oral traditions were not always reliable or comprehensive. The central issue, though, relates to the huge body of teachings found in the Talmud and in subsequent rabbinic literature that is based on the Talmud.

When I was a child learning in a Jewish day school, our teacher told us that the "Oral Torah is the Talmud." It is a prevalent notion among Orthodox Jews that the Talmud is the repository of the Oral Torah and that it therefore has divine sanction. I remember asking my teacher: How can the Talmud be the Oral Torah given by God at Mount Sinai when the Talmud includes so many names of rabbis who lived much later and when there are so many controversies in the Talmud? Unfortunately, my teacher was not able to answer this question properly, but only repeated the axiom that the Talmud is the Oral Torah. I suppose that Spinoza might have received similarly unsatisfactory answers from his rabbis and teachers!

What is the role of the Talmud in relation to the Oral Torah? The Talmud is not a systematic record of laws and traditions and does not have any tractate that is specifically dedicated to recording the oral teachings that Moses received from God at Mount Sinai. Rather, the first two categories of the Oral Torah listed by Rambam (such as translations of words or laws known as *halakha leMoshe miSinai*—laws given to Moses at Sinai) are scattered throughout the Talmud. The legal parts of the Talmud, including the ubiquitous controversies among the sages, are reflections of the *process* of the Oral Torah. Once the Great Court stopped functioning, the sages continued the process of analyzing the biblical texts and deriving laws through hermeneutical principles. During the days of the Great Court, such debates would take place, but then a vote would be called and the law would be established by majority vote. Once that mechanism was no longer in place, the rabbis of each generation continued the process of interpretation and debate, but they could no longer operate in the same way that the Great Court operated. Although attempts were made to emulate the Great Court system (for example, the academy in Yavneh established by Rabban Yohanan ben Zakkai after the destruction of the Second Temple in 70 CE), this system did not long endure. Rulings were established on the basis of the authority of individual rabbis; the earlier rabbis (*Tannaim*) were granted greater authority than the latter sages (*Amoraim*). The Talmud itself records discussions and debates spanning a period of about five hundred years, as well as later material that was added by sages during the following several centuries.

Thus the Talmud is a repository of discussions, debates, and legal interpretations of rabbis who functioned after the discontinuation of the Great Court in Jerusalem. To the extent that these discussions are part of the ongoing process of the Oral Torah, they are part of Rambam's third category of Oral Torah.

Rabbinic literature itself contains different ways of understanding the divine nature of the Oral Torah. One view posits that not only does it have divine sanction, but "even what an astute student will say before his teacher in the future—all was given as a halakha to Moses at Sinai."[10] According to this view, the Oral Torah in its entirety was given to Moses; the interpretations of future generations of sages were already known to Moses. The later rabbis, therefore, were not creating new knowledge but were merely rediscovering those divinely revealed truths that existed from the time of the original revelation of Torah.

This maximalist view of the Oral Torah was articulated in its extreme form by the twentieth-century rabbi Avraham Yeshayahu Karelitz, known as the Hazon Ish (1878–1953). He argued:

> Everything written in the Talmud, whether in the Mishnah or in the Gemara, whether in halakha or in aggadah, were things revealed to us through prophetic powers ... and whoever deviates from this tenet is as one who denies the words of our Rabbis, and his ritual slaughtering is invalid and he is disqualified from giving testimony.[11]

While the maximalist view argues that the entire Oral Torah in all its details was given to Moses, an intermediate position indicates that Moses was given much information but that God left it to the sages to determine the actual halakha. Rabbi Yannai taught that the words of the Oral Torah were not given as definitive rulings but that God gave Moses forty-nine arguments to declare something pure and forty-nine arguments to declare it impure. How, then, was the law to be established? This was left to majority vote among the sages.[12]

Another rabbinic statement indicates that "the Torah, its laws, and their details and explanations were given via Moses at Sinai."[13] Dr. David Weiss Halivni understands this passage to be saying that the Written Torah was accompanied by an Oral Torah that provided details and explanations necessary for the implementation of the laws. It does not claim that all possible interpretations of the Torah were already revealed to Moses at Sinai.[14]

The Talmud (*Menahot* 29b) tells a story in which God transported Moses into the future so that Moses attended a class given by Rabbi Akiva. Moses was dazzled by Rabbi Akiva's brilliant mind and had trouble following the lesson. Apparently, this story rests on the assumption that the Oral Torah had developed greatly since the time of Moses and that Rabbi Akiva derived new teachings based on the written text of the Torah and on the oral principles that had been passed down over the generations. Indeed, Rabbi Akiva's lesson was obviously not based on material that Moses had already known, since Moses had difficulty following Rabbi Akiva's argumentation. Nonetheless, Rabbi Akiva himself claimed that his lesson ultimately rested on principles of interpretation going back to Moses.[15]

The Talmud offers a far-reaching account of a debate between Rabbi Eliezer and the sages in regard to the ritual purity of "Okhnai's oven" (*Bava Metzia* 59b). Rabbi Eliezer was so certain that his view was correct that he caused miracles to happen to corroborate his opinion. The sages did not recant. At last, Rabbi Eliezer said, "If I am correct, let a voice come from heaven to prove it." Sure enough, a voice came from heaven proclaiming the law according to Rabbi Eliezer. However, the sages still did not change their minds. Their answer was: the Torah is not in heaven; it is up to us to decide the law according to our own reason and following the majority vote. This is a striking example of the view that the Oral Torah, that is, the halakhic decisions therein, was an ongoing process that was left in the hands of the sages of each generation. These sages were bound not by heavenly voices but to the dictates of reason. Laws and interpretations emerged as a result of new insights, not as rediscoveries of a body of ancient knowledge that had already been known by Moses. Rambam points out that prophets had no greater status than sages when interpreting the law, since it is reason—not prophecy—that is the determinant for the proper explication of Torah.

Rambam's opinion seems to be that the particular opinions and rulings of the Talmud—except where specifically indicated otherwise—do not date back to Moses at Sinai but are later analyses of Torah and halakha. In this same sense, the legal writings and rulings of post-Talmudic rabbis are also part of the Oral Torah, although these writings cannot claim to present material given to Moses by God at Mount Sinai.

For Rambam, then, the authority of the first two categories of the Oral Torah is on par with the authority of the Written Torah, as both were given to Moses at the same time. The subsequent development of the halakha, as recorded in Talmud and later rabbinic literature, is part of a divinely sanctioned process, but the specific content of the discussions and interpretations does not date back to Moses. The non-halakhic parts of the Talmud and rabbinic literature do not have any divine authority, even indirectly, but are simply reflective of the views of wise sages offering opinions based on their own intelligence and knowledge.

The Lasting Relevance of Jewish Law

Rambam viewed the entire corpus of Jewish law as having divine sanction. He devoted many years to the composition of his *Mishneh Torah*, so as to make God's law accessible and intelligible to the Jewish public. Through the *Mishneh Torah*, people would know what the halakha requires of them, and therefore they could fulfill their religious obligations appropriately.

Spinoza viewed Jewish law very differently. While he affirmed that laws teaching love of one's neighbor were, of course, essential for individual happiness as well as for the proper functioning of society, he regarded the ceremonial laws as merely devices to keep the ancient Hebrews under control. They existed so that "men should do nothing of their own free will, but should always act under external authority, and should continually confess by their actions and thoughts that they were not their own masters, but were entirely under the control of others."[16] In Spinoza's view, once the Jews lost sovereignty after the destruction of the Second Temple, the ceremonial law was no longer relevant.[17]

The fact that Jews continued to observe the ritual laws after the destruction of their political state was, for Spinoza, an anomaly. They simply succumbed to the authority of their rabbis, who continued to insist on the scrupulous observance of the ceremonial practices. Spinoza obviously felt that Jews were no longer bound by the dictates of Jewish law. If they would live righteous lives, they would attain blessedness without the halakha.

The Authority of Written and Oral Torah

When the Reform Movement gained momentum in the early nineteenth century, a new challenge to the Oral Torah emerged. The Reformers were proponents of the ideals of social justice taught by the ancient Hebrew prophets, but they thought that the ceremonial laws were not God-given and were no longer applicable. They sought to reshape Judaism into what they considered to be a modern, universal religion. To accomplish this, they called for the removal from Judaism of those rituals and nationalistic elements that tended to maintain Jews as a separate ethnic group. They argued that they were "Germans of the Mosaic persuasion," no different from other Germans except in their religious beliefs. To the extent possible, they sought to harmonize Jewish religious practices with those of the majority culture.

Early Reform Judaism, while sharing Spinoza's rejection of the Oral Torah/halakha, nonetheless did not follow Spinoza's logic to its conclusion. Proponents of the Reform Movement believed that Judaism—albeit with many changes—still had a mission in the world. It was important for Jews not to lose entirely their sense of distinctiveness, even if that distinctiveness was not reflected in rituals and social mores but primarily in the realm of religious ideas. The Reformers called for reform, not dissolution of Judaism.

In the ideal, Spinoza envisioned a humanity composed of philosophers who engaged in the intellectual love of God and in kind behavior toward their fellow human beings. Just as there was no spiritual need for Judaism in such a scenario, there was also no need for Christianity—or for any other religion that claimed a divinely revealed Scripture. If there was a need, it was simply to keep the masses under control, not to provide Truth or real blessedness.

Spinoza's views were diametrically opposed to those of Rambam. For Rambam, the divinely revealed Written and Oral Torahs were genuine sources of Truth and blessedness. God entered an eternal covenant with the people of Israel, and the laws of the Torah are applicable forever. By composing a thorough compendium of halakha, Rambam was underscoring the ongoing relevance of mitzvot, and of the obligation of Jews to maintain their religious practices, ethical and ceremonial.

For those with a traditional approach to Judaism and Jewish peoplehood, Spinoza's views are not a viable option. Indeed, Spinoza undermines the raison d'être of Judaism and the Jewish people. Although he grants that the Hebrew Bible teaches proper obedience and righteousness, he does not see the Bible (or the laws derived from it through the Oral Torah) as being necessary for living a fully satisfactory life. For Spinoza, it is the "neutral" philosopher—rather than one identified with a specific religion—who can reach the pinnacle of human experience.

Rambam laid the foundation for a sound, intellectual understanding of Judaism that rested on the divine authority of the Written and Oral Torah. While emphasizing the accurate historical transmission of halakha from generation to generation, he also recognized the human component in the ongoing development of Jewish law. For Rambam, Judaism and the Jewish people were eternal; the Torah and mitzvot were testaments to the covenant between God and Israel.

Authoritarianism and Obscurantism

A serious detraction to the authority of halakha is the authoritarian and obscurantist views that prevail among non-Maimonidean rabbis. We have already cited the opinion of the influential twentieth-century halakhic figure, the Hazon Ish, who claimed that every word of the Talmud had divine sanction. This generalization includes the irrational and scientifically incorrect statements of our sages—notions the ancient rabbis derived from their time and place. For the Hazon Ish, the sages of the Talmud were the transmitters of divine wisdom in a very literal sense; their words, as recorded in the Talmud, have unique authority. Later generations of rabbis derived their authority through their thorough knowledge of Talmud and through their absolute faith in the sages of the earlier generations (*emunat hakhamim*). Only those rabbis who shared this absolute faith in the earlier sages were deemed to be proper exemplars of Torah.

The Hazon Ish typified a relatively modern phenomenon—one that has roots in the teachings of earlier fundamentalist rabbis—that is encapsulated in the term *daas* (or *daat*) *Torah* (literally, "the Torah view"). This opinion posits that the great sages have the unique ability (and authority) to understand what the Torah *really* says. Only this elite group of sages can properly interpret Torah and guide the public in the Torah way of life.

This view has been articulated by Rabbi Eliyahu Dessler, an important rabbinic figure of the twentieth century:

> Our rabbis have told us to listen to the words of the Sages, even if they tell us that right is left and not to say, heaven forbid, that they certainly erred because little I can see their error with my own eyes. Rather, my seeing is null and void compared with the clarity of intellect and the divine aid they receive.... This is the Torah view [*daas Torah*] concerning faith in the Sages [*emunat hakhamim*]. The absence of self-negation toward our rabbis is the root of all sin and the beginning of all destruction, while all merits are as naught compared with the root of all—faith in the Sages.[18]

This view is elaborated by Rabbi Bernard Weinberger, another Orthodox rabbi of the twentieth century:

> *Gedolei Yisrael* [the great Jewish sages] possess a special endow-
> ment or capacity to penetrate objective reality, recognize the
> facts as they really are and apply the pertinent halakhic princi-
> ples. This endowment is a form of *ru'ah haKodesh* [divine inspi-
> ration], as it were, bordering, if only remotely, on the periphery
> of prophecy.... *Gedolei Yisrael* inherently ought to be the final
> and sole arbiters of all aspects of Jewish communal policy
> and questions of *hashkafa* [proper religious worldview]....
> [E]ven knowledgeable rabbis who may differ with the *Gedolim*
> on a particular issue must submit to the superior wisdom of the
> *Gedolim* and demonstrate *emunat hakhamim* [faith in our
> sages].[19]

The exponents of *daas Torah* promote a notion that gives exclusive
interpretive power to the so-called *Gedolei Yisrael*. They attribute an
almost prophetic power to these sages—and demand that the Jewish
public, including those learned in Torah, cede total authority to these
sages. Who decides who these *Gedolei Yisrael* are? The answer is that a
self-selected group of right-wing Orthodox rabbis decide who is in and
who is out of the "*Gedolim* club." Any scholar whose views do not correspond to the extreme right-wing view of Orthodoxy is excluded from
the inner circle.

The development of this concept—very much akin to the notion
of papal infallibility among Catholics—has been traced to the Hassidic
movement (beginning in the eighteenth century), where the rebbes
were given almost absolute power over their flocks, and where the
rebbe's followers were prone to attribute supernatural powers to their
spiritual head. This tendency of ascribing so much authority to the
rebbe later spread to the non-Hassidic Ashkenazic Orthodox community. (It is interesting to note that the very phrase *daas Torah* is generally given the Ashkenazic pronunciation, an indication of its roots and
development among the Orthodox Ashkenazim.) Agudas Yisroel, the
premier right-wing Orthodox organization begun in the early twentieth century, empowered a rabbinic governing board with the daunting
title *Moetzes Gedolei Yisroel*—the council of great sages of Israel. They

selected the rabbis to be on this board, and this council became (and continues to function as) the supreme religious authority for Agudas Yisroel and all those who turn to Agudas Yisroel for Torah guidance.[20]

Scholars have pointed out that this extreme turn to an authoritarian, quasi-infallible rabbinic leadership is a relatively modern phenomenon. It has appealed to a fundamentalist mindset, rather than to classic halakhic methodology. Professor Ephraim Urbach has written, "*Daat Torah* ideology has never been based upon authoritative halakhic sources, and, as far as I know, recourse has never been made to it in halakhic debate."[21]

By the latter half of the twentieth century, the *daas Torah* approach became increasingly popular among the Orthodox masses—Ashkenazic and Sephardic. Tremendous authority has been invested in a few individuals deemed to be *Gedolei Yisrael*, and this has applied not merely to questions of Jewish law but also to issues of religious worldview. This tendency has grown stronger through the early twenty-first century. The Orthodox masses, including its "non-*Gedolim*" rabbis, are called upon to defer to the judgments of the so-called *Gedolei Yisrael*. Diversity of opinion is quashed. Independent thinking is discouraged. Obedience to the *Gedolim* is the sign of true piety.

Although this approach to rabbinic authority has certainly attracted many followers, it is an approach that a great many modern religious Jews cannot accept. Indeed, the *daas Torah/emunat hakhamim* approach fosters an authoritarian system, where great power is given to few individuals—and where those individuals generally have a narrow conception of Judaism, limited secular education, and negative attitudes toward those whose beliefs and observances differ from theirs. They foster a view of the Oral Torah that invests in themselves the only legitimate power to interpret and apply Torah law and ideology.

If the advocates of *daas Torah* formed a harmonious, righteous, and compassionate community, this might serve to strengthen their claim to be the only true links in the chain of tradition of the Oral Torah. However, this is far from the case. The right-wing Orthodox community is torn by internal strife—between Hassidim and non-Hassidic Ashkenazim, among the various sects of Hassidim themselves, and between the Ashkenazic and Sephardic *Hareidim* (right-wing Orthodox). There are deep rifts and rivalries among various yeshivot in Israel and the Diaspora. If the squabbling rabbinic heads of the sects and yeshivot are supposed to be the authoritative *Gedolei Yisrael*, they do little to inspire confidence in the general Jewish public, including much of the Orthodox Jewish public.

If we contrast the image of Rambam to the image of the *Gedolei Yisrael* of our times, the differences are striking. Rambam valued reason and prized philosophy. The current *Gedolei Yisrael* restrict the individual's use of reason, demanding obedience to the *Gedolim* rather than free intellectual inquiry. The *Gedolei Yisrael* generally view philosophy as a source of heresy. Rambam thought that proper human development, including religious development, required us to be thinking individuals committed to discovering Truth. Current *Gedolei Yisrael* prize obedience and intellectual conformity. Rambam believed that the bulk of the Oral Torah was a process rather than a body of knowledge. In post-Talmudic times, the Oral Torah/halakha had to be rooted in the classic rabbinic texts. Authority was not invested in "infallible" rabbinic authorities, but in scholars who drew reasonable conclusions from the Talmud and rabbinic literature. In his many discussions of the Oral Torah and halakha, Rambam does not refer to *Gedolei Yisrael* or *Gedolim* in the sense of rabbis who have quasi-divine intuition and insight. Indeed, Rambam would be shocked and even appalled at the way the ideology of *daas Torah/emunat hakhamim* has come to prevail in certain Orthodox circles. Current *Gedolei Yisrael* espouse a viewpoint that stresses the uniqueness of the *Gedolim*, their superhuman powers, their divine (or quasi-divine) intuition. Although texts are important, the law depends on the charismatic *Gadol* more than on the text itself.

Rambam called on us to read the Bible and rabbinic texts with literary tact and with faithfulness to reason and truth. He believed that when we come upon statements that are philosophically or scientifically proved to be incorrect, we must not accept them literally but find other means of interpretation. Judaism does not demand that we believe statements that are clearly false, or based on incorrect science, or rooted in superstition. Current *Gedolei Yisrael*, following in the footsteps of the Hazon Ish, generally call on adherents to accept literally the words of the Bible and our rabbis, even when those words are not in accord with reason and with philosophical/scientific proofs.

At a time when fundamentalism and obscurantism are features of Christianity and Islam, it is not surprising that some religious Jews are also attracted to the views of the proponents of *daas Torah/emunat hakhamim*. Religious extremism is a means of retreating from a secular, technological world that seems to be out of control and without meaning or moral direction. By insulating oneself within a religious cult/group, a person can find escape from the unpleasant features of contemporary life.

Rambam eschewed the approach of fundamentalism, obscurantism, and retreat from reason. He himself participated actively in the intellectual life of his time and also worked as a medical doctor and Jewish communal leader. As head of the Jewish community in Egypt, he represented the interests of his community to the government officials. He was the model of a rabbinic sage who embodied the best teachings of the Torah and rabbinic tradition.

Rambam would call upon us to take personal responsibility, to study Torah and rabbinic literature, to remain faithful to the mitzvot and to the halakha as it has developed through the Oral Torah, to study philosophy and science, to participate in the society in which we live, and to foster a grand vision of Judaism as a world religion with a message for all people.

For many contemporary Jews, including Orthodox Jews, the Oral Torah/Talmud/halakha framework seems to have been co-opted by extremists, literalists, and fundamentalists. It has fallen into the control of a small clique of so-called *Gedolim* who represent a narrow and misguided view of Judaism. In the spirit of Rambam, it is essential that we reclaim the Oral Torah tradition as an authentic aspect of Judaism and that we view it as a powerful and meaningful pattern of life that brings adherents closer to God.

6

RELIGION AND
SUPERSTITION

Spinoza opens his *Theologico-Political Treatise* with a clear message: If human beings would govern their lives according to pure reason, they would not succumb to superstitious beliefs and practices. The problem is that human beings very often do not follow reason.

> The human mind is readily swayed this way or that in times of doubt, especially when hope and fear are struggling for the mastery, though usually it is boastful, over-confident, and vain.... Anything which excites their astonishment they believe to be a portent signifying the anger of the gods or of the Supreme Being, and mistaking superstition for religion, accounting it impious not to avert the evil with prayer and sacrifice.[1]

Essentially, superstition is engendered, maintained, and fostered by fear. When people do not understand a certain phenomenon, they feel the need for supernatural explanations to fill their void in knowledge. "All the portents ever invested with the reverence of misguided religion are mere phantoms of dejected and fearful minds."[2] Indeed, prophets or shamans are most powerful when people are most afraid. The masses will listen to those holy men and women who claim supernatural knowledge, who perform rituals that purport to be able to save people from the things they fear.

It is not just fear that engenders superstition; it is also the desire to find approval in the eyes of God. People want to be loved, favored, and blessed by God; therefore, they go to great lengths to curry God's favor. They seek some sort of reciprocal relationship, in which they provide something to God (such as sacrifices or ritual observances) and, as a result, receive something back in return. This, for Spinoza, is not religion but superstition. It is simply a means of bargaining for personal advantages.[3]

Intelligent, reasonable individuals are rightfully scornful of superstition. But where does superstition end and religion begin? For Spinoza, true religion is equated with true rationality. There is no room in such a religion for supernaturalism, miracles, prophecy, prayer, or divine providence. There is no room for religious rituals that exist basically to appease the divinity. For Spinoza, much of what popularly passes for religion is, in fact, superstition! In writing his *Theologico-Political Treatise*, Spinoza was interested in sharing his thoughts with sophisticated readers who governed their lives by reason; he did not think the general public would be receptive to his words.

> I know how deeply rooted are the prejudices embraced under the name of religion; I am aware that in the mind of the masses superstition is no less deeply rooted than fear; I recognize that their constancy is mere obstinacy and that they are led to praise or blame by impulse rather than by reason. Therefore the multitude, and those of like passions with the multitude, I ask not to read my book....[4]

Spinoza's *Theologico-Political Treatise* is the attempt of a philosopher to confront biblical religion rationally; to purge it of its superstitious nature; to get to its essence, that is, love of God and kindness to human beings. Spinoza thought that since the multitudes were so steeped in irrational superstition, it was not likely they would appreciate or even understand his work. Nevertheless, Spinoza believed there was an elite intellectual audience ready to shake the Bible from its lofty throne. This group would see the value of living according to reason and of freeing true religion from the grips of age-old superstitions.

Rambam's Opposition to Superstition

Five centuries before Spinoza, Rambam had striven to free religion of the baggage of superstition. Whereas Spinoza pared religion's legitimate domain to a strict rationalistic framework, Rambam took Judaism in its fullness—with all its laws and beliefs—and sought to remove superstitious elements from it.[5]

For Rambam, Judaism seeks to bring us closer to God through proper thought and deed. On the other hand, superstition seeks to circumvent God's power through the use of magical formulas or rituals. Whereas Judaism demands intellectual and moral excellence and a direct relationship with God, superstition provides purported means of bypassing or manipulating God in order to ward off evil or to achieve some other desired goal.

Rambam emphasized that since religion and superstition both transcend the domain of human reason, it is important not to blur the lines between them. Religion reflects Truth, the word of God. Superstition reflects falsehood, the fears and fantasies of human beings.

The Torah itself is emphatic in commanding that we not turn to shamans or wonder-workers but that we stay focused on our personal relationship with God. "There shall not be found among you anyone … who uses divination, a soothsayer, or an enchanter, or a sorcerer, or a charmer, or one who consults a ghost or a familiar spirit, or a necromancer. For whoever does these things is an abomination unto the Lord" (Deuteronomy 18:10–12).

For Rambam, the source of superstitious belief is ignorance of the true nature of God. Idolaters held erroneous ideas about the Divinity and ascribed divine/supernatural attributes to venerated objects (idols) or to multiple gods/powers. Idolatry was at the root of religious confusion; the Torah and its mitzvot aimed at ridding the Israelites of idolatry and its derivatives.[6]

Rambam clarifies the boundaries between religion and superstition in his discussion about using incantations to heal a wound:

> Anyone who whispers a charm over a wound and reads a verse from the Torah, or one who recites a biblical verse over a child lest he be terrified, or one who places a Torah scroll or tefillin over an infant to enable him to sleep, are not only included in the category of sorcerers and charmers, but are included among those who repudiate the Torah. They use the words of the Torah as a physical cure, whereas they are exclusively a cure for the soul, as it is written "they will be life to your soul." On the other hand, one who is enjoying good health is permitted to recite biblical verses, or a psalm, that he may be shielded and saved from affliction and damage by virtue of the reading.[7]

What are the characteristics of those individuals who "repudiate the Torah"? (1) They treat biblical verses as though they are magical formulas that can effect a cure; (2) they use religious objects, such as Torah scrolls or tefillin, as though they are endowed with independent magical powers; and (3) they resort to incantations and magical rituals, rather than turning directly to God. In short, they behave superstitiously, rather than religiously.

If we were to confront these individuals, though, they would be surprised to be placed in the category of those who "repudiate the Torah." They might well think of themselves as being pious, Torah-true Jews. After all, they have not gone to soothsayers or diviners for help; they have recited the holy words of the Bible and have used religious items of our own Jewish tradition. In what way have they sinned? Rambam would answer: Even if a person employs Torah words and symbols, he or she may yet be guilty of sinful behavior. To use the Torah's words and symbols in a superstitious way is also superstition! Indeed, such behavior repudiates the Torah's express teaching that we turn directly to God and that we not engage in magical practices.

Rambam notes that if a healthy person chants biblical verses in the hope that the merit of this mitzvah will invite God's protection, this is still on the correct side of the line separating religion from superstition. The person is not attributing intrinsic supernatural power to the biblical verses; rather, he or she is directing thoughts to God and hopes that the merit of the biblical readings will engender God's protection. Although this may not be an example of religion at its best, it is permissible—and not in the category of repudiating the Torah.

In his *Mishneh Torah*, Rambam cites another case in which he distinguishes between religious and superstitious behavior:

> There is a widespread custom to write the word *Shaddai* on the outer side of the mezuzah, opposite the blank space between the two sections. Since it is written on the outside, there is no harm done. On the other hand, those who write inside the mezuzah names of angels or names of saintly men, some biblical verse or some charms—they are included among those who have no share in the world to come. Those fools not only fail to fulfill the commandment, but they treat an important precept, which conveys God's Oneness as well as the love and worship of God, as if it were an amulet to benefit themselves, since they foolishly believe that the mezuzah is something advantageous for the vain pleasures of this world.[8]

Here, too, Rambam chastises those who treat a religious object as though it were a magical charm. People are included among "those who have no share in the world to come" even if they themselves may think they are acting piously. Rambam makes it clear that superstitious behavior—even if cloaked in traditional religious symbols—is a serious transgression of the Torah's teachings.

What leads people to superstitious behavior? Why doesn't everyone realize the foolishness of employing magical incantations and rites? Why would people rely on superstitious behavior rather than turning directly to God with their prayers? Let me suggest a few reasons:

1. True religion demands a lot from us. Superstition demands very little. True religion requires that we confront God

directly. Superstition offers shortcuts, ways to bypass that awe-inspiring confrontation with God.

2. When people are afraid and desperate, they may suspend their reason in order to adopt superstitious practices—"just in case" these might be efficacious. Why take chances by not trying everything?

3. Superstitious practices have been sanctioned by generations of people who seem to have religious credibility. If these great ones believed in demons and made amulets, then these things must be permissible (in spite of Rambam's rulings).

Let us elaborate a bit on this third point. The *Shulhan Arukh* follows the Rambam's lead in permitting the recitation of incantations on the Sabbath in order to minister to the psychological needs of a very sick person:

> If someone is bitten by a scorpion, it is permitted, even on the Sabbath, to recite a charm over the victim, although such a thing is of no benefit whatsoever. Still, since a life is in danger, they [the rabbis] permitted it lest the victim suffer mental anguish.[9]

In this passage, the *Shulhan Arukh* agrees with Rambam's assessment that charms and magical incantations have no objective value. However, since the victim of the scorpion's bite is in desperate straits—and the victim may believe these incantations have efficacy—it is permitted to recite these charms as a way of alleviating the victim's anxieties.

In his comments on the *Shulhan Arukh's* ruling, the Gaon of Vilna, known as the Gra, writes an impassioned critique of Rambam's views and an ardent defense of the belief in charms, amulets, and other such things:

> This opinion [of the *Shulhan Arukh*] is the Rambam's as expressed in his *Hilkhot Avoda Zarah*. But all subsequent author-

ities disagreed with him because of the numerous charms recorded in the Talmud. He, however, was drawn by the accursed philosophy, and that is why he wrote that witchcraft, names, charms, demons, and amulets are all deception. But he has been thoroughly refuted on the strength of the innumerable stories found in the Talmud.... [P]hilosophy with her blandishments misled him to explain all such stories allegorically and to uproot them from their literal meaning. As for me, Heaven forbid that I should accept any of those allegorical explanations.[10]

If a rabbinic authority of the magnitude of the Gaon of Vilna repudiated Rambam's views on magical amulets and incantation, it is certainly easy for the masses of Jews to rely on him rather than on the Rambam. After all, the Gra not only disagrees with Rambam but indicates that "all subsequent authorities" disagreed with him. Indeed, says the Gra, the Rambam was seduced by philosophy and therefore his opinions on this topic are tainted. Rather, the Gra advises us to follow the teachings recorded in the Talmud, where we learn that amulets are efficacious, that demons and witches exist, and that magical incantations work.

To reasonable, rational moderns, the words of the Gaon of Vilna are shocking examples of a defective, superstitious worldview. Does religious piety truly demand that we suspend reason so that we adopt belief in witches, demons, and magic incantations because rabbis in the Talmud believed in such things? The Gaon of Vilna seems to think so. The Rambam, however, disagrees completely with this. Is Rambam's view to be dismissed because he was "tainted" by philosophical study? The answer, I believe, is an emphatic *no*. Rambam was teaching us to be thinking human beings. He was pointing to an intellectual methodology that allowed for development of knowledge over the ages. Just because ancient rabbis and sages believed in demons does not mean we are bound to do likewise. On the contrary, we are obligated to take into account the intellectual and scientific developments of humanity and to revise our views as new, more accurate knowledge is discovered. The Rambam's position allows us to learn and grow.

Religious Leadership Today

A great challenge for religious leadership is to wean people from superstitious tendencies and bring them closer to God. People need to be reminded to use their reason, rather than to surrender to a mindless supernaturalism. The Torah itself was well aware of the human weakness of turning to diviners and magicians, and the Torah strictly forbade such practices that obstruct a direct relationship with God. Religion teaches responsibility, careful thinking, and reliance on God. Superstition promotes avoidance of personal responsibility, suspension of rational thinking, and reliance on supernatural forces other than God.

In spite of Rambam's powerful efforts to purge superstition from religion, the folk spirit (encouraged even by many within the rabbinic elite) has not given up its attachment to superstitious beliefs and practices. The popular religious culture continues to seek out holy men (or women) who can perform magical cures and persists in utilizing sacred texts and objects in a superstitious manner. These tendencies often pass themselves off as religiously valid expressions of Hassidism, or of Kabbalah, or even of mainstream Jewish teaching.

Spinoza's rigorous rationalism challenges all people, including religious people, to think carefully before accepting something as true. He argues that superstition stems from human ignorance and fear and that much of what passes for religion is, in fact, superstition. While this viewpoint negates the validity of religions based on divinely revealed Scriptures, prophecy, and miracles, it serves as an important corrective for religionists who too easily sink into supernaturalism as a way of dealing with the challenges of life. If Spinoza goes too far in one direction, some "religious" people go too far in the direction of superstition.

Rambam provides a framework for maintaining a rationalistic outlook while still adhering to the teachings of Judaism, including the belief in divinely revealed Scriptures, prophecy, miracles, and so forth. It is ludicrous to expect educated, thinking moderns to believe in demons, amulets, shamans, and evil spirits. Yet, these things have become so integrated into popular religion that traditionalists often think these are basic ingredients of Judaism that cannot be dismissed. It is instructive to study how careful Rambam was to remove superstitious notions from his writings and how he reinterpreted halakhic practices accordingly.

Examples of Rambam's Methodology

Many of our sages in earlier generations believed in demons, malevolent metaphysical forces, astrology, and other such things, as did many of the wise and learned non-Jews of those times. These beliefs are not only cited in the Talmud, but in some cases also have entered into standard halakhic codes. What are we to do when halakhic practice is built upon a "superstitious" foundation?

Let us consider the concept of *ruah ra'ah* as an illustration of how to address this problem. The *Shulhan Arukh* records the halakha that we must wash our hands ritually upon awakening in the morning. This is done in order to remove the *ruah ra'ah,* the evil spirit that clings to the hands. The *Shulhan Arukh* goes on to state that we must not touch the mouth, nose, ears, or eyes before washing our hands. Since the unwashed fingers have a *ruah ra'ah* on them, touching these sensitive organs is dangerous.[11]

This halakha is the subject of much discussion among codifiers and commentators. Some say that the *ruah ra'ah* comes from touching unclean parts of the body while sleeping. Others suggest that a metaphysical spirit adheres to the hands while sleeping, since sleeping is akin to dying, and death is the source of spiritual impurity. It thus has become halakhic practice in many Orthodox circles to have a pitcher of water and a basin placed near the bed, so that a person may wash the hands ritually immediately upon awakening. In this way, the evil spirit is removed promptly, and a person can then proceed with the activities of the day in purity.

These laws and explanations are recorded in authoritative halakhic texts, and yet, the rational mind is troubled by them. What exactly is a *ruah ra'ah*? Are we obliged to believe in supernatural evil spirits that cling to our hands when we sleep? If we don't wash our hands but touch our mouth, nose, ears, or eyes, will anything harmful really happen to us? After all, billions of people throughout the world touch these organs without requiring prior ritual hand washing, and they seem to be unharmed. Does the evil spirit only come onto the hands of religious Jews and is only a danger to them?

When we go to Rambam's *Mishneh Torah*, we find no reference at all to the *ruah ra'ah*. We find no warning against touching sensitive organs before hand washing. We do find the obligation to wash hands in the morning as a preparation for prayer.[12] This washing of hands (and legs as well) is part of the proper preparation for coming before the Almighty in prayer. Rambam apparently believed that the obligation to wash before prayer was a matter of physical cleanliness and ritual purification but was not connected to the concept of *ruah ra'ah*. Rambam has maintained the halakhic practice of hand washing but has eliminated superstitious/supernatural elements from the rite. He has made possible a reasonable and meaningful explanation.[13]

Another example of Rambam's approach relates to the blowing of the shofar (ram's horn) on Rosh Hashanah. The Talmud (*Rosh Hashanah* 16b) states that the shofar is blown "to confuse Satan." Other sources indicate that the shofar is used to scare demons and upset their plans, so that they will not bring evil charges against us to God (Talmud, *Hullin* 105b; Rashi on *Rosh Hashanah* 28a). Rambam omits reference to Satan or to demons in his discussion of the shofar. He explains that the shofar is blown as a way of calling the people to awaken from their spiritual slumber, to examine their deeds and change their ways.[14]

Similarly, Rambam omits mention of certain ritual practices that were (and still are) widely observed among Jews. There is a custom to cast one's sins into the water on Rosh Hashanah in a ceremony known as *tashlikh*. People usually toss some bread crumbs into the body of water, as a way of casting off their sins. This practice may be rooted in a superstitious belief that the bread crumbs serve as a bribe to Satan so that he won't report our evil deeds to God.[15]

Rambam was emphatic that Judaism does not countenance belief in supernatural powers other than God. These are superstitious notions that crept into Jewish thought but must be discarded by truly religious people. In the *Mishneh Torah*, he writes:

> All of these things are lies and untruths with which the ancient idol worshippers deceived the people, to entice them to follow them. It is not fitting for Israel, who are a really wise nation, to be attracted by such vanities, or to suppose that they have any value.... Whoever believes in these things and their like, and thinks that they are genuine and a kind of wisdom, but that the Torah forbids them [even though they are efficacious] belongs to the fools and the deficient in knowledge.[16]

In his commentary on the Mishnah (*Avodah Zarah* 4:7), Rambam reiterates the falseness of superstitious practices in sharp terms:

> You need to know that the perfected philosophers do not believe in talismans. They laugh at them and at the people who believe that they have an influence [on the physical].... [The deception is so great] that even the best of our pious Torah scholars think that they are true but are forbidden because the Torah prohibits them. They do not realize that they are nonsensical false things that the Torah warned against, just as it warned against falsehoods.

Rambam wants to make clear that idolatry and superstition are not only forbidden, but they lack truth and efficacy.

Rambam inveighed against astrology, even though it was considered a legitimate science by many Jewish and non-Jewish sages of his time. He argued that astrology is false from both a scientific point of view and a religious point of view. In his *Letter on Astrology*, he faulted the ancient Israelites for turning to astrology rather than relying on their own reason and common sense:

> That is why our kingdom was lost and our Temple was destroyed and why we were brought to this; for our fathers sinned and are

no more because they found many books dealing with these themes of the stargazers.... They did not busy themselves with the art of war or with the conquest of lands, but imagined that these [astrological] studies would help them.[17]

According to Rambam, astrology is akin to magic rather than science. Although practitioners of astrology sometimes make correct predictions, they also make incorrect predictions. Their method is not based on logical reasoning and is not worthy of credence. Not only is astrology not an objective, true science, it also rests on incorrect assumptions from a religious vantage point. Since Judaism teaches unequivocally that human beings have free will, we must absolutely reject astrology, since it posits a deterministic worldview. Astrologers teach that our lives are governed by the movements and forces of the stars and planets; but if this is true, human beings lack free will and are mere puppets in a cosmic melodrama.

Superstition, Religion, and Us

Rambam strove to present a halakhic Judaism that is intellectually sound. Since the halakha ultimately is a reflection of God's will as expressed in the Written and the Oral Torah, it is vital to our spiritual and physical well-being. Halakhic Judaism, though, has been corrupted by the introduction of irrational, superstitious, and supernatural elements. While some Talmudic literalists believe that piety demands total fidelity to the beliefs and practices of our halakhic authorities, Rambam believed that this is not so. Indeed, calling on people to maintain superstitious beliefs and customs is the height of sacrilege. Reasonable people are repelled by superstition; if they see religion as a conglomeration of superstitious ideas and practices, they will abandon religion altogether. That has happened among many Jews. They have been presented with an irrational, superstitious form of Judaism and have found it intellectually unsatisfying.

Let us consider a few contemporary examples of how Judaism is debased by so-called pietists who foster a superstitious religious worldview. A significant Orthodox charitable organization provides assistance to needy individuals and families. On a regular basis, it sends glossy brochures to potential donors, soliciting contributions. These brochures include abundant pictures of saintly looking men with long white beards, engaged in Torah study and prayer, and signing their names on behalf of this charitable organization. The brochures promise donors that the *Gedolei haDor* (the great sages of our generation) are official members of the organization. One of the rabbinic sages associated with this charity is quoted to say, "All who contribute to [this charity] merit to see open miracles." Moreover, donors are told that the *Gedolei haDor* will pray on their behalf and are actually given a choice of blessings they would like to receive from these prayers: to have pleasure from their children, to have children, to find a worthy mate, to earn an easy livelihood. "Urgent requests are immediately forwarded to the homes of the *Gedolei haDor*." Those who are willing to contribute a specified sum per name are guaranteed that a quorum of outstanding rabbinic scholars will pray for these names at the Kotel, the Western Wall in Jerusalem. If a lesser amount is contributed, then only one rabbinic scholar will recite the prayer. Potential donors are informed that they may write their requests on paper (*kvitel*) and these *kvitels* will be placed in the cracks of the Kotel for forty days; prayer requests may be transmitted by telephone hotline once a contribution has been made by means of a credit card.

This charity purports not only to be Torah-true, but to have the involvement and support of the *Gedolei haDor*. Anyone looking at the brochure would see this as an Orthodox Jewish charity operated by highly religious individuals.

Let us grant that this is indeed a worthy charity that provides assistance to needy Jews. Let us grant that the people who operate this charity see themselves as pious Jews of the highest caliber, literally linked to the *Gedolei haDor*. However, the method of solicitation used by this charity is not an example of true religion at all, but of something far more akin to superstition.

Is it appropriate for a *Gadol haDor* to assure contributors that they will be worthy of open miracles? Can anyone rightfully speak on behalf of the Almighty's decisions relating to doing open miracles? Doesn't this statement reflect a belief that prayers uttered by so-called sages (similar to incantations uttered by shamans!) can control God's actions, even to the extent of making God do miracles?

Moreover, why should people be made to feel that they are not qualified to pray to God directly? Why should religious leaders promote the notion that if people will pay money, some pious individual will recite a prayer at the Kotel—and that the prayer uttered by such an individual at the Kotel is more efficacious than our own prayers? How tasteless and contrary to religious values is the notion that a minyan of outstanding *talmidei hakhamim* will pray if you pay enough, but that only one will pray for you if you choose to contribute less than the recommended sum?

In this brochure, dressed as it is in the garb of Torah-true religion, we have a blatant example of superstition-tainted Judaism. The leaders of this organization assume: (1) *Gedolei haDor* (we are not told who decides who is a *Gadol haDor*, nor why any *Gadol haDor* would want to run to the Kotel to pray every time a donor called in an "urgent request") have greater powers to pray than anyone else; (2) a *Gadol haDor* can promise us open miracles if we send in a donation; (3) a prayer uttered at the holy site of the Kotel has more value than a prayer uttered elsewhere, that is, the Kotel is treated as a sacred, magical entity; and (4) A *kvitel* placed in a crevice in the Kotel has religious value and efficacy. This brochure relies on the public's gullible belief in the supernatural powers of *Gedolei haDor* and the Kotel.

Lest one think this charity is the only Orthodox Jewish group that promotes a superstitious (rather than truly religious) viewpoint, one may do a Google search and find others who do pretty much the same thing. The Wailing Wall *Kvitel* Service advertises that it will deliver your personal prayers or requests to God "even if you cannot travel to the holy land to visit Jerusalem in person." We are assured that once this organization receives our *kvitel* and donation, the *kvitel* will be placed between the stones of the Kotel, and "you will receive a postcard from the Wailing Wall."

Nor is this behavior restricted to the Hareidi sector of Orthodoxy. One website informs us that Jews and non-Jews have long had the practice of writing their private thoughts and prayers and having them inserted into the cracks of the Kotel "in the firm belief that at this holiest of locales God is always present and listening." (Doesn't Judaism believe that God is always present and listening everywhere?) The sponsors of this website, which promises to insert the *kvitels* "on a same day basis," have also arranged with a *kollel* in Jerusalem to have psalms recited for the ill or to have Torah studied in someone's memory. This program is staffed by volunteers of the Orthodox Union, a mainstream Orthodox organization!

Certainly, those who write *kvitels* do so with a sense of piety, with a sincere desire to get their prayers to God. Yet, shouldn't religious leaders be telling people that they ought to bring their prayers to God directly from their mouths and hearts? There is no need whatsoever to write out prayers for deposit in the Kotel. On the contrary, this practice smacks of superstition, relying on magical powers that are attributed to the Kotel rather than on direct prayer to God.

Defenders of the *kvitel* practice will argue: this is an age-old custom, approved or tolerated by great sages; this is a harmless custom that doesn't hurt anyone; this is a way for people to feel that their words will have a better chance of reaching God. In response, we can say that there have been various beliefs and practices approved or tolerated by great sages in the past that are more akin to superstition than religion, much like the belief in demons, the writing and wearing of magical amulets, or the ceremonies conducted to ward off evil spirits. The fact that great people believed or did these things does not make them correct. Rambam condemned those who used Torah scrolls, tefillin, or mezuzot as magical charms—and I would assume that there were rabbis before (and after) his time who approved or tolerated these practices.

Superstitious practices *do* cause harm. According to Rambam, severe punishments (including loss of one's portion in the world to come!) are meted out to those who engage in superstitious rites. Moreover, Rambam believed that a superstitious approach to Judaism undermines its intellectual foundations, treating it more as a cult than a religion. This is a vast disservice to Judaism and turns reasonable people away from Torah.

If the public has a tendency toward superstitious belief and practice, it is the responsibility of religious leaders to guide them away from these things. How sad it is when *"Gedolei haDor"* actually stand at the forefront of misguiding the public into thinking superstitiously and magically. Torah leaders must teach the public the right and responsibility of personal, direct prayer to God; the inappropriateness of writing or placing *kvitels* in the Kotel; the need to observe Torah and mitzvot in the spirit of religion, not superstition.

The line between religion and superstition often becomes blurred in connection with illness and death. I have known many otherwise rational people who have turned to "wonder-workers" and "kabbalists" for help when they, or loved ones, have confronted serious illness. People have sought "spiritual" protections and cures, such as red string tied around the wrist, or food and drink blessed by a holy person. There has also been a growing tendency of groups to gather for the recitation of psalms as a *segulah* (magical cure) for those who are ill. If these sessions were conducted as an expression of prayer to the Almighty for the recovery of a sick loved one, they would be within the boundaries of religion; but when they are promoted specifically as a *segulah*, then they cross the line into superstition. Although we may understand, and even sympathize, with those who turn to such practices due to fear and desperation, we must also recognize that this represents a turn away from true religion and a turn to superstition. People should be reminded to turn their hearts, minds, and souls entirely to God, and not to red strings, or amulets, or holy men who claim supernatural powers.

The *Kaddish* prayer, recited in memory of a loved one, has also taken on some superstitious features. In itself, it is a beautiful prayer praising God's greatness. Since the Middle Ages, the *Kaddish* has become associated with praying on behalf of the souls of the departed. A supernatural belief arose that the repose of the deceased was dependent on the daily recital of *Kaddish* by mourners. This has led to a tendency to view the *Kaddish* as a magical incantation that must be recited daily; otherwise the deceased will suffer punishments from the Almighty. Mourners go to great lengths to be sure to say *Kaddish* each day, so as to bring merit to the soul of the departed and not to cause suffering to that soul.

While the recitation of *Kaddish* is virtuous, it slips into the realm of superstition if the mourner views it as a magic formula that can control God's treatment of the soul of the deceased. God alone deals with the souls of the departed and surely does not withhold justice or compassion depending on whether a relative recites *Kaddish*.

Rambam stressed the need for human beings to use their power of reason and to eschew superstition. Although philosophers surely would agree with Rambam, what are we to do about the masses who are more prone to fall into the ways of superstition? The answer is: We must teach the masses a philosophically sound and rational approach to religion. We must wean people from false beliefs and superstitious behaviors.

Rambam and Spinoza both located superstition in the realm of ignorance and irrational fear. As human knowledge advances, human reason overcomes ignorance and allays fear. Rational people will learn to overcome the tendency toward superstition and will root their lives in reason and in an intellectual love of God.

7

ISRAEL AND HUMANITY

Reason is a human quality, available equally to Jews and non-Jews. A "religion of pure reason," such as that advocated by Spinoza, has no particularistic or ethnic component. Any human being, regardless of race or ethnic origin, can attain Truth by proper application of reason.

The religion of Israel, based on the revealed word of God in the Bible, is rooted in the historical experience of a particular people. Although the teachings of the Bible have universal meaning, they were originally delivered to humanity through the children of Israel and have a definite Israel-centric flavor. With its many laws and cere-monies, the religion of Israel is specifically geared to the people of Israel. Non-Jews may convert and join the Israelite nation, but this group will constitute only a small percentage of the non-Jewish world. According to ancient rabbinic teaching, the non-Jews who do not con-vert to Judaism are obligated to keep the Seven Noahide Laws (the pro-hibitions against blaspheming God, engaging in idolatry, murdering, stealing, committing sexual immorality, and eating the flesh taken from a living animal; and the positive commandment to set up a system for the administration of justice).

In Rambam's view, although Judaism has a historical foundation in a particular people, the teachings of Judaism[1] are relevant to all human beings in search of Truth and who wish to draw on the sources of both reason and revelation.

For Spinoza, the religion of the Jews was a localized system developed by a specific group of people to relate to an eternal deity.[2] The ancient Hebrews in their pre-monarchical era made important and valuable observations about religion and developed a society committed to proper behavior and obedience. They followed various rules and ceremonies that conduced to maintaining an orderly society. Their religion related only to themselves and was not concerned with those living outside their society. Although they established a system of self-government, they were far from reaching a philosophically correct understanding of God. Once the Jewish commonwealth was crushed by the Romans and came to an end in 70 CE, Jewish history should have come to an end. The Hebrew theocracy no longer existed, since there was no longer a Jewish country ruled by a Jewish government. As far as Spinoza was concerned, the Jews might best have let their religion/nation disappear once they had lost their homeland and government. They should simply have become philosophers, happy to find ultimate Truth and fulfillment in universally accessible rationalism.

But, of course, Judaism and Jewish history did not come to an end with the loss of sovereignty over the land of Israel. Jews went into exile, but they managed to keep their religious and national identity in the midst of their host countries. Jews were a historical anomaly. How did they survive for so many centuries in exile? Why did they struggle so intensely to maintain their religious traditions? Spinoza may have seen this survival as a sign of stubbornness or ethnic pride. But Rambam, along with all traditional Jews, saw this survival as an expression of divine providence. The Jews had a God-given way of life; they had a mission that God had chosen them to fulfill. They established communities based on Torah and halakha, and they continued the Jewish march through history against all odds and in spite of the seemingly endless oppressions that they suffered.

The tiny Jewish people has made inordinately great contributions to humanity. The Bible has been the foundation of Western civilization. Through Judaism's daughter religion, Christianity, many millions of human beings throughout the world have been influenced by the Hebrew prophets and psalmists. Judaism has also played an important role in the emergence of Islam, a religion that recognizes the sanctity of the Hebrew Scriptures. Even during their many centuries of exile, Jews have contributed vastly to the spiritual, intellectual, cultural, and economic life of the nations of the world.

Are Jews inherently different from other people? Do they have an essential God-given quality that distinguishes them from non-Jews? Or is there no ontological difference between Jews and non-Jews, so that the uniqueness of Jewish history is to be viewed in naturalistic, sociological terms?

Professor Menachem Kellner has pointed out:

Many post-rabbinic texts teach that there is some essential difference between Jews and non-Jews. This teaching is not to be found in the Hebrew Bible at all, nor is it easy to find in post-biblical rabbinic writings. One of the first Jewish thinkers to emphasize that the distinction resides in a property shared by Jews and lacking in non-Jews is Judah Halevi.[3]

Halevi (c. 1075–1141), in his influential book *The Kuzari*, argued that Jews were distinguished by an inherent spiritual sense that allowed them to reach the pinnacle of human experience. He believed that Jews differ from non-Jews by virtue of a special divine distinctiveness; God is connected to the Jews more directly and more intimately than to the non-Jews. For the most part, prophecy is a Jewish phenomenon. According to Halevi even if a non-Jew were to convert to Judaism, he or she would still not be "equal" to a born Jew, since the convert is not a blood descendant of the chosen seed of Abraham, Isaac, and Jacob. Thus, the Jewish spiritual distinctiveness is linked to the Jewish genetic distinctiveness.

Halevi's views were shared by the classic kabbalistic work the *Zohar*, which was first published during the thirteenth century. The notion of Jews' essential spiritual difference from non-Jews spread with the popularization of Kabbalah.

Rambam: A Foundation of Torah

Professor Kellner has demonstrated convincingly that Rambam's view on the nature of Jews and non-Jews was radically opposed to that of Halevi and the kabbalists.[4] Rambam thought that all human beings, Jews and non-Jews alike, were essentially the same. The differences emerged not due to some inherent ontological factors, but due to different historical experiences. The Jews received the Torah from God, which gave them access to the will of God as found in the Torah. Through their observance of the commandments of God, Jews have the opportunity to attain great spiritual heights. Rambam believed, however, that non-Jews can also attain great spiritual heights and that a non-Jew who converts to Judaism has precisely the same access to Torah as a born Jew.

Rambam makes this clear in his *Mishneh Torah*:

> Not only the tribe of Levi but every single individual from among the world's inhabitants, whose spirit moved him and whose intelligence gave him the understanding to withdraw from the world in order to stand before God to serve and minister to Him, and to know God, and who walked upright in the manner in which God made him, shaking off from his neck the yoke of the manifold contrivances which men seek—behold this person has been totally consecrated, and God will be his portion and inheritance forever and ever.[5]

According to Rambam, each human being—Jewish or non-Jewish—has access to ultimate Truth by virtue of his or her wisdom and understanding, and the commitment to walk in God's ways. Indeed, Rambam valued wisdom for its own sake and insisted that wisdom was manifested by non-Jews as well as Jews. In the introduction to his commentary on the *Ethics of the Fathers*, Rambam informs his readers that his commentary is based on the wisdom drawn from midrashim and the Talmud and other rabbinic works, "as well as from the words of the philosophers, ancient and recent, and also from the works of various authors, as one should accept the truth from whatever source it proceeds." This latter phrase refers to works of non-Jewish philosophers and authors. They, too, had developed ideas that were important to those seeking truth. Truth is not restricted to one ethnic group but is the universal heritage of humanity. Rambam believed we can and should learn from everyone who has something important to teach.

Rambam's argument goes further. Not only is wisdom accessible to all human beings, but the Torah itself cannot be fully grasped without taking into account the universal wisdom of physics and metaphysics. In some sense, the Torah—as the word of God—must encompass the Truth that God has made available to humanity as a whole. To be a true scholar of Torah, then, entails a thorough knowledge of universal wisdom—including the wisdom taught by non-Jewish philosophers, scientists, and thinkers.

Professor Marvin Fox has written eloquently about this powerful feature of Rambam's intellectual outlook:

> This lesson could be learned with profit by those among our contemporaries who reject out of hand every non-Jewish source of knowledge and truth. Against this kind of self-defeating intellectual obscurantism Maimonides stands out as a beacon of light, showing us that Judaism has nothing to fear from the best and most advanced sources of knowledge in any given age. In fact, it has much more to fear from an attitude that deliberately builds a protective wall around us, denies the legitimacy of independent thought and inquiry, and shuts out the world in order to protect Judaism from the seemingly dangerous ideas that abound in contemporary science, philosophy, and theology.[6]

Although Rambam valued wisdom taught by non-Jewish sages, he also believed that the non-Jewish world needed to recognize God—the giver of the Torah—as the ultimate source of Truth. In a striking passage (whose meaning has been misunderstood frequently due to an error in transcribing the text), Rambam explains:

> One who accepts the seven [Noahide] commandments and
> observes them scrupulously is a righteous gentile and has a
> share in the world to come, on condition that he accept them
> and perform them because the Holy One blessed be He com-
> manded them in the Torah and made known to us through
> Moses our Teacher that Noahides had been commanded to
> obey them before [the giving of the Torah]. But if one observed
> them because his reason compels him, he is not a resident alien
> nor one of the righteous gentiles, but one of their wise men.[7]

Although it is preferable for non-Jewish sages to be righteous (that is,
believers) as well as wise, Rambam does not belittle their wisdom even
if they are not believers in God's Torah. We are to seek truth from whatever source, whether Jewish or non-Jewish, whether from a believer or
a nonbeliever.

The Excellencies of the Jews

Rambam denied any ontological difference between Jews and non-
Jews, but he did believe that Jews had developed certain positive character traits due to their adherence to the laws of the Torah. These
qualities were not innate; Jews were not born with them. Rather, these
qualities were culturally conditioned by centuries of devotion to Jewish
tradition.

For example, in various passages of the *Mishneh Torah*, Rambam
describes Jews as being more compassionate and righteous than non-
Jews. In *Hilkhot Teshuvah* 2:10, he notes that "forgiveness is natural to
the seed of Israel, characteristic of their upright heart. Not so are the
gentiles of uncircumcised heart." He says that Jews have pity and forgive others, and non-Jews are hard-hearted and resentful. In *Hilkhot
Issurei Biah* 19:17, Rambam states that the distinctive traits of the people of Israel are modesty, mercy, and loving-kindness. If a person
lacked these qualities, this was grounds for questioning his or her
Jewish ancestry. In *Hilkhot Matanot Aniyim* 10:1–2, Rambam indicates
that "giving charity is the mark of righteous individuals who are of the

seed of our father Abraham." He goes on to say that "whoever is cruel and merciless lays himself open to suspicion as to his descent, for cruelty is found only among the gentiles." In *Hilkhot Avadim* 9:8, Rambam tells us that the Jews "are merciful people who have mercy upon all."

Some writers have tried to explain the above passages in the sense that Rambam did in fact believe Jews were innately different—and superior—to non-Jews. Professor Kellner has argued convincingly, though, that these writers have misunderstood Rambam.[8] Rambam's point was not that Jews were born with superior moral qualities, but that they developed these qualities as a result of following the commandments of the Torah and by emulating God's ways. In the words of Professor Kellner:

> *Verus Israel* thus turns out to be, not all the descendants of Abraham, Isaac, and Jacob, as Judah Halevi would have it, and not adherents of Jesus, as Christianity would have it, but all humans who sincerely and correctly attach themselves to God. The overwhelming majority of those are indeed descendants of Abraham, Isaac, and Jacob. But that is a temporary condition. Rambam confidently expected that by the fruition of the messianic era, the terms "Israel" and "human being" would be coextensive.[9]

Israel: The Chosen People

The Torah itself indicates that God chose the people of Israel from among all the nations (Exodus 19:5–6). This idea is well-entrenched in the Bible, Jewish liturgy, and Jewish consciousness. The question is: What does it mean to be the chosen people?

As we have already seen, Rambam rejected the notion of any inherent difference between Jews and non-Jews. So why were the Jews chosen to be God's messengers on earth? What was so special about this tiny people that led God to choose the Israelites from among all nations to receive His revelation at Mount Sinai?

Before answering this question, it is important to note that Rambam did not list belief in the chosenness of Israel among his thirteen principles of faith. Indeed, he did not expound in great length or detail on this topic in any of his writings. He obviously knew that the Israelites were the chosen people; yet he did not offer a full-scale explanation of what chosenness means.

In the first chapter of the *Mishneh Torah*, *Hilkhot Avodah Zarah*, Rambam describes how humankind fell into idolatrous errors. He goes on to delineate the spiritual career of Abraham, who apprehended God by means of philosophical speculation. Abraham arrived at his faith in God through intellectual exertion, not because he had received any prophetic message from God. Only later did God appear to him. From this description of Abraham's career, Rambam teaches that it was Abraham who first chose God, rather than the other way around. Abraham passed on his insights to his son, Isaac, who passed them on to his son Jacob, who passed them on to his children—the children of Israel. Through the merit of Abraham, Isaac, and Jacob, their descendants found themselves in a relationship with God. Because Abraham had chosen God and transmitted the ways of God to his descendants, so God chose the children of Israel to receive the Torah.

That the Israelites received the Torah at Mount Sinai is, for Rambam, historical fact, and the "chosenness" of Israel is not subject to debate. Every rational and honest human being will acknowledge that the Torah came to humanity via the people of Israel. People may be happy or unhappy with this fact; yet it remains a fact. Rambam suggested that the chosenness of Israel originated in Abraham's choosing to seek God and develop a relationship with Him. While humanity as a whole had drifted into idolatry, Abraham alone formulated an ethical monotheism that made him the forerunner of the people of Israel.

Insight into Rambam's position may be drawn from a letter he wrote to Obadiah, the proselyte. Obadiah inquired whether he—as a convert to Judaism—was allowed to recite the Hebrew prayers that included the words "Our God and God of our fathers," "You who have sanctified us through Your commandments," "You who have separated us," "You who have chosen us," "You who have inherited us," "You who have brought us out of the land of Egypt," "You who have worked miracles for our fathers," or other phrases of this nature. Since Obadiah had not been born Jewish, was he allowed to utter these prayers that referred to God's relationship with "our" ancestors? Rambam's response was powerful and emphatic:

> Yes, you may say all this in the prescribed order and not change it in the least. In the same way as every Jew by birth says his blessing and prayer, you, too, shall bless and pray alike, whether you are alone or pray in the congregation. The reason for this is, that Abraham our Father taught the people, opened their minds, and revealed to them the true faith and the unity of God.... Ever since then whoever adopts Judaism and confesses the unity of the Divine Name, as it is prescribed in the Torah, is counted among the disciples of Abraham our Father, peace be with him.
>
> ... There is no difference whatever between you and us ... for the Creator, may He be extolled, has indeed chosen you and separated you from the nations and given you the Torah. For the Torah has been given to us and to the proselytes.... Do not consider your origin as inferior. While we are the descendants of Abraham, Isaac, and Jacob, you derive from Him through whose word the world was created.[10]

Rambam viewed proselytes as the equals—in some sense even the superiors—of born Jews. By adopting the teachings of Abraham and the commandments of the Torah, proselytes became integral members of the Jewish people. Their connection was not genetic, but spiritual.

What were the Israelites chosen to do? The simple answer is that God chose Israel to receive the Torah and the later biblical books; to live their lives according to the teachings of Torah; to create a model human society that could serve as "a light unto the nations," to rid humanity of idolatry and immorality, and to lead humanity to a messianic age when all human beings will recognize the One God and live moral, spiritual lives inspired by knowledge of the Lord.

These are tremendous responsibilities—and privileges. But they have exacted a terrible toll on the Jews. It has not been easy to have been chosen. The Bible itself is quite candid in relating the sins and punishments of the ancient Israelites and their failures to live up to the requirements of God's commandments. Moreover, the nations of the world have not always appreciated the role of the Jewish people in the unfolding of humanity's spiritual history. Jews have been targets of attack since antiquity; they embodied a way of life and a spiritual philosophy that many non-Jews did not understand and did not want to understand. The chosenness of Israel led to resentment, hatred, violence, and cruelty of the worst sort. Jews have suffered isolation, persecution, forced conversion, and murder. Anti-Jewish sentiment is rooted in antiquity and has continued as an ever-present reality for the Jewish people. So why have Jews opted throughout the ages to stay chosen? Why haven't they abandoned their covenant with God?

Spinoza's approach essentially undermined the notion that the Jews had any special role in the ongoing history of humanity. In his view, they might just as well blend into humanity and abandon any trace of ethnic, national, and religious identity. Spinoza himself—an outcast from Amsterdam's Jewish community—lived as a philosopher and left behind no Jewish progeny. He seems to have shed his Jewishness without much remorse and may have seen himself as a prototype of what Jews (and all other human beings) should become: just plain human beings devoted to rational philosophy.

It is interesting that Spinoza sought to be a universal human being rather than a specifically Jewish human being. In spite of his universalism, his detractors were not shy to refer to him disparagingly as "the Jew Spinoza" or "the heretic Jew." Moreover, he was clearly aware of how the Christian society in the Iberian Peninsula continued to persecute Jews who had abandoned Judaism to convert to Christianity. Spanish and Portuguese Christians insisted on a distinction between the pure-blooded Christians and the new Christians of Jewish stock. Even Jews who sincerely adopted Christianity were subject to discrimination for having Jewish blood. Did Spinoza really believe that Jews could simply drop their identities and become fully accepted by the non-Jewish world?

Spinoza's approach to Jewish peoplehood is fundamentally irrelevant to those of us who choose to live as Jews and who continue to see ourselves as having a God-given mission to be a light unto the nations. In spite of the difficulties and hostilities that we may face, we embrace our Jewishness as an essential and inseparable aspect of our humanity. We must turn to Rambam, not to Spinoza, for guidance.

Rambam's Advice to Persecuted Jews

Rambam's *Epistle on Martyrdom*, probably written in 1165, was his response to a crisis that had struck Jews in Morocco. Due to the fanaticism of the Muslim rulers, Jews had been coerced into making a public affirmation of Islam or to suffer death. While some chose martyrdom, others made the profession of Islam but tried to maintain their Jewish lives in secret. One of the forced converts had asked a rabbi whether it was meritorious to observe the mitzvot under such conditions; the rabbi answered that any Jew who had publicly accepted Islam was not only guilty of apostasy, but was committing additional sins each time he observed a commandment of the Torah. Observing mitzvot as an apostate, according to this rabbi, compounded one's guilt.

In his letter, Rambam refuted the position of this rabbi and urged the forced converts to maintain as many mitzvot as they could; they would surely receive merit from God for their fulfillment of the commandments. He also prodded them to leave for safer lands whenever they could do so, even at great financial sacrifice, so that they could practice Judaism openly.

Rambam reminds his readers that God rewards everyone for the good deeds they perform. Even wicked people such as Eglon, Nebuchadnezzar, and Esau were granted reward for whatever good actions they did:

> If these well-known heretics were generously rewarded for the little good that they did, is it conceivable that God will not reward the Jews, who, despite the exigencies of the forced conversion, perform commandments secretly? Can it be that

He does not discriminate between one who performs a commandment and one who does not, between one who serves God and one who does not?[11]

Rambam points out the virtue of martyrdom in times of duress. Yet, the current crisis in Morocco had extenuating circumstances that did not demand martyrdom. The rulers insisted that Jews make a verbal profession of faith in Islam but did not enforce behavior patterns. A Jew might utter some words to appease the Muslim fanatics but then could continue to observe the mitzvot of the Torah secretly without a risk to his or her life. A Jew who chose martyrdom under these circumstances was certainly praiseworthy and would deserve great reward from God. But one who chose to verbalize acceptance of Islam while maintaining Judaism in secret was not culpable for words uttered under duress. Indeed, Rambam writes, "But if anyone comes to ask me whether to surrender his life or to acknowledge, I tell him to confess and not choose death."[12]

Rambam indicates that even Jews who sin are to be loved and brought closer—not scorned or pushed away. In a particularly meaningful passage, he writes:

It is not right to alienate, scorn, and hate people who desecrate the Sabbath. It is our duty to befriend them, and encourage them to fulfill the commandments. The rabbis regulate explicitly that when an evil-doer who sinned by choice comes to the synagogue, he is to be welcomed and not insulted.[13]

Rambam obviously believed with all his soul that it was imperative for Jews to stay devoted to Judaism, even in times of duress. He offered advice to strengthen the will to survive among the persecuted Jews of Morocco. He called on them to observe as many mitzvot as possible and to believe that God would reward them for their devotion. He urged them to leave for freer lands at their earliest opportunity and not persist in living under an oppressive regime any longer than necessary.

In his *Epistle to Yemen*, written in 1172, Rambam offers his guidance and consolation to the persecuted Jews of that country. Fanatical

Muslims were attempting to force the conversion of all non-Muslims, and Jewish life became precarious.

Rambam reminded the Jews of Yemen that

> ours is the true and divine religion, revealed to us through Moses, chief of the former as well as of the later prophets. By means of it God has distinguished us from the rest of mankind, as He declares: "Yet it was to your fathers that the Lord was drawn in His love for them, so that He chose you, their lineal descendants, from among all the peoples" (Deuteronomy 10:15). This choice was not made thanks to our merits, but was rather an act of grace, on account of our ancestors who were cognizant of God and obedient to Him....[14]

If we are the chosen people of God, why do we suffer so much? Rambam explains that the nations of the world persecute us because they are motivated by envy and impiety, injustice, and enmity.

> They wanted to thwart God, but He will not be thwarted. Ever since the time of revelation every despot or rebel ruler, be he violent or ignoble, has made it his first aim and his final purpose to destroy our Law, and to vitiate our religion by means of the sword, by violence, or by brute force.[15]

Rambam notes that aside from the anti-Jewish despots, Jews have also suffered from educated non-Jews who sought to undermine Judaism through their arguments and controversies. These individuals have tried through their writings and preachings to destroy Israel. But just as the despots have failed to destroy us through their violence, so the intelligentsia has failed to undermine us through their arguments. "Every disputant who will attempt to demonstrate the falsity of our Law, the Lord will shatter his arguments and prove them absurd, untenable, and ineffective."[16] For Rambam, the eternity of the Jews was guaranteed by a divine promise.

Rambam refers to another group, more dangerous than the despots and the anti-Jewish propagandists. This group consisted of those who combined both methods, violence and controversy. Rambam states that Jesus and Mohammed founded religions that sought to undermine the Torah and that also came to foster violence against Jews. These religions attempted to distort the biblical record by making false interpretations; then they accused the Jews of stubbornness for not accepting their corrupt readings of Jewish Scriptures! Rambam assures his readers that Judaism would ultimately be vindicated:

> The three parties that warred against us will ultimately perish: the one that sought to overpower us with the sword, the second that claimed it had arguments against us, and the third that claims to have a religion similar to ours. Though they shall appear to be triumphant for a while and be in the ascendancy for a longer or shorter period of time, they shall neither last nor endure. We have a continuous divine assurance that whenever a decree of apostasy is passed against us and wrath breaks out, God will ultimately terminate it.[17]

Rambam reminds the Yemenite Jews that Moses was the greatest prophet and that the Torah was spoken to Moses from beginning to end. The Torah would never be supplanted nor superseded. Although Christians and Muslims distorted the clear meaning of the Torah by making false interpretations, the Jews should not be deluded by them. Rather, they should hold fast to the Torah.

Rambam then discusses the days of the Messiah, when the truth of Judaism would finally be acknowledged by all:

> For while the gentiles believe that our nation will never consti-tute an independent state, nor will it ever rise above its present condition, and all the astrologers, diviners, and augurs concur in this opinion, God will prove their views and beliefs false, and will order the advent of the Messiah…. This is the correct view that every Israelite should hold, without paying any attention to the conjunctions of the stars, of greater and smaller magnitude.[18]

Rambam warned the Jews of Yemen to pay no heed to a certain individual who was passing himself off as the promised Messiah, for he was a fraud. The true Messiah would descend from King David and would restore the glory of Torah and the sovereignty of Israel. History had produced a number of false messiahs, all of whom had perished and had been unable to make good their claims.

The Messianic Era

We learn from Rambam's teachings that the chosenness of Israel has its roots in our forefather Abraham, but the purpose of its chosenness is to bring humanity to a true understanding of God. The culmination of this process will be reached during messianic times. Among his thirteen principles of faith, Rambam listed belief in the ultimate redemption of Israel with the arrival of the Messiah.

Rambam viewed the messianic era in naturalistic terms. The laws of nature would not be set aside; the world would follow its normal course. The only difference between our times and messianic times is that the Messiah would deliver the people of Israel from servitude to foreign powers. Moreover, the nations of the world would accept the true religion—Judaism—and would no longer persecute the Jewish people. For Jews, the messianic ideal was simply to be left alone—not to be harassed and treated meanly by others—so that life could be devoted to the intellectual love of God and the righteous fulfillment of His commandments. Rambam writes:

> The sages and prophets did not long for the days of the Messiah that Israel might exercise dominion over the world, or rule over the heathens, or be exalted by the nations, or that it might eat and drink and rejoice. Their aspiration was that Israel be free to devote itself to the Torah and its wisdom, with no one to oppress or disturb it, and thus be worthy of life in the world to come.[19]

For Rambam, the goal of Israel—its raison d'être—had always been to serve God and to bring humanity into a proper belief in God and into a moral way of life. The people of Israel had not sought, and would not seek in messianic times, to rule over other nations. The role of Israel was in the realm of theology and righteousness.

According to Rambam, the Messiah would restore the monarchy of David, rebuild the Holy Temple, and gather all the exiles of the Jewish people into the land of Israel. In the messianic era, sacrifices would once again be offered in the Temple, and the people would observe the Sabbatical and Jubilee years as in former times. "The essential point is as follows. This Torah with all its statutes and ordinances is eternal. We may not add to it, nor may we subtract from it (*Hilkhot Melakhim* 11:1, 3)."[20] What is the role of non-Jews in the messianic drama? In the uncensored version of the end of *Hilkhot Melakhim* 11:4, Rambam suggests that Christianity and Islam play a role in the unfolding of the mission of Israel. On its own, Israel apparently would have been unable to teach monotheism to the entire world.

> But it is beyond the human mind to fathom the designs of the Creator; for our ways are not His ways, neither are our thoughts His thoughts. All these matters relating to Jesus of Nazareth and the Ishmaelite (Mohammed) who came after him, only served to clear the way for King Messiah, to prepare the whole world to worship God with one accord, as it is written, "For then will I turn to the peoples of pure language, that they may all call upon the name of the Lord to serve Him with one consent" (Zephaniah 3:9). Thus the Messianic hope, the Torah, and the commandments have become familiar topics—topics of conversation (among the inhabitants) of the far isles and many peoples, uncircumcised of heart and flesh. They are discussing these matters and the commandments of the Torah. Some say, "Those commandments were true, but have lost their validity and are no longer binding"; others declare that they had an esoteric meaning and were not intended to be taken literally; that the Messiah has already come and revealed their occult significance. But when the true King Messiah will appear and succeed, be exalted and lifted up, they will forthwith recant and realize

that they have inherited naught but lies from their fathers, that their prophets and forebears led them astray.[21]

Rambam understood that Christianity and Islam have attracted billions of adherents—all of whom are aware of the Torah and the special role of Israel in the unfolding of humanity's spiritual history. Although these religions have distorted the teachings of Judaism, they have nevertheless introduced vast numbers of people to ethical monotheism. They have primed the way so that the masses of humanity will ultimately be ready to accept the undiluted teachings of Torah in messianic times.

Would all non-Jews convert to Judaism in the messianic era? Professor Menachem Kellner's reading of Rambam is that indeed all humanity would become Jewish. Since there is no innate difference between Jews and non-Jews, all humanity would one day come to realize the Truth of Torah and choose to live by its teachings. The historic rivalries and antagonisms among the world's religions would come to an end. All people would live in harmony, righteousness, and love of God.[22]

Choosing Harmony and Righteousness

We who have been raised in Western civilization place a premium on the values of human equality and freedom of expression. We are taught to be nonjudgmental, to seek the wisdom that is manifested in traditions other than our own. We can appreciate Rambam's commitment to truth and his insistence that we learn from all sages—whether they are Jewish or non-Jewish.

We are comfortable with Rambam's view that Jews and non-Jews are basically the same, sharing universal human qualities. Jewish distinctiveness does not stem from an innate metaphysical characteristic of the Jews, but from the transmission of values and observances taught by the Torah and our rabbis. Jewish distinctiveness is from nurture, not nature; therefore, non-Jews may also choose to adopt the Jewish way of life. Rational-minded Jews are uncomfortable with the kabbalistic notion that Jews have souls that are qualitatively different from the souls of non-Jews; Rambam offers us a meaningful way of understanding ourselves not simply as Jews, but as human beings.

Modern Jews are sometimes uncomfortable and apologetic about the phrase "chosen people." This phrase seems to imply spiritual superiority, whereby somehow God loves Jews more than other people. Rambam's insights are instructive. He argues that it was, in fact, Abraham who chose God; it is the Israelite people who chose to follow in Abraham's ways and ultimately to accept the Torah in the days of Moses. Israel was chosen not due to any superior spiritual gift, but as God's reaction to a people who had chosen Him.

Even during periods of intense persecution, Jews have been steadfast in pursuing their devotion to ethical monotheism. In spite of the fact that many Jews perished or were forcibly converted over the centuries, a remnant of Israel has always survived. This survival must be based on a deep-seated belief that we are responsible to God, that we have been elected by God to bring humanity to a messianic age. If Jews see themselves merely as another ethnic or national group, what is the point of suffering so much persecution and hostility? Why not—as Spinoza would have suggested—simply give up the Jewish enterprise and become a plain human being with no Jewish affiliation? The root reason why Jews persist is that they understand themselves—consciously or unconsciously—to be leading humanity to a messianic era.

Even if we choose not to share the view that all non-Jews will ultimately convert to Judaism, we can still hope that all non-Jews will one day become ethical monotheists who will live in harmony with Jews. When all people seek God, when all people live moral and upright lives, when all people recognize their kinship with all other human beings—that, too, might fairly be described as the messianic age. Those who share this dream and who work for it, these are the chosen people of our time.

8

CONVERSION TO JUDAISM

I n the previous chapter, we touched upon the issue of conversion to
Judaism. This topic is of great importance in contemporary Jewish
life, with serious ramifications for the future of the Jewish people in
Israel and the Diaspora. In this chapter, we will discuss this issue in
greater detail and underscore the ongoing significance of Rambam's
teachings on this subject. (Since Spinoza essentially had given up on the
future of the Jewish people, this chapter and the next one will focus on
Rambam's teachings, since they have continued relevance for modern-
day Jews and Judaism.)

The Bible does not describe a formal procedure for conversion.
The biblical word *ger* literally means "stranger" and refers to a non-
Israelite who lived among the Israelite nation. Rabbinic tradition interpreted the word *ger* also to refer to proselytes who actually became
members of the Israelite community through conversion. The midrash
traces the origin of conversion to Abraham and Sarah, the founders of
what became the Jewish tradition:

> Said Rabbi Hunya: Abraham converted the men, and Sarah the
> women. And what does the Torah teach when it refers to "the
> souls they made in Haran"? This teaches that Abraham our

father would bring them into his house, feed them, and give them drink, and demonstrate love toward them and bring them near and convert them and bring them under the wings of the Divine Presence. From this we learn that one who brings one person under the wings of the Divine Presence, it is as though he created him and formed him and fashioned him.[1]

As the Torah teaches, circumcision of males was a requirement for entry into the Abrahamic covenant (Genesis 17:10–14). Jacob's sons insisted that the men of Shekhem be circumcised, stating, "We cannot do such a thing to give our sister to a man who is uncircumcised" (Genesis 34:14).

When the Israelites were redeemed from their slavery in Egypt, the Torah informs us that a mixed multitude of non-Hebrews accompanied them. We are not given details about if or how this group assimilated into and became part of the Israelite people.

The most famous biblical account of a convert pertains to Ruth, who followed her mother-in-law Naomi to the land of Israel. In expressing her commitment, Ruth stated, "For whither you go I will go; and where you lodge I will lodge. Your people will be my people and your God my God" (Ruth 1:16). Her statement reflects loyalty both to the people of Israel and to the religion of Israel, the essential ingredients of a proper conversion.

The book of Esther refers to non-Jews who were *mityahadim*—Judaizing—but it is not clear if they actually converted to Judaism or merely feigned Jewishness out of fear (Esther 8:17). The Book of Ezra tells of the large number of Jewish men in Jerusalem who had married non-Jewish wives. Ezra ordered them to separate from their "foreign women" (Ezra 10:11). It is not known whether Ezra was ideologically opposed to conversion for the sake of marriage or was simply taking an extreme measure that was needed in this particular situation.

The Talmud and midrashim reflect different attitudes toward conversion. A positive disposition to conversion is evident in passages that remind us that King David, from whose line the Messiah will emerge, was a descendant of Ruth—a righteous proselyte. Great sages such as

Shemaya and Avtalyon were converts. Rabbi Akiva and Rabbi Meir are said to have descended from non-Jews who had been enemies of the Jewish people. Rabbinic tradition mentions that Roman nobles had become Jewish.[2]

Other rabbinic passages indicate that the Jews were sent into exile in order to gather converts to Judaism. Non-Jewish communities who produced even one righteous proselyte per year were granted great merit from God.[3]

On the other hand, rabbinic literature also reflects negative attitudes toward conversion and converts. The most notorious statement is attributed to Rabbi Helbo, who said that "converts are as difficult to Israel as a scab" (Talmud, *Kiddushin* 70b). Rabbi Yitzhak warned that many problems will befall those who receive converts into Judaism (Talmud, *Yevamot* 109b). One Talmudic statement goes so far as to say that converts cause the delay of the arrival of the Messiah (*Nidah* 13b).

As long as Jews had sovereignty over their own land, conversion was akin to naturalization. The non-Jewish resident decided to become Jewish in order to be part of the dominant national culture. However, once the Romans razed the Temple in Jerusalem in 70 CE, the Jews embarked on a long period of exile when they lacked sovereignty over their own land. There was no more Temple or Sanhedrin. Jews were scattered in many countries. When a non-Jew wished to convert, the emphasis would necessarily shift to the religious component of the Jewish people rather than the political/national aspects.

With the rise of Christianity and then Islam, new issues arose relating to conversion to Judaism. Both of these religions issued sanctions—including the death penalty—forbidding Jews from engaging in proselytizing. Nonetheless, conversions to Judaism took place, albeit in a very limited fashion and only after the Jewish authorities had confidence that the converts would be fully loyal to Judaism and the Jewish people. An upsurge in conversions to Judaism began in the eighteenth century, when European Jews were gaining political rights through Emancipation and were interacting more freely with non-Jewish fellow citizens.

A number of rabbinic sages of the nineteenth and twentieth centuries were positively disposed to receive converts, even in cases where the initial impetus for the conversion was the desire on the part of the would-be convert to marry a Jewish spouse. Some of these rabbis called for the acceptance of converts even if it was suspected (or even known) that the converts would not be fully observant of all the mitzvot. Other rabbis, though, were emphatically opposed to conversion, unless the would-be convert was totally committed to Judaism and to the observance of all the commandments of the Torah.[4]

Talmudic Sources for Conversion

The primary sources for the laws of conversion are in the Talmud. The basic description of the conversion process is recorded in *Yevamot* 47a–b:

> Our rabbis taught: If at the present time a person desires to become a proselyte, he is to be addressed as follows: "Why do you come to be a proselyte? Do you not know that Israel at the present time is persecuted and oppressed, despised, harassed, and overcome by afflictions?" If he replies, "I know and yet am unworthy [but still wish to convert]," he is accepted forthwith, and is given instruction in some of the minor and some of the major commandments…. And as he is informed of the punishment for the transgression of the commandments, so is he informed of the reward granted for their fulfillment…. He is not, however, to be persuaded or dissuaded too much. If he is accepted, he is circumcised forthwith…. As soon as he is healed, arrangements are made for his immediate ablution [in a mikvah]. When he comes up after his ablution, he is deemed to be an Israelite in all respects. In the case of a woman proselyte, women make her sit in the water up to her neck, while two [three] learned men stand outside and give her instruction in some of the minor commandments and some of the major ones.

The candidate for conversion is first told of the dangers confronting the Jewish people in order to ascertain whether he or she is willing to be subjected to these risks as a Jew. This harks back to biblical Ruth, whose conversion declaration began with "your people will be my people" and only afterward went on with "your God will be my God."

The Talmud requires us to inform the would-be proselyte of some of the mitzvot—not all of them. Indeed, we are not supposed to belabor the issue of mitzvot, so as not to scare off the person who has already expressed a desire to become a member of the Jewish people. We may neither persuade nor dissuade too much. Rather, we want the person to know that our religion makes demands on us—demands that entail rewards and punishments. It is up to the person to decide, based on the limited information we have presented, whether or not to become Jewish.

The Talmud makes no reference to the need for the would-be proselyte to devote years to studying Torah before being accepted for conversion. It makes no demand that the candidate even know what all the mitzvot are! On the contrary, the Talmudic conversion process is fairly straightforward. Once the candidate has expressed willingness to join the Jewish people, and once he or she has been told some of the mitzvot, the person is accepted forthwith, without delays.

What if the candidate for conversion has ulterior motives, for example, he or she wishes to marry a Jew? In this case, the motivating factor is not purely religious (or not religious at all). Is such a conversion valid? The Talmud discusses this issue (*Yevamot* 24b):

> Mishnah: If a man is suspected of [intercourse] … with a heathen who subsequently became a proselyte, he must not marry her. If, however, he did marry her, they need not be separated. Gemara: This implies that she may become a proper proselyte. But against this a contradiction is raised. Both a man who became a proselyte for the sake of a woman and a woman who became a proselyte for the sake of a man … are not proper proselytes. These are the words of Rabbi Nehemiah, for Rabbi Nehemiah used to say: Neither lion proselytes nor dream

proselytes nor the proselytes of Mordecai and Esther are proper
proselytes unless they become converted as at the present
time…. Surely concerning this it was stated that Rabbi Isaac
bar Samuel bar Martha said in the name of Rab: The halakha is
in accordance with the opinion of him who maintained that
they are all proper proselytes.

Rabbi Nehemiah argued that conversions with ulterior motives (for
example, to marry a Jew) are not valid. Only conversions motivated by
pure spiritual considerations are acceptable. However, the Talmud
rejects Rabbi Nehemiah's opinion. The halakha follows Rab—conversions by those who had ulterior motives are, in fact, valid. These converts are halakhically Jewish.

Rabbi Nehemiah viewed conversion primarily as an unsullied
acceptance of Judaism; thus, one whose motives were suspect would
not be a suitable proselyte. Rab, though, seemed to view the conversion process as a means of bringing the non-Jew into the Jewish peoplehood. Even if the decision to become Jewish did not stem from
purely religious considerations, the proselyte became a full member of
the Jewish people by undergoing the conversion procedure. Although
this Talmudic passage is discussing a de facto situation (bedi-avad),
great modern-day halakhic authorities have argued that it is appropriate to accept such converts even initially, due to the unique exigencies
of the modern period.

The Talmud (Shabbat 31a) records three instances where individuals expressed the desire to convert to Judaism and who came both to
Shammai and Hillel. Since each of the three began his inquiries with
improper assumptions—one accepted to follow the Written Torah but
not the Oral Torah, one wanted to learn the entire Torah while standing on one foot, and one wanted to convert in order to become the
High Priest—Shammai turned them away. Hillel, on the other hand,
accepted each of them lovingly, and through his patient and wise
instruction he was able to bring them into Judaism. The Talmud relates
that these three proselytes faulted Shammai's strictness and praised the
kindness and humility of Hillel for having allowed them to come

"under the wings of the Divine Presence." The point of these stories is that even if candidates come with mistaken ideas and improper motives, they should be received kindly. By teaching them lovingly, the hope is that they will indeed come to a proper understanding of Jewish traditions and will eventually develop pure motives for conversion.

What if a convert's knowledge of Torah and mitzvot was seriously deficient? Could such a convert be deemed to be Jewish? The Talmud (*Shabbat* 68a) rules that a person who unknowingly transgresses Sabbath laws many times is obligated to bring only one sin offering, rather than one offering for each transgression. Rab and Shemuel, the leading sages of their generation, explained that this rule refers to "a child who was captured among non-Jews and a convert who was converted among the gentiles." Since these individuals simply did not know the Sabbath laws because they had been raised or converted among non-Jews, they could not be held responsible for all their transgressions. Here we have a case of a non-Jew who became a valid proselyte—but who did not even know the laws of Shabbat! The Talmud never questions the Jewishness of such a proselyte nor even faintly suggests that the conversion was not valid or could be retroactively annulled. As long as the proselyte underwent the technicalities of conversion (which obviously did not include a full knowledge of mitzvot), the proselyte was a full-fledged Jew.

One Talmudic passage (*Bekhorot* 30b) is frequently quoted to prove that a proselyte must accept every mitzvah and that a rejection of even one mitzvah disqualifies him or her from being accepted as a convert:

> Our rabbis taught ... If a heathen is prepared to accept the Torah except one religious law, we must not receive him. R. Jose son of R. Judah says: Even [if the exception be] one point of the special minutiae of the Scribes' enactments.

This passage seems to go against the previously mentioned Talmudic passages, which clearly do not require the proselyte to know and commit to observe every mitzvah, let alone each point of special minutiae of the Scribes' enactments. Neither Rambam nor the *Shulhan Arukh* cites this passage as authoritative halakha in regard to the conversion process. Indeed, Rambam did not believe this passage is referring to a righteous proselyte at all, but rather to a resident alien (*ger toshav*).[5]

Even if we were to apply this passage to righteous proselytes (although neither Rambam nor the *Shulhan Arukh* did so!), it could still be understood in light of the other Talmudic passages cited earlier. Rabbi Hayyim Ozer Grodzinski explained: We are supposed to inform the would-be proselyte of the mitzvot. As long as the candidate gives general assent to accept the mitzvot, that is sufficient. If the would-be proselyte specifically rejects a particular mitzvah, only then should he or she not be accepted. "But in the case of one who accepts all the mitzvot, while his intention is to transgress for his own pleasure [*letei'avon*] this is not a deficiency in the law of *kabbalat hamitzvot*."[6]

Rabbi Benzion Uziel ruled:

> If a convert accepts the Torah and the rewards and punishments of the commandments but continues to behave in the way he was accustomed before conversion, he is a sinning convert, but we do not hesitate to accept him because of this.[7]

In other words, what is required is a general statement from the proselyte indicating an acceptance of mitzvot. It is not incumbent upon us to probe too deeply, nor to receive a promise that each and every mitzvah will be fulfilled without exception. As long as the candidate for conversion does not make a formal declaration rejecting a particular halakha, that is sufficient as *kabbalat hamitzvot*.

Rambam's Rulings

In describing the procedure for accepting converts, Rambam basically follows the protocol recorded in *Yevamot* 47a–b. However, he adds the requirement of informing the candidate of the basic principles of our faith, such as the unity of God and the prohibition of idolatry.[8] Rambam, like the Talmud, indicates that we inform the candidate of some of the mitzvot and some of the rewards and punishments—but we do not overly prolong this nor give too many details "lest we cause him anxiety and thereby turn him from the good path to the bad path."[9] We are supposed to draw the potential convert to Judaism with goodwill and soft words.

Rambam did not require—or expect—that would-be converts be given thorough instruction in Torah and mitzvot. This is reflected in Rambam's discussion of the *hakhel* commandment, when the people of Israel gathered in Jerusalem once in seven years to hear the king read from the Torah. Men, women, and children were to attend this event—even those who could not understand the Torah reading. Rambam seems to take it for granted that proselytes were among those who would not understand the Torah reading. He writes:

> As for proselytes who do not know the Torah, they must make ready their heart and give ear attentively to listen in awe and reverence and trembling joy, as on the day when the Torah was given on Sinai.[10]

Rambam noted that potential converts should be examined to see if they have ulterior motives.[11] In the days of King David and King Solomon, the official rabbinical court did not accept proselytes, since it was assumed that non-Jews came for personal gain rather than religious reasons. Nonetheless, Rambam points out, numerous converts were made in the days of David and Solomon through *hedyotot*, ad hoc courts of non-experts that were not the official courts of the land. Such converts were neither pushed away nor brought close until it was seen how they turned out, that is, whether they were truly serious in their desire to be Jewish. Having said this, though, Rambam instructs us not to believe that Samson or Solomon married non-Jewish women. Rather, their "non-Jewish" wives were actually converted by the courts of *hedyotot*, so that they were in fact Jewish. Yet, we know that these wives did not convert from religious motivations. We also know that they continued to worship idols after their conversions. Wouldn't this be a clear indication that their conversions were not valid? Isn't it obvious that they turned out to be idolaters rather than Jews?

Rambam rules:

> A proselyte who was not examined [as to his motives] or who was not informed of the mitzvot and their punishments, and he was circumcised and immersed in the presence of three laymen, is a proselyte. Even if it is known that he converted for some ulterior motive, once he has been circumcised and immersed he has left the status of being a non-Jew and we suspect him until his righteousness is clarified. Even if he recanted and worshipped idols, he is [considered] a Jewish apostate; if he betroths a Jewish woman according to halakha, they are betrothed; and an article he lost must be returned to him as to any other Jew. Having immersed, he is a Jew.[12]

According to Rambam, a person who undergoes the technical procedures of conversion (circumcision and immersion for a man, immersion for a woman) in the presence of a *bet din* (even one made up of laymen) is a valid convert. Even if the motives for conversion were dubious, and even if the convert reverted to idolatry, the conversion remains valid. We may not want this person to marry into our family. We may suspect his or her sincerity and uprightness of character—but he or she is Jewish all the same.

The Talmud, Rambam, and the *Shulhan Arukh* (*Yoreh Deah* 268) provide a general framework for the acceptance of converts but do not give a detailed list of guidelines. These classic halakhic sources recognize that each conversion case is unique, and each must be evaluated by those overseeing the conversions. In the Talmud's words, *ein leDayan ela ma sheEinav ro'ot*: each judge must take responsibility for the cases that come before him, based on his own evaluation. Classic halakha eschewed uniform standards in the area of conversion, leaving it to the individuals in charge to use their own judgment in dealing with each would-be proselyte.

Rambam issued a far-reaching ruling in one of his responsa, pointing the way to how individual rabbis might deal with difficult cases.[13] The question related to an unmarried Jewish man who had purchased a maidservant. He was suspected of having immoral relations with her. Did the *bet din* have an obligation to have her removed from his house? In his response, Rambam states categorically that the maid certainly should be removed from this man's house. The *bet din* should exert its power to have the maid sent out or to have the Jewish master free her and then marry her. However, the Talmud rules (*Yevamot* 24b) that a man suspected of having immoral relations with his maid is not allowed to marry her, even if he were to free her. In spite of this clear Talmudic law, Rambam states that he has judged in such cases that the man should set his maid free and then marry her. He justifies his decision by stating that it is necessary to make things easier for those who wish to repent. He relies on the famous rabbinic formulation "It is time to serve the Lord, go against your Torah" (Talmud, *Berakhot* 9:5). There are emergency situations that call for rulings that may go against one law but that prevent greater evils. Rambam closes his responsum: "And the Lord in His mercy will forgive our transgressions."

Rambam realized that his decision violated the ideal halakhic practice. Nonetheless, he allowed his human insight to deal with the problem in a realistic way. The Talmud itself offers guidance in this direction, indicating that it is preferable to choose the lesser of two evils, even when the choice is not ideal (*Kiddushin* 21b; *Shabbat* 31b). In the above case, if the court realized that it would be unable to separate the man from the maidservant, it is preferable that she be freed and then married to him according to Jewish law rather than remaining in an immoral relationship.

Rabbi Uziel and other sages have applied this ruling of Rambam to problematic cases of conversion. Although some candidates for conversion may not fulfill the ideal requirements, the rabbinic court needs to determine whether it is better to convert such individuals or to turn them away. Given the serious issues we face today relating to intermarriage and to establishing Jewish status in the State of Israel, we might well see the contemporary scene as a period of "emergency" when Rambam's ruling can be an important precedent.

Contemporary Stringencies

The Talmud, Rambam, and the *Shulhan Arukh* (1) do not demand nor expect a candidate for conversion to learn all the mitzvot prior to conversion; (2) do not demand nor expect a candidate for conversion to promise to observe all the mitzvot in specific detail; (3) do not demand an extended period of study before conversion; (4) do not equate conversion with a total acceptance to observe Torah and mitzvot, but rather see conversion as a way for a non-Jew to become a member of the Jewish people; (5) do recognize the validity of conversions even when the convert came with ulterior motives, even when the convert was ignorant of basic laws of Judaism; (6) do not allow for the retroactive annulment of a conversion, even when the convert continued to worship idols after converting to Judaism.

Since the classic halakhic sources allow so much leeway in the acceptance of converts, why have important nineteenth- and twentieth-century halakhic authorities adopted stringent positions that are so antithetical to these sources? Indeed, why has the stringent view become so prevalent within Orthodoxy?[14]

One answer is that the Orthodox rabbinate has been vastly influenced by the rise of Reform and Conservative Judaism and by the increasing number of Jews who have defected from the halakhic way of life. In seeing Orthodoxy as a bastion of Torah-true Judaism, Orthodox sages have insisted on policies that clearly distinguish between "us" and "them." "We" are the ones who demand scrupulous observance of halakha. "They" are the ones who have betrayed Torah tradition by undermining mitzvah observance. This attitude carries into the area of acceptance of converts. "We" only want converts who will be like us—truly dedicated to Torah and mitzvot. "We" don't want to create more nonobservant Jews in our communities.

Another possible answer is that some in the Orthodox community have a mystical view of Jewishness that deems it quite difficult for a non-Jew to become Jewish. Rabbi Abraham Isaac Kook, for example, believed that the act of conversion requires the convert to join the soul of *Kenesset Yisrael*, a metaphysical representation of the congregation of Israel. This can be accomplished only through a total acceptance of the mitzvot, since mitzvot are the essence of the Jewish soul. This is not an easy transition, according to Rabbi Kook, since Jewish souls and non-Jewish souls are ontologically different. For a non-Jew to transform his soul into a Jewish soul requires a tremendous connection to Torah and mitzvot.[15] Without belaboring the point, Rabbi Kook's line of thinking can be used to buttress feelings of Jewish "superiority" as well as latent xenophobic tendencies. Rabbi Kook was deeply steeped in Kabbalah and obviously absorbed the notion of the ontological uniqueness of Jewish souls as distinguished from the souls of non-Jews. This view not only pervaded the thought of Rabbi Kook, but also vastly influenced—directly and indirectly—other rabbinic sages of the modern period.

Rambam, of course, sharply rejected the concept that Jewish souls are intrinsically different from non-Jewish souls. He did not subscribe to the mystical view that Jewish souls had inherent spiritual powers that were lacking in the souls of other human beings. Because of his philosophical stance, Rambam understood conversion as a means for non-Jews to become part of the Jewish people. By being Jewish, they would have greater opportunity to observe Torah and mitzvot, and hence develop their spiritual lives and come to a closer relationship with God. A non-Jew does not need to overcome any metaphysical obstacles in order to convert to Judaism; he or she simply needs to accept to become Jewish and to become familiar with basic mitzvot of the Torah.

If Rabbi Kook is a modern representative of the kabbalistic view of conversion, Rabbi Benzion Uziel is a modern representative of the Rambam's approach. Rabbi Uziel (1880–1953), late Sephardic Chief Rabbi of Israel, shared Rambam's outlook that Jews and non-Jews have the same essential qualities.[16] Conversion to Judaism does not entail a metaphysical transformation of a non-Jewish soul, but a practical commitment by the non-Jew to become a member of the Jewish people.

This commitment should ideally stem from a religious quest for truth. But even if a non-Jew chooses to convert for ulterior motives, such as in order to marry a Jewish person, the conversion is valid. This is true even if it is unlikely that the convert will become a fully observant religious Jew. Rabbi Uziel saw himself as being very stringent in applying the prohibitions against intermarriage. Therefore, he believed that rabbis must do everything in their power to prevent intermarriage situations. When a Jew and non-Jew were intending to marry each other, or already were married to each other, Rabbi Uziel urged that rabbis convert the non-Jewish partner to Judaism. He made this ruling even when it was expected that the couple would not be observant of all the mitzvot. He ruled that performing such conversions was not only permitted, but was a mitzvah!

> From all that has been stated and discussed, the ruling follows that it is permissible and a mitzvah to accept male and female converts even if it is known to us that they will not observe all the mitzvot, because in the end they will come to fulfill them. We are commanded to make this kind of opening for them; and if they do not fulfill the mitzvot, they will bear their own iniquities, and we are innocent.[17]

Rabbi Uziel was deeply concerned about the fate of children born to a Jewish father and a non-Jewish mother. He believed that such children, although of Jewish stock (*zera Yisrael*), were in fact not halakhically Jewish. Children raised in such intermarriages would be lost to the Jewish people entirely. Thus, it should be obligatory for rabbis to convert the non-Jewish mother in order to keep the children in the Jewish fold. Rabbi Uziel noted:

> And I fear that if we push them [the children] away completely by not accepting their parents for conversion, we shall be brought to judgment and they shall say to us: "You did not bring back those who were driven away, and those who were lost you did not seek" (Ezekiel 34:4).[18]

In another responsum, Rabbi Uziel wrote:

> I admit without embarrassment that my heart is filled with
> trembling for every Jewish soul that is assimilated among the
> non-Jews. I feel in myself a duty and mitzvah to open a door to
> repentance and to save [Jews] from assimilation by [invoking]
> arguments for leniency. This is the way of Torah, in my hum-
> ble opinion, and this is what I saw and received from my par-
> ents and teachers.[19]

Certainly Rabbi Uziel would have liked all Jews—born Jews and converted Jews—to live fully religious lives devoted to Torah and mitzvot.
However, we live in an imperfect world, and we therefore need to make
halakhic judgments based on the realities we face. Since intermarriage
is a great sin and leads to the loss of children to the Jewish people, Rabbi
Uziel deemed these concerns to outweigh considerations about how
religiously observant the converts would be. Surely, he pointed out,
candidates for conversion should be taught some of the major and some
of the minor mitzvot, and should come to feel as members of the Jewish
people. But if they live as nonobservant Jews, this is their sin—not ours.
By preventing intermarriage situations, we can hope that these couples
and their children will be part of the Jewish people and will ultimately
come closer to our Torah traditions. If, however, we turn such converts
away, we allow intermarriages to persist, and we undermine the possibility of keeping children of such marriages within the Jewish people.
Unlike the kabbalistic notion of different souls, the Maimonidean argument is that conversion is available to any non-Jew who wishes to join
the Jewish people and adopt the Jewish religion in general terms. It is
more a philosophical/sociological/communal phenomenon than a mysterious metaphysical phenomenon.

Welcoming Conversion

In our times, many thousands of non-Jews seek conversion to Judaism.
Some live in the State of Israel and want to become part of the dominant

national religion. Others live throughout the world and are attracted to Judaism's teachings and observances, or they wish to marry a Jew or are already married to a Jew.

The conversion issue today is complicated by the fact that alternative forms of conversion are available. Non-Orthodox rabbis perform conversions with varying faithfulness to halakhic norms. Within Orthodoxy, as has been seen in the different views of Rabbi Uziel and Rabbi Kook, there is no unanimity in what the halakha does or does not require for conversion. In actual fact, though, the Orthodox conversion process has become increasingly extreme. The Israeli Chief Rabbinate has refused to accept conversions performed by Orthodox rabbis in the Diaspora unless those rabbis are on an approved list— that is, they agree to submit to the stringent standards typical of right-wing Orthodoxy. The mainstream Orthodox rabbinic groups in the Diaspora have basically ceded authority to Israel's Chief Rabbis. To make things more confusing, conversions accepted by Israel's Chief Rabbinate are not necessarily accepted by the *Hareidi* (right-wing) Orthodox rabbis in Israel or the Diaspora.

At a time when thousands of non-Jews seek entry into Judaism, the Orthodox rabbinic establishment has become increasingly extreme and obstructionist. Candidates for conversion are turned away unless they are ready to adopt a fully Orthodox lifestyle.

Rambam's views on conversion provide a framework for addressing the current situation in a proper halakhic manner. Like Rambam, we must combat the kabbalistic notion that Jewish souls are ontologically different from non-Jewish souls. This belief is at the root of negative and restrictive views relating to conversion. We must see conversion primarily as a process by which non-Jews join the Jewish people. Surely we must teach them Torah and mitzvot, and surely their conversion will be greatly enhanced by their commitment to Torah and mitzvot; however, converts need not promise to observe the entire Torah in every detail before they can actually be accepted as members of the Jewish people. Rambam makes it very clear that even a convert who comes with ulterior motives, who has little or no instruction in Judaism, and who does not observe Judaism properly after conversion—such a person is still a valid convert as long as he or she underwent the technical procedures of conversion.

Given the many challenges faced by the Jewish people today, it is incumbent for us to promote a meaningful and accessible halakhic process for conversion. This is not the time to seek unnecessary stringencies, nor to rely upon problematic kabbalistic beliefs about the nature of our souls. This is the time to draw on the insights of Rambam. This is surely the time to rely on the halakhic authority of sages such as Rabbi Benzion Uziel who apply the teachings of Rambam to the situations confronting us in our era.

9

ETERNAL TORAH, CHANGING TIMES

Rambam wrote his works to serve as a foundation and guide to his and future generations for their understanding of Judaism. The eternal Torah is relevant to all generations. Yet, new ideas, discoveries, and sociological conditions develop over the ages. Rambam provides a framework with which we may apply the teachings of an ancient Torah tradition to the new exigencies of the changing times. We need to apply these same critical faculties to our understanding of Rambam's own writings.

First, let us examine Rambam's views on human perfection. This will provide not only a "curriculum" for what we should be studying, but also an approach to educational methodology. We will then discuss issues relating to religion and science and to the radical changes of the past century relating to the role of women in society.

Human Perfection

Rambam presents a parable in his *Guide of the Perplexed* that indicates his educational philosophy:

> The ruler is in his palace, and all his subjects are partly within the city and partly outside the city. Of those who are within the

city, some have turned their backs upon the ruler's habitation, their faces being turned another way. Others seek to reach the ruler's habitation, turn toward it, and wish to enter it and to stand before him—but up to now they have not yet seen the wall of the habitation. Some of those who seek to reach it have come up to the habitation and walk around it searching for its gate. Some of them have entered the gate and walk about in the antechambers. Some of them have entered the inner court of the habitation and have come to be with the king, in one and the same place with him, namely, in the ruler's habitation. But their having come into the inner part of the habitation does not mean that they see the ruler or speak to him. For after their coming into the inner part of the habitation, it is indispensable that they should make another effort; then they will be in the presence of the ruler, see him from afar or from nearby, or hear the ruler's speech or speak to him.[1]

Rambam then proceeds to explain this parable. Those outside the city are individuals without doctrinal belief, akin to irrational animals. Those inside the city but facing away from the palace are those who hold incorrect doctrinal belief. The further they walk, the further they move away from the palace. Those who seek to enter the palace but have not yet seen it are the Jewish masses who are "ignoramuses who observe the commandments." Those who have reached the king's habitation, circling it to find a way in, are halakhists who hold true beliefs but "who do not engage in speculation concerning the fundamental principles of religion and make no inquiry whatever regarding the rectification of belief." Those who have entered the gate and walk in the antechambers are those "who have entered into speculation concerning the fundamental principles of religion" and who have "understood the natural sciences."

Those who have entered the inner court and are with the ruler include the individual "who has achieved demonstration, to the extent that that is possible, of everything that may be demonstrated; and who has ascertained in divine matters, to the extent that that is possible, everything that may be ascertained; and who has come close to certainty in those matters in which one can only come close to it." These are "the men of science" who achieve different grades of perfection. A higher level is attained by prophets who, after attaining perfection in the study of metaphysics, turn their intellects toward God. Moses was the highest of the prophets and attained the most direct access to God.

This parable has been variously interpreted. The bitterest critique of it came from those who believed that Rambam placed philosophers (even non-Jewish thinkers who did not accept or know the truth of Torah) on a higher level than religiously observant Jews and halakhists who were not also philosophers. Professor Menachem Kellner has explained convincingly that this was not the intent of Rambam's parable. Rather, Rambam was relating specifically to Jews when he discussed halakhists and philosophers, that is, halakhists who studied philosophy were on a higher level than those who did not engage in philosophical speculation.[2]

The ultimate goal of attaining wisdom is not merely to have intellectual knowledge of God, but to imitate God's attributes of compassion and righteousness. Rambam sums up his view in the last paragraph of the *Guide*:

> It is clear that the perfection of man that may truly be gloried in is the one acquired by him who has achieved, in a measure corresponding to his capacity, apprehension of Him, may He be exalted, and who knows His providence extending over His creatures as manifested in the act of bringing them into being and in their governance as it is. The way of life of such an individual, after he has achieved this apprehension, will always have in view loving-kindness, righteousness, and judgment, through assimilation to His actions, may He be exalted, just as we have explained several times in this Treatise.

According to Rambam, then, the perfect Jew must be not only a halakhist but a philosopher; not only a person of ideas but a paragon of compassion, righteousness, and judgment. This is, of course, a tall order. Nonetheless, it provides a framework within which each Jew can strive for as high a level as he or she can attain. If we are devoted only to halakha but do not engage in philosophical analysis, our religious attainments are defective. Likewise, if we engage in speculation but ignore the commandments of the Torah, we are deficient religiously. If we devote ourselves entirely to study and speculation but not to the performance of good deeds, then we are also falling short of the ideal.

Rambam had harsh words for those students of Torah who eschewed labor, preferring to be supported by charity. In his view, such individuals were guilty of desecrating the name of God, humiliating the Torah, and extinguishing the light of religion. Although they might think they were being pious by devoting themselves to full-time Torah study, they were in fact disgracing the Torah. Rambam believed it is highly virtuous for people to earn an honest living through their own labors.[3]

Given these prescriptions, it follows that the ideal religious education should include study of Bible, Mishnah, and Talmud—the foundational texts of Jewish belief and religious observance. It should also include the sciences, logic, mathematics, and philosophy—so that students can develop the rational faculties needed to enter the "throne room of the king." It should aim at perfecting their moral qualities, so that they will be humble, righteous, and compassionate. Moreover, it should teach students those skills needed to earn a living so that they do not become dependent on charity. Underlying the particular subjects of study should be a philosophy that guides the students—gradually and at their own pace—to human perfection. Education must not only teach facts, figures, and skills; it must be imbued with a religious worldview that can inspire and guide students along the proper path.

Rambam wanted Jews to follow the ways of Torah not from blind obedience, but from intellectual understanding and commitment. Proper Torah education seeks to empower students to think clearly and critically. We must push our reason as far as it will take us and draw on the truths of revelation in areas that transcend the powers of reason.

We ought to take a cue from the example set by Rambam himself. He was thoroughly steeped in all aspects of Torah knowledge and wisdom. At the same time, he was thoroughly trained in philosophy and logic, was a medical doctor, was a communal leader, was a highly regarded model of moral excellence and integrity, and was perfectly fluent in Hebrew and Arabic.

Torah Education and Reason

Since the role of religious education is to guide us toward human perfection, it must address the needs of individuals at all stages of their lives. A proper educational philosophy must imbue our intellectual and moral development from the time we are children through our old age. The nature of education is an ongoing process, a striving, an advancement from one level to the next.

We noted in chapter 1 of this book that Rambam sought to harmonize religion and reason; he reinterpreted the Bible to conform to the dictates of philosophy. He scorned those who maintained a literalist understanding of rabbinic statements when those statements were irrational or philosophically incorrect. In his introduction to *Perek Helek*, he branded the literalists as being "of impoverished understanding—one must pity their foolishness." These people felt obligated to defend the literal veracity of every word of our sages, without understanding that the sages often spoke in parables and symbolic language, never expecting that their words would be taken at face value. These misguided pietists were not thus honoring our sages but were "dissipating the glory of the Torah and clouding its lights, placing the Torah of God opposite of its intention." Rambam's son, Abraham, underscored his father's disdain for the literalists. He wrote about those who "interpret these scriptural verses and homiletical passages literally. For this our heart is faint and for these things our eyes are dim."[4] He criticized those who spoke of secret things about which they have no knowledge and that they do not understand:

> They believe in the simple interpretation of some midrashic and aggadic passages. But if we were to accept the simple interpretation of those midrashic and aggadic passages, we would

be denying our faith like those whose faith is perverted.... We would be distrustful of the sages, of blessed memory, and would, Heaven forbid, view them as heretics or fools....[5]

In his essay on the nature of rabbinic homilies, printed in the introductory section of some editions of *Ein Yaacov*, Rabbi Abraham son of Rambam made the following observation, very much in the spirit of the teachings of his father:

We, and every intelligent and wise person, are obligated to evaluate each idea and each statement, to find the way in which to understand it; to prove the truth and establish that which is worthy of being established, and to annul that which is worthy of being annulled.... We see that our sages themselves said: If it is a halakha [universally accepted legal tradition] we will accept it; but if it is a ruling [based on individual opinion], there is room for discussion.

Rambam's philosophy of religious education demanded that we approach the classic texts of Judaism with reverence and with a clear commitment to reason. Reverence entails respect for the authority of Scriptures, the Talmud, and other ancient rabbinic literature. Commitment to reason requires that we read the texts in a reasonable fashion and interpret them in light of the dictates of reason. Striking the proper balance between reverence and reason is not a precise science, and different scholars will arrive at different conclusions.

Throughout this book, we have seen how Rambam sought to maintain religion on a proper philosophical basis. His goal was not merely to reconcile reason and revelation; he wanted to undermine the fundamentalist, obscurantist, and superstitious elements that had crept into Judaism.[6] He believed that his approach purified Judaism of negative accretions that had seeped in through the incorrect teachings of fundamentalist rabbis.

On the one hand, Rambam would not favor Jewish schools that teach Judaism without due reverence to the holiness of the Bible and the wisdom of our rabbinic sages. He would argue that Torah needs to be conveyed by teachers who believe in it, who live by its laws and traditions, and whose primary mission is to transmit the Torah way of life to the new generations. Rambam reasoned that Torah and mitzvot are the foundation of Jewish life and cannot properly be taught as legends, quaint customs, or optional practices. Rambam's manifest commitment to mitzvot is powerfully reflected in his *Mishneh Torah*, where he meticulously recorded the entire body of halakha. He obviously took this responsibility very seriously—and expected his readers to do likewise. Mitzvot are not "good deeds" or "suggestions" or "cultural behaviors," but are commandments from God and rulings established by our authoritative rabbinic sages.

On the other hand, Rambam would be highly critical of Jewish education that teaches the sacred texts in a literalist, obscurantist fashion. He would insist that children be taught in a reasonable, sophisticated manner; the text material should be taught based on the ages and capacities of the students.

A staple of Orthodox Jewish education today is teaching the Torah with the commentary of Rashi (Rabbi Solomon Yitzhaki). Rashi, born in Troyes in northern France, became the single most important commentator on the Bible and the Talmud. His works continue to be standard fare for all Jews who study these texts. Since Rashi often draws on midrashic interpretations, his words need to be explained to students so that they can appreciate the deeper meaning of these midrashim. Rambam would insist that students be taught to differentiate between what the Torah text states and what the rabbis relate in their midrashim. Let us consider several examples of problems that arise when teaching Torah with Rashi's commentary and try to resolve these problems using reason and literary skills.

Rashi on Genesis 25:20, following midrashic calculations, notes that our forefather Isaac was forty years old when he married Rebecca—who was three years old at the time! This calculation assumes that Abraham sent his servant to find a wife for Isaac immediately after the episode of the *Akeidah* (the binding of Isaac). However, the Torah itself does not specify if this occurred immediately after the

Akeidah or if there had been a lapse of years between stories. The *Tosafot* commentary on the Talmud (*Yevamot* 61b, on the words "*veKhein hu omer*") reports a rabbinic calculation that has Rebecca being fourteen years old at the time she watered the camels for Abraham's servant. Thus, even within classic rabbinic literature there is a difference of opinion about Rebecca's age when she was married to Isaac.

It is problematic to teach Rashi's midrashic comment that Rebecca was three at the time of her marriage to Isaac without some sort of further explanation. Wouldn't students find it highly irregular if a biblical hero aged forty were to marry a baby girl aged three? What sort of moral lesson would they draw from such a teaching? How does such a midrash deepen the religious life of students?

If the marriage of a forty-year-old man to a three-year-old girl is so odd, why does Rashi include this midrashic statement in his commentary? What might the author of the midrash have intended? Here is a suggestion: The author of the midrash was using a midrashic technique that underscores the unusual qualities of biblical heroes. Rebecca is described as being three years old as a way of highlighting how precocious she was. Likewise, a midrashic statement has it that Abraham was three years old when he discovered God. When the midrash says "three years old," it is not referring to a specific chronological age, but to a quality—the quality of precociousness. The midrashim have no objective way to know how old Abraham was when he discovered God or how old Rebecca was when she married Isaac. The midrashim aren't interested in establishing historical facts, but in underscoring the unique qualities of Abraham and Rebecca.

Rashi on Genesis 26:5 cites a midrashic teaching that our forefather Abraham observed all the laws of the Torah, including the Oral Torah and rabbinic rules. This is, of course, quite amazing given that Abraham lived long before the giving of the Torah at Mount Sinai! Obviously, the author of this midrash had no way of ascertaining whether or not Abraham observed all the laws of the Torah and the rulings of our rabbis. He was not presenting us with a historical fact—because he himself did not have access to the facts. What, then, does this midrash mean, and how should it be taught to our children?

Here is a suggestion: The midrash is teaching us that the laws of the Torah and our rabbis are accessible to the human mind. Even before the revelation at Mount Sinai, great minds—such as Abraham's—were able to penetrate the inner meaning of Torah. So too can we, who live after the revelation, apply our minds to the Torah and seek to find the inner meanings of its commandments; we can carefully analyze the words of our sages and try to plumb the depths of the meaning of their rulings.

When midrashic commentaries are taught as though they are integral parts of the biblical text, this does violence to the text—and also to the midrashim and their composers. Students should always be able to differentiate between what is stated in the text and what is later rabbinic interpretation. This is especially true when midrashim present supernatural or odd details; students may come to believe that these midrashic elements are actually part of the Bible. If they later reject these strange midrashim, they may feel they are actually rejecting the Bible itself, and this may lead to much spiritual turmoil.

In order to teach midrash and midrashic commentaries properly, Rambam would insist that we first understand the literary and homiletical methods of the authors of the midrashim; that we explain "irrational" midrashim in a way that reflects rabbinic wisdom and insight; that we do not take the midrashim literally, but as vehicles for conveying deeper meanings and religious lessons.[7]

Rambam's views were in line with those of earlier rabbinic figures. Hai Gaon (939–1038) taught that the aggadah and midrash included statements by rabbis in which "each one interpreted whatever came to his heart." He thought that we do not rely on these words, but view them as personal opinions.[8] Sherira Gaon (c. 900–1000) taught that aggadah, midrash, and homiletical interpretations were in the category of personal opinion and speculation.[9] The Gaon Shemuel ben Hofni (d. 1013) stated, "If the words of the ancients contradict reason, we are not obligated to accept them."[10]

During the nineteenth century, Rabbi Zvi Hirsch Chajes, one of the great rabbinic figures of his day, wrote:

> There are several subjects in the Gemara whose meaning can-not be taken in a literal sense, because the text expounded lit-erally would depict God as a corporeal being, and would also at times involve an act of blasphemy.... [W]e are, indeed, duty-bound to believe that the transmitters of the true tradition (*kabbalah*), who are known to us as righteous and saintly men and also as accomplished scholars, would not speak merely in an odd manner. We must therefore believe that their words were uttered with an allegorical or mystical sense and that they point to matters of the most elevated significance, far beyond our mental grasp.[11]

Another outstanding nineteenth-century figure, Rabbi Samson Raphael Hirsch, noted that "aggadic sayings do not have Sinaitic origin.... Nor must someone whose opinion differs from that of our sages in a mat-ter of aggadah be deemed a heretic, especially as the sages themselves frequently differ."[12]

Rabbi Haim David Halevy (1924–98), one of the great rabbinic sages of the twentieth century, noted that the rabbis of the midrash often offered different interpretations that were mutually exclusive.[13] For example, the Torah reports that after the death of Joseph, a "new Pharaoh arose over Egypt who did not know Joseph" (Exodus 1:8). Rashi cites the debate between Rav and Shemuel on the meaning of this phrase. Rav suggested that an actual new Pharaoh came to power who had not had a personal connection with Joseph. Shemuel, though, interpreted the phrase to mean that it was the same Pharaoh—who indeed did know Joseph—but who acted as though he did not know Joseph and issued decrees against Joseph's people. Neither Rav nor Shemuel had any objective way to determine the historical facts. It is impossible for them both to be correct. The student of these rabbinic interpretations needs to look for the deeper meaning that Rav and Shemuel were trying to convey. Rav believed that it was not possible for a Pharaoh who knew Joseph, and who had benefited so greatly from Joseph's astute policies, to turn against Joseph's people. Thus, the situation must have arisen because a new Pharaoh came to power, who owed no allegiance to Joseph. Shemuel suggested that the same Pharaoh did indeed betray Joseph; tyrannical leaders are not necessarily loyal to their underlings and can turn against them in a whimsical, irrational manner.

Rabbi Halevy pointed out that we must revere the wisdom of our ancient rabbis and treat their words with deep respect. Nonetheless, this does not mean accepting the literal veracity of all their midrashic and aggadic statements. We must read these passages with due reverence, but also with a clear mind.

Torah Education and Science

Professor Warren Zev Harvey has well described Rambam's view on the relationship between Torah and science:

> The lesson of *Sefer haMadda* is that Torah directs us to science, and science to Torah. The Torah directs us to science, for its first commandment is to know God (*Yesodei haTorah* 1:1–6), and it is impossible to know Him except by knowing His creation, which means science (ibid., 2:2, 4:12; *Hilkhot Teshuvah* 10:6). Conversely, science directs us to Torah, for when we contemplate the infinite wisdom manifest in the physical universe, we are filled with love and awe for its Creator, and seek a way of life which will enable us to know Him to the extent humanly possible, and such a way of life is the Torah (*De'ot* 3:2).[14]

Religion and science are inseparably intertwined, and each plays a vital role in the human quest for knowledge of God. For Rambam, the deepest levels of Torah—*ma'aseh bereishit* (acts of creation) and *ma'aseh merkavah* (acts of the "Chariot")—are equated with physics and metaphysics. Thus, profound knowledge of Torah is dependent upon a profound knowledge of science and philosophy.[15]

Since One God created both Torah and science, it is axiomatic for Rambam that Torah and science can never be in fundamental conflict. In modern times, religionists have had to cope with dramatic discoveries in science that have eclipsed earlier scientific notions held sacrosanct by much of the Western world, including rabbinic sages. When a conflict arises between new scientific knowledge and ancient rabbinic teaching, how should religious people respond?

Professor Menachem Kellner tells of a lecture he heard from a scientist affiliated with the Chabad sect of Hassidim.[16] That lecturer stated as a matter of fact that Rambam wrote his *Mishneh Torah* with divine inspiration; therefore, we must accept every word of this work as being correct and authoritative, even those sections that include the Ptolemaic description of the universe.

Professor Kellner wondered, "This may be the Chabad view of Rambam, but is it Rambam's view of Rambam?" Did Rambam himself believe that the scientific information he presented had been granted to him by divine inspiration and was infallibly true? Or did he write his opinions based on the best scientific information available to him, fully realizing that this information was subject to further evaluation based on future developments in scientific research? Professor Kellner concluded that Rambam would never have made the claim about his work that had been made by the Chabad lecturer. Rambam recognized that even our Talmudic sages were sometimes mistaken in matters of science. That does not denigrate their wisdom but only makes the obvious point that they were limited by the scientific information available in their historical context. Rambam would not dispute this observation even as it would relate to his own work; surely he would want his scientific statements updated to reflect the results of new discoveries. He would hardly expect—or condone—that we maintain the truth of Ptolemaic astronomy when it has been fully demonstrated that the earth orbits around the sun and that the earth is not the center of the universe.

In *Guide of the Perplexed*, Rambam notes that our Talmudic sages believed—along with other philosophers of antiquity—that the motion of the spheres of the universe produces fearful and mighty sounds. Pythagoreans believed that these mighty sounds were pleasant, even musical. The problem was, if the spheres make these sounds, why don't we hear them?

Avoiding this problem, Aristotle posited that the heavenly bodies make no sound. The Aristotelian view prevailed. Our sages' view was in conflict with Aristotle. The ancient rabbis, though, were willing to admit when their scientific views were shown to be incorrect. Rambam writes:

> You know, on the other hand, that in these astronomical matters they [the rabbis] preferred the opinion of the sages of the nations of the world to their own. For they explicitly say: The sages of the nations of the world have vanquished (*Pesahim* 94b). And this is correct. For everyone who argues in speculative matters does this according to the conclusions to which he was led by his speculation. Hence the conclusion whose demonstration is correct is believed.[17]

In another passage in the *Guide*, Rambam makes it clear that our ancient sages based their scientific statements on the information available to them:

> Do not ask me to show that everything they [the sages] have said concerning astronomical matters conforms to the way things really are. For at that time mathematics was imperfect. They did not speak about this as transmitters of the dicta of the prophets, but rather because in those times they were men of knowledge in those fields or because they had heard these dicta from the men of knowledge who lived in those times.[18]

Since Rambam well understood that scientific knowledge is subject to ongoing development, he would not want Judaism to be tied to scientific notions that have been proved incorrect.[19] Rambam worked with the best scientific information available to him, for example, the geocentric Ptolemaic system of astronomy. Since this system has been eclipsed by later scientific developments, Rambam would surely not expect us to continue to operate on the basis of Ptolemaic theories. Indeed, it would be the height of folly for us to reject new scientific knowledge out of the mistaken notion that our ancient sages—and even Rambam himself—made their scientific statements with divinely inspired authority.

Yet, there is a stream of thought within right-wing Orthodoxy that is quite uncomfortable setting aside the scientific statements of our revered sages—even when later scientific development has proved those statements to be incorrect. Like the Chabad rabbi heard by Professor Kellner, they argue that our sages (including Rambam) wrote with divine inspiration and simply could not be wrong. If our rabbis stated that the earth is the center of the universe and that the sun orbits around the earth, then we are obligated to believe them—in spite of what modern science teaches. An important twentieth-century rabbinic figure went so far as to say that anyone who accepts the heliocentric position is a rejecter of rabbinic tradition and is "a denier of our faith."[20] Rabbi Avraham Karelitz (1878–1953), known popularly as the Hazon Ish, stated that the heliocentric position is incorrect, since it goes against the words of our sages; nevertheless, he was "liberal" enough to concede that those who accepted heliocentrism were not to be considered as outright heretics.[21]

This obscurantist stream of thought also manifests itself in religious discussions relating to the age of the universe. Ancient Jewish sages calculated the age of the world by adding up the ages of biblical characters from the time of Adam and then adding six days to this number—the six days of creation described in the opening passages of the Torah. This would mean that the world was created less than six thousand years ago. It follows, then, that nothing on this planet can be older than six thousand years. Although physicists, geologists, and paleontologists have concluded that our universe is billions of years old and that life on planet earth has existed for many millions of years, these scientific views are discarded as heresies by the ultra-right wing fundamentalists. According to them, there never were dinosaurs; all scientific evidence pointing to an older universe is false.

Rabbi Nosson Slifkin, himself a very traditional Orthodox rabbi, has written books in which he accepted the scientific data indicating a universe that is billions of years old. A group of Ashkenazic rabbis in Israel and the United States, describing themselves as *Gedolei haDor* (the great rabbis of our generation), issued a proclamation banning Rabbi Slifkin's books. The ban claims that Slifkin's books "present a great stumbling block to the reader. They are full of heresy, twist and misrepresent the words of our sages, and ridicule the foundations of our *emunah* [faith]." The ban states that it is "forbidden to read, own, or distribute" his books. "There can be no room or justification whatsoever for spreading these books." It closes with a plea to the author to "burn all of his works and publicly retract all that he has written." This ban was issued in the fall of 2004.[22]

These "great sages" have not only vilified Rabbi Slifkin. They have cast aspersions on any rabbi who thinks the world is more than six thousand years old. At a conference of right-wing Orthodox rabbis in the fall of 2007, one of their leaders quoted a *Gadol haDor* in Israel who told him, "Any rabbi who believes that the world is more than approximately six thousand years old is a heretic and may not perform conversions." Thus, according to this stream of right-wing Orthodoxy, it is forbidden to accept the findings of modern science when those findings are in conflict with statements of our ancient sages. There can hardly be a more anti-Maimonidean view than this.

Since these fundamentalist statements are issued as rulings of the *Gedolei haDor*, many otherwise thinking people feel compelled to accept these positions, or at least not to object to them openly. These anti-science notions seep into Orthodox schools, since the teachers themselves have been indoctrinated with belief in the infallibility (or near infallibility) of the so-called *Gedolim*. New generations of students are trained in a fashion that would make Rambam shudder.

Several years ago, students in an Orthodox Jewish day school in New Jersey were told by their teacher that dinosaurs never existed. When a student told the teacher that he and his family recently visited the Museum of Natural History in New York City and saw dinosaur bones, the teacher replied, "You did not see dinosaur bones; you saw dog bones that became swollen during Noah's flood."

Do the Torah and Jewish religious tradition really require us to deny scientific evidence in order to justify outdated and erroneous views held by our ancient rabbis? Do we really need to believe that dinosaurs never existed, even though there is an abundance of evidence showing that they did indeed roam the earth millions of years ago? Is it proper religious education to teach children that dinosaur bones are just swollen dog bones from the time of Noah's flood? Rambam held that the opposite is true, namely that we must seek truth; if the statements of our sages have been shown to be false, we must reject or reinterpret those statements. If science has demonstrated beyond reasonable doubt that dinosaurs existed millions of years ago and that the universe is billions of years old, then we need to dismiss the literalist view that insists the universe is less than six thousand years old.

The obscurantist view flourishes due to the mistaken belief that we must uphold the infallibility—or quasi-infallibility—of our sages. It is feared that if their statements on science are cast aside, then people may come to cast aside their statements relating to Jewish law; that once doubt is thrown on their divinely inspired wisdom, their overall authority will be diminished. Rambam rejected this view outright. He argued that it was foolish—and religiously detrimental—to adhere to irrational, incorrect statements of our sages.

There are intellectually sound and religiously valid ways of approaching questions relating to the age of the universe that do not entail denying the findings of modern science. It has been pointed out, for example, that the six days of creation were not twenty-four-hour days. Indeed, the sun was not created until the fourth day, so there could not have been a sunset or sunrise on the first three "days." The word "days" might better be understood to mean "periods" of indeterminate length. At each period of the creation, there was a development from a simpler stage to a more complex stage. Since these six "days" of creation could have lasted billions of years by human calculation, then dinosaurs had ample time to live and become extinct before Adam and Eve were created on the sixth "day."

Rabbi Aryeh Kaplan, a remarkable twentieth-century rabbinic figure, cited classic rabbinic texts asserting the world is far older than six
thousand years. The *Sefer haTemunah*, attributed to the Talmudic sage
Rabbi Nehunya ben haKanah, suggested that God created other worlds
before creating Adam. The *Midrash Rabbah* on Genesis 1:5 teaches that
there were "orders of time" prior to the first day of creation recorded
in the Torah. Most interesting is the view of Rabbi Yitzhak of Akko, a
student and colleague of Nahmanides and one of the foremost kabbalists of the thirteenth century. In examining one of Rabbi Yitzhak's
important works, *Otsar haHayyim*, Rabbi Kaplan discovered that Rabbi
Yitzhak adduced that the universe is a bit over 15.3 billion years
old! This theory by a medieval kabbalist, based on interpretations of
biblical and rabbinic texts, is remarkably close to the calculations of
modern science that date the "Big Bang" at approximately 15 billion
years ago.[23]

Rabbi Yitzhak felt no need to offer far-fetched explanations to
keep the universe within the six-thousand-year range. He and his
many pious colleagues and students had no problem at all positing a
universe that was billions of years old; they did not see this calculation
as in any way impinging on the truth of Torah. It is clear, then, that
there are legitimate traditions in Torah Judaism that view the universe
as being far older than six thousand years.

To cloak falsity in the clothing of religion is to undermine true
religion. How could any thinking person have respect for the opinions
of "*Gedolei haDor*" who are not only bereft of scientific and philosophical knowledge, but whose very worldview precludes an open and
intellectually sound approach to the attainment of knowledge?
Judaism does not—and according to Rambam cannot—demand that
we turn off our brains or that we deny the best available scientific
information.

Just as it is an enormous intellectual error to deny the clear and
proven findings of science, it is an enormous intellectual error to
assume that science can answer our ultimate questions about the
meaning of life. Science has indeed advanced over the centuries, and
we may assume safely that it will continue to advance in the years

ahead. Things that we believe true today may well be shown to be false at some future period, when scientific knowledge advances. We must have the humility to recognize the limits of modern science.

Professor Menachem Kellner has stated the matter quite well:

> In the final analysis, if we are really to use the eyes God gave us, we can do no other but revert to a qualified Maimonideanism: The Torah cannot contradict that which has been *proven* scientifically, but science often proves less than what some scientists think they have proven. We must live in a world of fewer absolutes than many thinkers (rabbis and scientists alike) would like. The Torah cannot teach what science rejects as false, but the evidence of science is not yet fully in, so we do not yet know what the Torah really teaches.[24]

Women, Rabbinic Texts, and the Western World

The classic rabbinic texts dealing with the role of women were articulated in a premodern era, when women generally were relegated to particular functions, such as taking care of the household, having babies, and raising children. Although some women achieved a high educational level, most did not. While some women engaged in economic activity, most were precluded from pursuing occupations and professions. Women were generally excluded from voting or holding public office or positions of communal leadership. This was true for the world at large, as well as for the Jewish community. In 1917, for example, only five countries in Europe allowed women to vote.

During the twentieth century, a radical transformation took place relating to the role of women in the Western world. Women gained equal rights in almost every area of political, economic, and cultural life. Education became equally available for male and female children, with the number of women receiving university degrees skyrocketing. Women today are active and equal participants in nearly all aspects of contemporary society in the Western democracies.

This dramatic change in the status of women has obviously led to conflicts with traditional religion based on traditional texts. One response has been to opt for modernity and egalitarianism and to reject the authority of the classic religious texts. This has been the general response of non-Orthodox Jewish movements. Another response has been to cling to the ancient texts and reject modernity to the extent possible. This has been the general response of right-wing, *Hareidi* Orthodoxy. The Modern Orthodox community has tried to find a middle road, one that is reverent toward classic religious texts while at the same time is sensitive to the demands of modernity. The non-Orthodox assume that everything has changed; the right-wing Orthodox assume (or pretend to assume) that nothing has changed. The Modern Orthodox know that things have changed but want to find ways in which change can be mediated by tradition.

Rambam on the Role of Women

A surface reading of Rambam's work will reveal that he subscribed to the commonly held stereotypes of women. A more careful reading will demonstrate that he actually was far in advance of his times on some significant issues.

Rambam seemed to agree with the prevailing view of his time that a woman's place is in the home. However, he also recognized that a woman has the right to leave her home in order to visit her parents or to go to the homes of mourners or those celebrating a happy occasion. In the *Mishneh Torah*, he notes that a husband must provide his wife with a suitable head covering and modest garb,

> so that she can visit her father's home or the house of a mourner or the house of celebration, since every women may go and come from her father's house to visit him, and to the house of mourning or celebration in order to show kindness to her friends, so that they will [also] visit her. For a woman is not in a prison preventing her from going and coming.[25]

Having stated that a woman is not to be held prisoner in her own home, Rambam then offers some advice to husbands:

> It is unseemly for a woman constantly to be going abroad and in the streets, and the husband should prevent his wife from this. He should not let her leave [the home] except once or twice per month, according to the need. There is no beauty for a woman except in dwelling in the corner of her home, for so it is written, "All the glory of the king's daughter is within" [Psalm 45:14].[26]

Rambam cites the teachings of the Talmudic sages that a woman should behave and dress modestly, should not engage in levity or frivolity in the presence of her husband, and should avoid situations that might lead to any trace of scandal. Moreover, Rambam says that a wife must honor her husband exceedingly, considering him to be an officer or a king. In return, a husband must honor his wife more than his own self and love her as he loves himself. He should support her according to his financial means and speak with her gently, avoiding sadness and anger. "This is the custom of holy and pure Jewish women and men in their marriages. And these ways will make their marriage pleasant and praiseworthy."[27]

Rambam, following the Talmudic rabbis, places women in a subservient role to their husbands and sharply limits their ability to leave their own homes. Virtue is equated with staying indoors, out of public view. These prescriptions negate the modern view that women are equal members of society, with as much right as men to determine how they dress and where they go.

If we understand these passages as being reflections of attitudes of a former time, we can classify them as "advice" rather than as legal rulings. And since this "advice" is no longer fully relevant, we are free to draw on what makes sense to us. We can and should maintain the values of modesty and decency, but we may choose to define these terms in light of our contemporary situation—where women are equal members of society and expect to be equal partners in marriage.

A useful methodological insight may be drawn from the halakhic ruling in the *Shulhan Arukh* that states that it is forbidden for a man to walk behind a woman, since this can provoke immoral thoughts. If a man finds himself in such a situation, he must rush to the side of the road in order to avoid walking behind a woman.[28] Rabbi Haim David Halevy asserted that this law was intended for those earlier times when women generally remained home and were not often found walking in public. In our times, when public thoroughfares are frequented by many women, the situation is different. If a man would run away every time he found a woman in front of him, people would think he was a fool. In his seeming piety, he would actually be causing religion to be subjected to ridicule. Rabbi Halevy ruled, therefore, that a man who found himself walking behind a woman should simply keep his eyes from looking at her. He should not follow the *Shulhan Arukh*'s ruling that he must rush to the side of the road.[29]

Rabbi Halevy's opinion makes eminent sense. It underscores the need to maintain the value of modesty and purity of thought while recognizing that current realities are far different from those in Talmudic times or the Middle Ages. The problem arises: If we are allowed to discard or reinterpret halakhic texts to meet contemporary needs, where does this process stop? Won't this lead to a complete unraveling of the halakha? The answer is: We must recognize the eternal teachings of Torah and halakha and uphold the basic foundations and observances of Judaism. At the same time, we must be able to differentiate between the immutable eternal teachings and the historically conditioned accretions that are reflected in some of our classic texts. It may be objected that this leads to a slippery slope. Possibly it does. But this is a risk that must be taken if religion is to remain alive and meaningful to the ongoing generations. To freeze religion is not an acceptable alternative.

Rabbinic leaders of the *Hareidi* community are not comfortable veering from the classic texts of our ancient and medieval rabbis, even when modern sociological conditions are so radically different from earlier times. The role of women is a prime example of the dilemma that faces them. They argue that instead of modifying traditional practice to adapt to current realities, we need to reject current realities in order to conform to traditional texts. The result of this attitude is to forbid women from assuming positions of communal authority over men; to sharply limit social interactions between men and women; to confine women, to the extent possible, to the domains of bearing and raising children and maintaining the household; and to limit women's access to advanced education, even in Torah studies.

The *Hareidi* world attempts to maintain its viewpoint through the policies it fosters. Men and women are separated as much as possible, with separate seating at all public events. In some *Hareidi* areas, there are separate shopping hours for men and for women. Even on public buses under *Hareidi* influence, men and women are seated separately with a partition between the genders. In *Hareidi* neighborhoods, immodest billboards are defaced; women who walk through these neighborhoods in clothing that is deemed inappropriate are spat upon. A number of these communities have "modesty patrols" that enforce communal norms of dress. Women are not allowed to sing in public, where men may hear their voices. The prohibition against hearing a woman's singing voice has been applied to synagogues and to Shabbat tables, so that women must either sing in an undertone inaudible to men or refrain from singing altogether. This prohibition has gone to such an extreme that *Hareidi* rabbis in Israel have forbidden listening to recordings of a particular religious male singer—because his voice is "too feminine."[30]

Even with all the above restrictions, though, the *Hareidi* world cannot totally conform itself to the classic halakhic texts. For example, women in the *Hareidi* community do leave their homes more frequently than the once or twice per month permitted by Rambam. It is also not altogether uncommon for *Hareidi* women to have jobs in the public workplace and to interact in some social contexts with men. Moreover, a number of women in the *Hareidi* world do achieve higher levels of education.

There always must be a mediation between the flow of life and the teachings of ancient religious texts. Even extreme fundamentalists cannot avoid making some accommodation to new realities.

Women and Education

For much of human history, women have received far less formal education than men. This has had vast ramifications on the overall status of women in society. In the Jewish world, most women (until the modern era) received minimal education. Although some women did achieve high levels of education, they were the exception rather than the rule. This was true not only in regard to general education, but also to religious education. Girls learned basic religious laws from their mothers but received little or no formal instruction in the halakhic texts. The Talmud (*Sotah* 20a) records the opinion of Rabbi Eliezer that whoever teaches his daughter Torah teaches her *tiflut* (foolishness or obscenity). Although this opinion is disputed in the Mishnah by Ben Azzai, Rambam, in the *Mishneh Torah*, cites the view of Rabbi Eliezer as law:

> A woman who learns Torah receives a reward, but not the same reward as a man, since she was not commanded [to learn Torah]; and anyone who does something for which he was not commanded does not receive reward on the same level as someone who was commanded and who performed it, but rather receives less than he. And although she does have a reward, our sages commanded that a man must not teach his daughter Torah, since the intelligence of the majority of women is not geared to be instructed; rather, they reduce the words of Torah to matters of foolishness according to the poverty of their understanding. Our sages said: One who teaches his daughter Torah is as though he taught her foolishness. To what does this refer? To the Oral Torah; but as concerns the Written Torah, he should not teach her; but if he did teach her it is not as though he taught her foolishness.[31]

Rambam codifies the notion that the intelligence of most women is deficient and that most women cannot be properly instructed due to their poverty of understanding. The result of this position is that men should not teach their daughters Torah, at least not the Oral Torah.

Girls apparently should learn only those laws and customs they need to know to function as religious Jews; but they do not need—and would probably not benefit from—more formal education.

What are we to do with this passage of Rambam, based on an opinion in the Mishnah? One response is: If the authoritative texts say this, we must accept it. Indeed, this would seem to be the basic *Hareidi* view. They forbid girls and women from studying the Oral Torah, except for the *Ethics of the Fathers* and other texts that relate to ethics and faith. At the same time, *Hareidim* have established schools for girls, so that almost all girls do receive formal education. Some of these students do go on to more advanced Jewish studies, including the study of halakhic texts.

In the Modern Orthodox community, it is not uncommon for girls and boys to study the same curriculum, which includes the study of Talmud and halakha. A new generation of Orthodox women, highly trained in rabbinic literature, is emerging in Israel and the Diaspora. The Modern Orthodox rabbinic leadership has essentially set aside Rambam's statements on women and education, placing them into the category of outdated "advice" rather than accepting them as authoritative halakhic rulings.

There is an obvious gap between Rambam's text and current reality. Women today do receive fine educations and are able to succeed quite well. Women serve in the top echelons of contemporary intellectual, professional, and political life. If women's intellects are able to grasp the whole range of academic topics, why should they be prevented from studying Talmud?

Rabbi Haim David Halevy suggested that in earlier times, girls received no formal education at all; thus, to teach them Talmud would have been beyond their ken. They lacked the rudimentary intellectual training required for proper analysis of Talmud. Since in our times women do receive formal education, Talmud may be taught to girls and women who have demonstrated their ability to grasp the material.[32]

It has been argued that in spite of Rambam's words relating to women's intellectual abilities and education, he actually had a far higher opinion of women's intellects. His statement in the *Mishneh Torah* reflected his understanding of how things were, but not how they could or should be. Throughout his writings, Rambam describes women as being akin to children, in the sense that they had potential to learn but had not yet fulfilled that potential. Indeed, some women did achieve prophecy, which for Rambam was predicated on attaining philosophical truth through intellectual exertion. Moreover, Rambam rules that all Jews—men and women—must fulfill the commandments of knowing, loving, and fearing God. Furthermore, in his view, these commandments presuppose a prior knowledge of physics and metaphysics. Thus, embedded in the overall corpus of Rambam's work are passages that indicate that (1) women have the intellectual ability to reach the greatest spiritual heights, (2) women have an obligation to study physics and metaphysics as a means of fulfilling commandments of faith for which they are obligated, and (3) in Messianic times, all people—men and women—will be imbued equally with the spirit of God and will be able equally to reach the pinnacle of human perfection.[33]

Other Issues Relating to Women

Dr. Joel Kraemer, in his extensive study of Rambam's works, has found that Rambam's rulings "often elevated the status of women."[34] Rambam sought ways to enhance their legal rights and give them greater freedom. Dr. Kraemer offers an example from a case involving a woman whose first two husbands died. According to Talmudic precedent, such a woman was considered a "killer wife" and shouldn't be allowed to marry again. Rambam rejected this view as being superstitious. After all, husbands die for a variety of reasons, and it is not rational or fair to blame a woman because she had the misfortune to be widowed twice. He noted that rabbinic sages in Spain had permitted such women to remarry, lest they turn to nonsanctioned relationships. Although Talmudic precedent and kabbalistic teachings forbade such women from remarrying, Rambam served as a powerful halakhic authority to allow such women to marry again and go on with their lives.[35]

Another problematic area of law deals with divorce. According to halakha, a divorce may only be given with the consent of the husband.

If a marriage has fallen apart but the husband refuses to agree to a divorce, the wife is put in an untenable situation. She is alienated from her husband and wants out of the marriage, but without her husband's consent to give the divorce, she is still legally married to him and cannot marry anyone else. She is an *agunah*, a woman chained to a recalcitrant husband. As can easily be understood, this situation can lead to unspeakable suffering.

The halakha does indicate instances where a wife has the right to sue for divorce—if she finds her husband to be repulsive or abusive. However, rabbis have been reluctant to press on behalf of the woman's rights, unless the husband clearly consents to the divorce. They do not want to exert undue pressure on the husband, for fear this will result in a "forced bill of divorce" (a divorce issued against the husband's will), since such a divorce is not legally valid.

Rambam discusses the case where the husband is obligated by law to issue the divorce because the wife's claims against him are valid. If such a man does not give the divorce, "the court should have him beaten until he consents, at which time they should have the divorce written. The divorce is valid. This applies at all times and in all places."[36] The question arises: If the husband is being beaten into submission, why isn't this considered a "forced divorce," which is not valid? Rambam offers an ingenious answer:

> If a person's evil inclination presses him to negate [the observance of] a mitzvah or to commit a transgression, and he was beaten until he performed the action he was obligated to perform, or he dissociated himself from the forbidden action, he is not considered to have been forced against his will.... With regard to this man who refuses to divorce [his wife]—he wants to be part of the Jewish people, and he wants to perform all the mitzvot and avoid all the transgressions; it is only his [evil] inclination that forces him. Therefore, when he is beaten until his [evil] inclination has been subdued, and he consents [to the divorce], he is considered to have performed the divorce willfully.[37]

For Rambam, then, a person's real self wants to fulfill mitzvot and avoid sins. If he acts in an improper way—for example, if he withholds consent to divorce his wife who has a right to the divorce—this is not really a reflection of "himself" but of his "evil inclination." The beating suppresses the evil inclination, so that he can consent to do what he really knows he ought to do and wants to do. With this creative explanation, Rambam allows the courts to bring recalcitrant husbands to their senses until they "agree" to give the divorces.

Maimonidean Methodology versus Modernity

In this chapter, we have discussed areas in which classic halakhic texts—including the writings of Rambam—come into conflict with new realities. We have seen that the Maimonidean methodology brings us closer to truth by insisting on the use of reason and by drawing on the best available information. While staying firmly rooted in the Torah and rabbinic tradition, we must also stay alert to the ongoing scientific and sociological changes that characterize modernity. We need not—and should not—forsake religious tradition; we need not—and should not—close our eyes and minds to the lessons of modernity.

10

FAITH AND REASON

The modern period cannot be described fairly as an "age of faith." Although a great many human beings believe in God and follow the dictates of their religions, a large and growing number of educated people have drifted away from traditional religious faith and practice. This is true of Jews and non-Jews alike.

The modern period also cannot be described fairly as an "age of reason." Although a great many human beings espouse the supreme value of reason, a large and growing number of people have drifted away from a strictly rationalistic worldview. This is true of Jews and non-Jews alike.

"Old-time religion" does not satisfy those who place a premium on reason. "Cold rationalism" does not satisfy those who place a premium on emotion and spirituality. A balance must be found between the claims of faith and the claims of reason, the needs of the intellect and the needs of the soul.

Rabbi David Hartman has devoted enormous energy to forging ways in which faith can be maintained in a reasonable way. The intellectual currents of modern philosophy challenge the foundations of traditional religion. What are the available responses to these challenges? In *Maimonides: Torah and the Philosophic Quest*, Rabbi Hartman suggests four options: the way of insulation, the way of dualism, the way of rejection, and the way of integration.[1]

The Way of Insulation

We can meet the threat and challenges of alien philosophies by refusing to take them seriously. We have the Truth. We do not need or want integration with the external culture that could pose uncomfortable questions to our way of thinking and our way of life. We do not have to justify ourselves or defend our positions to others who are outside our community.

> This method of exclusion insulates an entire body of knowledge from all serious challenges. All problems are answered by denying legitimacy to the questions. In order to make this move of cultural insulation, one has to claim that one's culture not only defines what a person should do but also what is to count as genuine knowledge—a logical move of one who maintains that his body of knowledge and his way of life are guaranteed authenticity by divine revelation.[2]

Throughout this book, we have seen examples of the way of insulation as promoted by extreme right-wing Orthodox Judaism. This group generally eschews secular education, limits social contacts with individuals outside their group, and promotes norms of dress and behavior that separate themselves from others. Since they are sure that they have the Truth, they feel no need to enter into dialogues or discussions with those who believe differently from themselves. They attribute vast authority to their rabbinic leaders, and these rabbis decide what is permitted and what is not permitted for them to think and do.

The way of insulation also may be found on the opposite side of the religious spectrum. Extreme secularists are certain that they are pursuing the Truth. They reject religion with as much fervor as the fundamentalists blindly accept religion. The extreme secularists are unable to enter the "religious mind" in a sympathetic way and thus are unable to have honest intellectual interchange with people of faith. A great many people are shut off from faith because they reject faith blindly or because they have been brainwashed by their intellectual mentors to scorn religion. Those searching for a meaningful harmony between faith and reason will not find satisfaction in the way of insulation.

The Way of Dualism

Another method of dealing with conflicts between faith and reason is the way of dualism, that is, isolating each entity in a separate domain. By compartmentalizing, we avoid bringing the two worlds into direct conflict. Philosophy belongs to the mind, and we may think whatever we like. Religion belongs to the realm of ethics, communal norms, and behavior; we follow the practices prescribed by our religion, without introspecting too much about the metaphysical ideas that lay at the foundation of faith. As long as we keep thought separate from deed, we adhere to the way of dualism.

This strategy seems appropriate for those who believe that religion is the opiate of the masses. Intellectuals retain inner freedom of thought; but they espouse public obeisance to religious rules as a sop to the ignorant multitudes. The way of dualism entails that a person display "a combination of openness to truth—regardless of the source and the implications of that truth—and complete behavioral loyalty to the norms of his tradition."[3]

Obviously, the way of dualism smacks of intellectual dishonesty. It requires people to keep their thoughts to themselves and pretend to go along with religious precepts for the sake of communal harmony. It is condescending to the masses, assuming that they would only become confused if confronted with philosophical ideas. The way of dualism is unacceptable to a person of intellectual integrity, who refuses to fabricate a barrier between philosophical thought and religious action.

The Way of Rejection

The way of insulation rejects knowledge that is not confirmed by religious tradition. The way of dualism accepts the premises of philosophy, but also admits the practical demands of religion—keeping each domain from interacting with each other. A third option is the way of rejection. This is the way of a person who gives primacy to reason and philosophy and cannot find a way of putting religious faith on a suitable rational basis. This person does not wish to create an artificial split between thinking and action; rather, he or she wants to be an integrated, consistent person. This person's philosophy must govern his or her deeds. If faith cannot withstand the challenges of reason, then faith—and the religious rituals that go with it—is to be rejected.

Spinoza is a classic representative of the way of rejection. His pursuit of reason was the touchstone of his life. When conflicts arose between reason and faith, he sided entirely with reason. Although Spinoza acknowledged some value in the biblical religions, he found them to be philosophically deficient. He abandoned Judaism—and did not adopt Christianity—because his faith in reason prevented him from accepting supernatural postulates as being true.

Spinoza is widely—and justly—considered to be an intellectual hero and martyr. He paid whatever price was necessary in order to retain his devotion to Truth. He was willing to live as an outcast from his community rather than pretend to go along with traditional religious norms. He was scorned as a heretic and a destroyer of public morality. He aroused the fury of political leaders, the church hierarchy, and much of the intelligentsia of Europe. Yet he did not back down. He was content to live a humble life as a lens grinder, a loner with a small circle of friends and admirers. This quiet, unassuming philosopher changed the world.

Although we must respect Spinoza's remarkable intellectual courage and the dramatic impact of his teachings on subsequent generations, we must also recognize some clear shortcomings in his philosophy. His teachings were revolutionary during the seventeenth and eighteenth centuries; however, their luster has diminished with the passage of time.

By the twenty-first century, thinkers have come to recognize more clearly the limitations of human reason. It is not as reliable and foolproof as Spinoza believed. The pursuit of reason has not led us to a single pristine view of reality that all intelligent people accept as true.

Scientists have become increasingly aware of uncertainties and anomalies in nature that defy conventional reason. Psychiatrists have explored the "irrational" aspects of the human mind and have come to understand that human perceptions of reality are colored by subconscious forces not governed by reason. Many thinkers have sought to understand the "whole" human being: not just the rational component, but also the emotional, poetic, spiritual, aesthetic aspects. Reason is not the sum and substance of Truth—nor of our human reality.

Spinoza's trust in reason ultimately is itself based on "faith," not reason. He had to posit that the universe is—and always has been—entirely governed by the dictates of reason. Even God is encompassed by immutable laws from which He cannot deviate. Yet there is no proof—and can be no proof—that indeed the laws of science and reason are eternal and immutable. How can we be certain that the laws of physics, as we know them today, operated in exactly the same way 100 billion years ago and will operate in exactly the same way 100 billion years from now? Positing this, as Spinoza did, is essentially a leap of faith; it cannot be proved or verified by science or reason.

Just as we might question Spinoza's faith in reason, we also might question the validity of some of his critiques of religion in general, and Judaism in particular. Since his philosophy precluded such things as divine revelation, miracles, and providence, he could hardly give the Bible an objective reading. His philosophical assumptions disallowed the claims of biblical religion.

Although the way of rejection must itself be rejected by those who seek a healthy relationship between faith and reason, it offers important insights that must not be ignored. Spinoza, in his own way, helped advance the cause of religious and intellectual freedom. His critiques of Judaism and Christianity, including his critiques of the Bible, challenged religionists to rethink their religious traditions and come up with responses to his attacks. Religion actually becomes healthier and more robust if it faces challenges; otherwise, it can sink into self-righteous dullness. Even as a heretic, Spinoza performed a service for religion. Even as an excommunicated Jew, Spinoza performed a service for Judaism.

The Way of Integration

Rabbi Hartman describes a fourth option for dealing with the relationship between philosophy and religion, one that takes both knowledge claims seriously.

> Divine revelation need not be in discord with human understanding. In fact, where they share a common domain, in principle, they are never in discord. Man's rationality participates in the divine system of knowledge. There are not two truths.... The fourth way makes possible an integration between the claims of tradition and the claims of reason by expanding the possible meanings of religious language to include symbolic meaning.[4]

The classic Jewish representative of the way of integration is Rambam. He fully subscribed to the notion that faith and reason led to the identical Truth, albeit from different vantage points. For Rambam, it is not possible for reason to dislodge the truth of revelation. It also is not possible for reason to undermine faith in God, since reason cannot reach that far; it has a limited range that can never enter into the domain of an eternal and infinite God. Reason, although vitally important in the quest for Truth, is insufficient to bring us to the ultimate destination.

On the other hand, religion cannot teach falsehood. If philosophy or science has proved something to be true, religion cannot deny this truth; nor can religion affirm something that is demonstrably false. Thus, Rambam interpreted biblical anthropomorphisms in a symbolic way, so as not to conflict with the philosophical truth that God is incorporeal. He rejected superstitious beliefs and practices, because they had been proved false by philosophy and science.

Throughout this book, we have seen how Rambam sought to balance the claims of revealed religion with those of philosophy and science. He did not see his methodology as being a compromise or apologetic position, but rather as being the ideal expression of both religion and philosophy. Religion without philosophy is superstition;

philosophy without religion is sterile. Rambam's approach to Judaism provides guidance to those of all eras, including our own, who espouse a firm loyalty to the biblical and rabbinic traditions and who also insist on the use of their reason. For thinking Jews of faith, the way of integration is the way to enter the inner precincts of the palace of the King.

If we hope to experience an intellectually vibrant and compelling Judaism, we will need to avoid the extreme fire of fundamentalism and the extreme ice of philosophical skepticism. We will need a profound reverence for our sacred texts, along with a sophisticated way of approaching these texts. In seeking a balanced and focused religious philosophy, we have drawn heavily on the teachings of Rambam, who provided a rational framework for understanding Torah. We have also learned from the critiques and insights of Spinoza.

A rabbinic teaching has it that the way of Torah is a narrow path. Our ultimate goal as thinking Jews is to walk happily and meaningfully along this path. It is a challenge and an adventure of the profoundest significance.

Notes

1 Faith in Reason, Reason in Faith

1. Marvin Fox, *Interpreting Maimonides* (Chicago: University of Chicago Press, 1990), p. 24.
2. Ibid., p. 25.
3. Maimonides, *The Guide of the Perplexed*, trans. Shlomo Pines (Chicago: University of Chicago Press, 1963), p. 16. Quotations from the *Guide* in this book are drawn from Pines's translation.
4. *Guide* 2:13, p. 290.
5. *Mishneh Torah, Hilkhot Kiddush haHodesh* 17:24.
6. Isidore Twersky, ed., *A Maimonides Reader* (New York: Behrman House, 1972), p. 454.
7. Ibid., pp. 464–65.
8. Ibid., p. 472.
9. Ibid., p. 407.
10. *Mishneh Torah, Hilkhot Avodah Zarah* 1:3.
11. Richard Popkin, "Spinoza's Excommunication," in H. Ravven and L. Goodman, *Jewish Themes in Spinoza's Philosophy* (Albany: State University of New York Press, 2002), pp. 263ff.
12. Jonathan Israel, *Radical Enlightenment* (Oxford: Oxford University Press, 2001), p. 159.
13. Spinoza, *The Letters*, trans. Samuel Shirley (Indianapolis and Cambridge: Hackett Publishing Company, 1995), p. 151.
14. Spinoza, *A Theologico-Political Treatise*, trans. R. H. M. Elwes (Mineola, N.Y.: Dover Publications, 2004), p. 192.
15. Ibid., p. 228.
16. Ibid., p. 241.
17. Ibid.

18. Ibid., p. 257.
19. Ibid., p. 263.
20. Ibid., p. 264.
21. *Guide* 3:54, p. 638.
22. Spinoza, *The Ethics*, trans. R. H. M. Elwes (New York: Dover Publications, 1955), p. 270.
23. Maimonides, *Mishneh Torah, Yesodei haTorah*, chaps. 7–8.
24. *Ethics*, p. 255.
25. *Guide* 1:31, p. 65.
26. Quoted by Brian Greene, *The Elegant Universe* (New York: Vintage Books, 2003), p. 111.

2 The Nature of God, the God of Nature

1. This passage from the *Zohar* is quoted from *The Daily-Sabbath Prayer Book*, ed. and trans. David de Sola Pool (New York: Union of Sephardic Congregations, 2006), p. 209.
2. *Mishneh Torah, Yesodei haTorah* 1:1.
3. Ibid.
4. *Guide* 1:58, p. 137.
5. Ibid.
6. Ibid.
7. Ibid., 1:59, p. 139.
8. Ibid., p. 141.
9. Kenneth Seeskin, *Maimonides: A Guide for Today's Perplexed* (West Orange, N.J.: Behrman House, 1991), p. 34.
10. *Guide* 1:53, p. 121.
11. *Ethics*, proposition 20.
12. *Letters*, p. 277.
13. *Mishneh Torah, Yesodei haTorah* 2:2.
14. *Guide* 2:25, pp. 327–28.
15. Ibid., p. 329.
16. *Guide* 2:17, p. 295.
17. This section is largely based on chap. 8 of my book *The Rhythms of Jewish Living* (New York: Sepher Hermon Press, 1986).
18. *Sefer Hareidim* (Jerusalem, 5718 [1958]), p. 214.
19. Ibid., p. 215.
20. *Mishneh Torah, Hilkhot Tefillah* 4:15–16.
21. *Shulhan Arukh, Orah Hayyim* 98.
22. Fox, *Interpreting Maimonides*, p. 319.

23. Ibid., p. 319.
24. Ibid., pp. 320–21.
25. Ibid., p. 80.

3 Torah from Heaven

1. *Zohar, Va-et-hanan,* p. 261a.
2. *Sifri,* 357; Talmud, *Makot* 11a; Talmud, *Menahot* 30a.
3. See Marc Shapiro, *The Limits of Orthodox Theology* (Oxford: Littman Library of Jewish Civilization, 2004), p. 104.
4. For a discussion of "Torah from Heaven" and the various rabbinic understandings of this term, see Abraham Joshua Heschel, *Torah min ha-Shamayim be-Aspaklariah shel ha-Dorot,* 2 vols. (London and New York: Soncino Press, 5722 [1962]).
5. See David Weiss Halivni, *Breaking the Tablets* (Lanham: Rowman and Littlefield, 2007), chap. 2. See also B. Barry Levy, *Fixing God's Torah* (Oxford: Oxford University Press, 2001), chap. 1.
6. Heschel, *Torah min ha-Shamayim,* vol. 2, pp. 229–30.
7. Introduction to *Perek Helek.*
8. *Mishneh Torah, Hilkhot Teshuvah* 3:8.
9. Shapiro, *Limits of Orthodox Theology,* p. 120.
10. *Guide* 1:36, p. 85.
11. Ibid., 1:54, p. 125.
12. Ibid., 3:50, p. 613.
13. *Theologico-Political Treatise,* pp. 114ff.
14. *Letters,* p. 135.
15. *Theologico-Political Treatise,* p. 103.
16. *Letters,* p. 348.
17. *Theologico-Political Treatise,* p. 172.
18. *Letters,* p. 158.
19. *Theologico-Political Treatise,* p. 69.
20. Menachem Kellner, *Must a Jew Believe Anything?* (London and Portland, OR: Littman Library of Jewish Civilization, 2008).
21. Matthew Arnold, *Literature and Dogma* (New York: Home Library Edition, n.d.), p. 56.

4 Divine Providence

1. *Guide* 3:17, p. 474; see also 3:18.
2. Ibid., 3:17, p. 471.
3. Maimonides, *Shemonah Perakim,* section 8.

4. Ibid.

5. *Guide* 3:51, p. 625.

6. *Mishneh Torah, Hilkhot Taaniyot* 1:1.

7. Ibid., 1:9.

8. *Asei Lekha Rav* 7:69.

9. Rambam discusses this in his introduction to *Perek Helek.*

10. *Mishneh Torah, Hilkhot Teshuvah* 5:1.

11. Ibid., 5:5.

12. *Guide* 2:32, p. 361.

13. Maimonides, *The Essay on Resurrection*, in Abraham Halkin and David Hartman, *Crisis and Leadership: Epistles of Maimonides* (Philadelphia: Jewish Publication Society of America, 1985), p. 223.

14. *Guide* 2:29, p. 345.

15. *Mishneh Torah, Yesodei haTorah* 8:1.

16. Israel, *Radical Enlightenment*, p. 218.

17. *Ethics*, part 1, p. 78.

18. *Letters*, p. 338.

19. *Ethics*, part 1, proposition 32, corollary 1; proposition 33.

20. *Letters*, p. 284.

21. Ibid.

22. Ibid, p. 285.

23. Ibid., p.156.

24. *Ethics*, part 5, proposition 42.

25. Ibid., part 3, proposition 7.

26. *Guide* 3:10, p. 440.

27. See the discussion in my book *The Rhythms of Jewish Living*, pp. 124ff.

28. Lewis Thomas, *The Lives of a Cell* (New York: Penguin Group, 1975), p. 26.

5 The Oral Torah and Rabbinic Tradition

1. *Mishneh Torah, Hilkhot Mamrim* 1:1.

2. See Menachem Kellner, *Maimonides on the 'Decline of the Generations' and the Nature of Rabbinic Authority* (Albany: State University of New York Press, 1996), p. 67.

3. *Mishneh Torah, Hilkhot Mamrim* 2:1–4.

4. Ibid., 3:3.

5. The ensuing discussion is drawn from my book *Voices in Exile: A Study in Sephardic Intellectual History* (Hoboken, N.J.: Ktav Publishing House, 1991), chap. 4.

6. The *Kol Sakhal* is included in Isaac Reggio, ed., *Behinath ha-Kabbala* (Goeritz, 1852).

7. A classic in defense of the Oral Torah was written by Haham David Nieto (b. 1654), *Ha-Kuzari ha-Sheni hu Mateh Dan* (Jerusalem, 5718 [1958]). See also Jacob Petuchowski, *The Theology of Haham David Nieto* (New York: Ktav Publishing House, 1970). Nieto's work was composed long after Spinoza's excommunication from the Jewish community of Amsterdam.

8. *Theologico-Political Treatise*, p. 119.

9. Ibid., p. 107.

10. *Kohelet Rabbah* 5:9; see also Jerusalem Talmud, *Peah* 2:6.

11. *Kovetz Iggerot* 1:59. This is cited by David Weiss Halivni, "From Midrash to Mishnah: Theological Repercussions and Further Clarifications of 'Chate'u Yisrael,'" in *The Midrashic Imagination: Jewish Exegesis, Thought and History*, ed., Michael Fishbane (Albany: State University of New York Press, 1993), p. 40, n. 13.

12. *Midrash Tehillim* 12:4.

13. *Sifra, Behukotai* 2:8.

14. Halivni, "From Midrash to Mishnah," p. 28.

15. See David Weiss Halivni, "On Man's Role in Revelation," in *From Ancient Israel to Modern Judaism: Essays in Honor of Marvin Fox*, ed. J. Neusner, E. S. Frerichs, and N. M. Sarna (Atlanta: University of Florida Press, 1989), pp. 30–31.

16. *Theologico-Political Treatise*, p. 76.

17. Ibid., p. 69.

18. Eliyahu Dessler, *Mikhtav me-Eliyahu* I:75–77, cited by Lawrence Kaplan, "Daas Torah: A Modern Conception of Rabbinic Authority," *Rabbinic Authority and Personal Autonomy*, ed. M. Sokol (Northvale, N.J.: Jason Aronson, 1992), pp. 16–17.

19. Quoted by Kaplan, ibid., p. 17.

20. Kaplan, ibid., p. 54, n. 84.

21. Quoted by Kaplan, ibid., p. 50.

6 Religion and Superstition

1. *Theologico-Political Treatise*, preface.

2. Ibid., p. 4.

3. Ibid.

4. *Theologico-Political Treatise*, p. 11.

5. The following material is drawn from my article "Religion and Superstition: A Maimonidean Approach," *Conversations*, no. 3 (Winter 2009): 109–120. See also Marc Shapiro, "Maimonidean Halakha and Superstition," in *Studies in Maimonides and His Interpreters* (Scranton, Pa., and London: University of Scranton Press, 2008), pp. 95–150.

6. See David Guttmann, "*Avodah Zarah* as Falsehood—Denial of Reality and Rejection of Science," *Hakirah* 6 (Summer 2008): 119–38.

7. *Mishneh Torah, Hilkhot Avodah Zara* 11:12.

8. *Mishneh Torah, Hilkhot Mezuzah* 5:4.

9. *Shulhan Arukh, Yoreh Deah* 179.

10. *Biur haGra, Yoreh Deah* 179.

11. *Shulhan Arukh, Orah Hayyim* 4:2–3.

12. *Mishneh Torah, Hilkhot Tefillah* 4:2–3.

13. See my article, "Reflections on Torah Education and Mis-Education," *Tradition* 41, no. 2 (2008): 17–18.

14. *Mishneh Torah, Hilkhot Teshuvah* 3:7. See Israel Drazin, *Maimonides, The Exceptional Mind* (Jerusalem: Gefen Publishing Company, 2008), pp. 192–93.

15. Ibid., pp. 205–6.

16. *Mishneh Torah, Hilkhot Avodah Zarah* 11:16.

17. Twersky, *A Maimonides Reader*, p. 465. See also Y. Tzvi Langermann, "Maimonides' Repudiation of Astrology," in *Maimonidean Studies*, vol. 2, ed. Arthur Hyman (New York: Yeshiva University Press, 1991), pp. 123ff.

7 Israel and Humanity

1. I will be using the words *Judaism* and *Jews/Jewish* (although they emerged much later than the time of the giving of the Torah at Mount Sinai) to refer to the religion and people of Israel.

2. See Rosenthal, "Why Spinoza Chose the Hebrews," pp. 225–60.

3. Menachem Kellner, *Maimonides' Confrontation with Mysticism* (Oxford: Littman Library of Jewish Civilization, 2006), p. 216.

4. Ibid., chap. 7.

5. *Mishneh Torah, Hilkhot Shemitah veYovel* 13:13.

6. Fox, *Interpreting Maimonides*, p. 329.

7. The last phrase in the correct Hebrew text is *ela mehakhmeihem*, "but one of their wise men." The incorrect Hebrew text that has caused confusion as to Rambam's meaning is *velo mehakhmeihem* "and not one of their wise men." According to this latter erroneous reading, Rambam would be saying that a non-Jewish person who did not accept the divine Torah origin of the Noahide Laws was neither righteous nor wise. See M. Kellner's discussion of this text in his book *Maimonides on Judaism and the Jewish People* (Albany: State University of New York Press, 1991), pp. 75–76.

8. Kellner, *Maimonides' Confrontation with Mysticism*, pp. 250ff.

9. Ibid., p. 263.

10. I am quoting the text from Twersky, *A Maimonides Reader*, pp. 475–76.

11. Abraham Halkin and David Hartman, *Crisis and Leadership: Epistles of Maimonides*, p. 23.
12. Ibid., p. 30.
13. Ibid., p. 33.
14. Ibid., pp. 96–97.
15. Ibid., p. 97.
16. Ibid.
17. Ibid., p. 101.
18. Ibid., p. 117.
19. *Mishneh Torah, Hilkhot Melakhim* 12:4.
20. Fox, *Interpreting Maimonides*, pp. 340–41. Fox discusses Maimonides' belief that sacrifices will be restored in messianic times.
21. Twersky, *A Maimonides Reader*, pp. 226–27.
22. Kellner, *Maimonides on Judaism and the Jewish People*, pp. 38ff.

8 Conversion to Judaism

1. *Shir ha-Shirim Rabbah* 1:3.
2. Talmud, *Gittin* 56a; *Devarim Rabbah* 2:24; *Shemot Rabbah* 30:12. See also Louis H. Feldman, *Jew and Gentile in the Ancient World* (Princeton, N.J.: Princeton University Press, 1993), p. 311.
3. Talmud, *Pesahim* 87b; *Shir ha-Shirim Rabbah* 1:3 and 1:4.
4. This discussion is drawn from my article "Conversion to Judaism: Halakha, Hashkafa, and Historic Challenge," *Hakirah* 7 (Winter 2009): 25–49; and from my book *Choosing to Be Jewish: The Orthodox Road to Conversion* (Jersey City, N.J.: Ktav Publishing House, 2005), especially chap. 2 and 4.
5. *Mishneh Torah, Hilkhot Issurei Biah* 14:8.
6. *Ahiezer* 3:26, section 4.
7. *Mishpetei Uziel,* vol. 2, *Yoreh Deah* 58.
8. *Mishneh Torah, Hilkhot Issurei Biah* 14:2.
9. Ibid.
10. *Mishneh Torah, Hilkhot Hagigah* 3:6.
11. *Mishneh Torah, Hilkhot Issurei Biah* 13:14–16.
12. Ibid., 13:17.
13. *Pe'er haDor* (Amsterdam, 5525 [1765]), no. 132.
14. Avi Sagi and Zvi Zohar, in their book *Giyyur veZehut Yehudit* (Jerusalem: Shalom Hartman Institute and Mosad Bialik, 1997), indicate that the stringent view equating conversion with absolute commitment to observe all mitzvot only arose in the latter nineteenth century in Europe.

15. *Orot* (Jerusalem, 5745 [1985]), p. 156. See also Yoel Bin-Nun, "Nationalism, Humanity and Kenesset Israel," in *The World of Rav Kook's Thought* (New York: Avichai Foundation, 1991), pp. 210ff.

16. See my article "A Discussion of the Nature of Jewishness in the Teachings of Rabbi Kook and Rabbi Uziel," in *Seeking Good, Speaking Peace*, ed. Hayyim Angel (Hoboken, N.J.: Ktav Publishing House, 1994), pp. 112–23.

17. *Mishpetei Uziel, Even haEzer* (Jerusalem, 5724 [1964]), no. 20; see also my book *Loving Truth and Peace: The Grand Religious Worldview of Rabbi Benzion Uziel* (Northvale, N.J.: Jason Aronson, 1999), chap. 7.

18. *Mishpetei Uziel, Even haEzer*, no. 20.

19. *Mishpetei Uziel* (5698 [1938]), no. 26.

9 Eternal Torah, Changing Times

1. *Guide* 3:51, pp. 618ff.

2. Menachem Kellner, *Maimonides on Human Perfection* (Atlanta: Scholars Press, 1990), pp. 4ff, especially p. 20.

3. *Mishneh Torah, Hilkhot Talmud Torah* 3:10–11.

4. Abraham Maimonides, *War of the Lord*, trans. Fred Rosner (Haifa, Isr.: Maimonides Research Institute, n.d.), p. 85.

5. Ibid., p. 103.

6. Menachem Kellner, "Maimonides' Critique of the Rabbinic Culture of his Day," in *Rabbinic Culture and Its Critics*, ed. Daniel Frank and Matt Goldish (Detroit: Wayne State University Press, 2008), p. 84. See also Kellner's discussion in chap. 1 of his book, *Maimonides' Confrontation with Mysticism*.

7. See my article "Reflections on Torah Education and Mis-Education," *Tradition* 41, no. 2 (2008): 10–23.

8. B. M. Lewin, ed., *Ozar ha-Geonim*, vol. 4, *Hagigah* (Jerusalem, 5692 [1932]), pp. 59–60. See also Marvin Fox, "Nahmanides on the Status of Aggadot," *Journal of Jewish Studies* 40, no. 1 (Spring 1989): 95–109. *Aggadah* refers to the non-halakhic texts in the Talmud; *midrash* refers to rabbinic interpretations and homilies in books of midrashim, separate from the Talmud.

9. Lewin, ibid., p. 60.

10. Ibid., pp. 4–5.

11. Zvi Hirsch Chajes, *The Student's Guide to the Talmud* (London: Soncino Press, 1952), p. 201; and his discussion on pp. 208ff.

12. Joseph Munk, "Two Letters of Samson Raphael Hirsch, a Translation," *L'Eylah*, April 1989, pp. 30–35.

13. *Aseh Lekha Rav* 5:49.

14. Warren Zev Harvey, "Maimonides' First Commandment, Physics and Doubt," in *Hazon Nahum*, ed. Y. Elman and J. Gurock (New York: Yeshiva University

Press, 1997), p. 149. See also, in the same volume, the article by Rabbi Nachum L. Rabinovitch, "Rambam, Science and *Ta'amei haMitzvoth*," pp. 187–205.

15. Menachem Kellner, *Science in the Bet Midrash: Studies in Maimonides* (Brighton, Mass.: Academic Studies Press, 2009), pp. 223–24.

16. Kellner, *Maimonides on the 'Decline of the Generations'*, p. 92.

17. *Guide* 2:8, p. 267.

18. Ibid., 3:14, p. 459.

19. Kellner, *Science in the Bet Midrash*, chaps. 12–15.

20. Quoted by Chaim Rappoport, "*Ve-ha-arets le-Olam Omedet*," *Or Yisrael* 14:3, Nisan 5769, p. 207, n. 2.

21. Ibid.

22. Rabbi Slifkin discusses the charges lodged against him and offers a defense of his positions on his website: www.zootorah.com/controversy/science response.

23. Aryeh Kaplan, *Immortality, Resurrection and the Age of the Universe: A Kabbalistic View* (Hoboken, N.J.: Ktav Publishing House, 1993), p. 9. See also Nathan Aviezer, *In the Beginning* (Hoboken, N.J.: Ktav Publishing House, 1990).

24. Kellner, *Science in the Bet Midrash*, p. 245.

25. *Mishneh Torah, Hilkhot Ishut* 13:11.

26. Ibid.

27. Ibid., 15:18–20.

28. *Shulhan Arukh, Even haEzer* 21:61.

29. Haim David Halevy, *Mayyim Hayyim,* (Tel Aviv: Committee for the Publication of the Writings of Rabbi H. D. Halevy, 5755 [1995]), 2:45.

30. ynetnews.com/articles/0,7340,L-3417632.html, in a report about the singer Eliyahu Haim Fayzakov.

31. *Mishneh Torah, Hilkhot Talmud Torah* 1:13.

32. Halevy, *Mayyim Hayyim* 2:89.

33. Warren Zev Harvey, "The Obligation of Talmud on Women According to Maimonides," *Tradition* 19 (Summer 1981): 122–30; and Abraham Melamed, "Maimonides on Women: Formless Matter or Potential Prophet?" in *Perspectives on Jewish Thought and Mysticism*, ed. A. Ivry, E. Wolfson, and A. Arkush (Newark: Harwood Academic Publishers, 1998), pp. 99–134.

34. Joel L. Kraemer, *Maimonides: The Life and World of One of Civilization's Greatest Minds* (New York: Doubleday, 2008), p. 315.

35. Ibid., pp. 299–300

36. *Mishneh Torah, Hilkhot Geirushin* 2:20.

37. Ibid.

10 Faith and Reason

1. David Hartman, *Maimonides: Torah and Philosophic Quest* (Philadelphia: Jewish Publication Society of America, 1976), introduction.

2. Ibid., pp. 8–9

3. Ibid., p. 13.

4. Ibid., pp. 15–17.

Suggestions for Further Reading

Angel, Hayyim, ed. *Seeking Good, Speaking Peace: Collected Essays of Rabbi Marc D. Angel*. Hoboken, N.J.: Ktav Publishing House, 1994.

Angel, Marc D. *Choosing to Be Jewish: The Orthodox Road to Conversion*. Jersey City, N.J.: Ktav Publishing House, 2005.

———. "Conversion to Judaism: Halakha, Hashkafa, and Historic Challenge," *Hakirah: The Flatbush Journal of Jewish Law and Thought* 7 (Winter 2009): 25–49.

———. *Loving Truth and Peace: The Grand Religious Worldview of Rabbi Benzion Uziel*. Northvale, N.J.: Jason Aronson, 1999.

———. "Reflections on Torah Education and Mid-Education." *Tradition* 41, no. 2 (2008): 10–23.

———. "Religion and Superstition: A Maimonidean Approach." *Conversations*, no. 3 (Winter 2009): 109–20.

———. *The Rhythms of Jewish Living*. New York: Sepher Hermon Press, 1986.

———. *Voices in Exile: A Study in Sephardic Intellectual History*. Hoboken, N.J.: Ktav Publishing House, 1991.

Angel, Marc D., and Hayyim Angel. *Rabbi Haim David Halevy: Gentle Scholar and Courageous Thinker*. Jerusalem: Urim Publications, 2006.

Drazin, Israel. *Maimonides: The Exceptional Mind*. Jerusalem and New York: Gefen Publishing Company, 2008.

Fox, Marvin. *Interpreting Maimonides*. Chicago and London: University of Chicago Press, 1990.

———. "Nahmanides on the Status of Aggadot." *Journal of Jewish Studies* 40, no. 1 (Spring 1989): 95–109.

Goldstein, Rebecca. *Betraying Spinoza*. New York: Schocken, 2006.

Greene, Brian. *The Elegant Universe*. New York: Vintage Books, 2003.

Halivni, David Weiss. *Breaking the Tablets*. Lanham, Md.: Rowman and Littlefield, 2007.

————. "From Midrash to Mishnah: Theological Repercussions and Further Clarifications of 'Chate'u Yisrael.'" In *The Midrashic Imagination: Jewish Exegesis, Thought and History*. Edited by Michael Fishbane. Albany: State University of New York, 1993.

————. "On Man's Role in Revelation." In *From Ancient Israel to Modern Judaism: Essays in Honor of Marvin Fox*. Edited by J. Neusner, E. S. Frerichs, and N. M. Sarna. Atlanta: University of South Florida, 1989.

Halkin, Abraham, and David Hartman. *Crisis and Leadership: Epistles of Maimonides*. Philadelphia: Jewish Publication Society, 1985.

Hampshire, Stuart. *Spinoza and Spinozism*. Oxford: Clarendon Press, 2005.

Hartman, David. *Maimonides: Torah and Philosophic Quest*. Philadelphia: Jewish Publication Society of America, 1976.

Harvey, Warren Zev. "Maimonides' First Commandment, Physics and Doubt." In *Hazon Nahum*. Edited by Y. Elman and J. Gurock. New York: Yeshiva University Press, 1997.

————. "The Obligation of Talmud on Women According to Maimonides." *Tradition* 19 (Summer 1981): 122–30.

Heschel, Abraham Joshua. *Torah min ha-Shamayim be-Aspaklariah shel ha-Dorot*. 2 vols. London and New York: Soncino Press, 5722 [1962].

Israel, Jonathan. *Radical Enlightenment*. Oxford: Oxford University Press, 2001.

Kaplan, Lawrence. "Daas Torah: A Modern Conception of Rabbinic Authority." In *Rabbinic Authority and Personal Autonomy*. Edited by M. Sokol. Northvale, N.J.: Jason Aronson, 1992.

Kellner, Menachem. *Maimonides' Confrontation with Mysticism*. Oxford: Littman Library of Jewish Civilization, 2006.

————. "Maimonides' Critique of the Rabbinic Culture of His Day." In *Rabbinic Culture and Its Critics*. Edited by D. Frank and M. Goldish. Detroit: Wayne State University Press, 2008.

————. *Maimonides on Judaism and the Jewish People*. Albany: State University of New York Press, 1991.

————. *Maimonides on the 'Decline of the Generations' and the Nature of Rabbinic Authority*. Albany: State University of New York Press, 1996.

————. *Must a Jew Believe Anything?* London and Portland, Ore.: Littman Library of Jewish Civilization, 2008.

————. *Science in the Bet Midrash: Studies in Maimonides*. Brighton, Mass.: Academic Studies Press, 2009.

Kraemer, Joel L. *Maimonides: The Life and World of One of Civilization's Greatest Minds*. New York: Doubleday, 2008.

Levy, B. Barry. *Fixing God's Torah*. Oxford: Oxford University Press, 2001.

Maimonides. *The Guide of the Perplexed*. Translated by Shlomo Pines. Chicago: University of Chicago Press, 1964.

Melamed, Abraham. "Maimonides on Women: Formless Matter or Potential Prophet?" In *Perspectives on Jewish Thought and Mysticism*. Edited by A. Ivry, E. Wolfson, and A. Arkush. Newark: Harwood Academic Publishers, 1998.

Nadler, Steven. *Spinoza: A Life*. Cambridge: Cambridge University Press, 1999.

Popkin, Richard. "Spinoza's Excommunication." In *Jewish Themes in Spinoza's Philosophy*. Edited by H. Ravven and L. Goodman. Albany: State University of New York Press, 2002, pp. 263–79.

Ravven, Heidi M. "Some Thoughts on What Spinoza Learned from Maimonides about the Prophetic Imagination. *Journal of the History of Philosophy* 39 (2001): 193–214, 385–406.

Ravven, Heidi, and Lenn Goodman, eds. *Jewish Themes in Spinoza's Philosophy*. Albany: State University of New York, 2002.

Seeskin, Kenneth. *Maimonides: A Guide for Today's Perplexed*. West Orange, N.J.: Behrman House, 1991.

Shapiro, Marc. *The Limits of Orthodox Theology*. Oxford: Littman Library of Jewish Civilization, 2004.

———. *Studies in Maimonides and His Interpreters*. Scranton, Pa., and London: University of Scranton Press, 2008.

Spinoza. *The Letters*. Translated by Samuel Shirley. Indianapolis and Cambridge: Hackett Publishing Company, 1995.

Spinoza. *On the Improvement of the Understanding, The Ethics, Correspondence*. Translated by R. H. M. Elwes. New York: Dover Publications, reprint of 1955 edition of *Works of Spinoza*, vol. 2.

Spinoza. *A Theologico-Political Treatise*. Translated by R. H. M. Elwes. Mineola, N.Y.: Dover Publications, 2004.

Stewart, Matthew. *The Courtier and the Heretic: Leibniz, Spinoza, and the Fate of God in the Modern World*. New York: W. W. Norton and Company, 2006.

Twersky, Isidore. *Introduction to the Code of Maimonides*. New Haven, Conn., and London: Yale University Press, 1980.

———, ed. *A Maimonides Reader*. Springfield: Behrman House, 1972.

Zohar, Zvi, and Avi Sagi. *Giyyur veZehut Yehudit*. Jerusalem: Shalom Hartman Institute and Mosad Bialik, 1997.

———. *Transforming Identity: The Ritual Transformation from Gentile to Jew, Structure and Meaning*. London: Continuum, 2007.

Bar/Bat Mitzvah

The JGirl's Guide: The Young Jewish Woman's Handbook for Coming of Age
By Penina Adelman, Ali Feldman, and Shulamit Reinharz
This inspirational, interactive guidebook helps pre-teen Jewish girls address the many issues surrounding coming of age. 6 x 9, 240 pp, Quality PB, 978-1-58023-215-9 **$14.99**
Also Available: **The JGirl's Teacher's and Parent's Guide**
8½ x 11, 56 pp, PB, 978-1-58023-225-8 **$8.99**

Bar/Bat Mitzvah Basics: A Practical Family Guide to Coming of Age Together
Edited by Cantor Helen Leneman 6 x 9, 240 pp, Quality PB, 978-1-58023-151-0 **$18.95**

The Bar/Bat Mitzvah Memory Book, 2nd Edition: An Album for Treasuring the Spiritual Celebration *By Rabbi Jeffrey K. Salkin and Nina Salkin*
8 x 10, 48 pp, Deluxe HC, 2-color text, ribbon marker, 978-1-58023-263-0 **$19.99**

For Kids—Putting God on Your Guest List, 2nd Edition: How to Claim the Spiritual Meaning of Your Bar or Bat Mitzvah *By Rabbi Jeffrey K. Salkin*
6 x 9, 144 pp, Quality PB, 978-1-58023-308-8 **$15.99** *For ages 11–13*

Putting God on the Guest List, 3rd Edition: How to Reclaim the Spiritual Meaning of Your Child's Bar or Bat Mitzvah *By Rabbi Jeffrey K. Salkin*
6 x 9, 224 pp, Quality PB, 978-1-58023-222-7 **$16.99**; HC, 978-1-58023-260-9 **$24.99**
Also Available: **Putting God on the Guest List Teacher's Guide**
8½ x 11, 48 pp, PB, 978-1-58023-226-5 **$8.99**

Tough Questions Jews Ask: A Young Adult's Guide to Building a Jewish Life
By Rabbi Edward Feinstein 6 x 9, 160 pp, Quality PB, 978-1-58023-139-8 **$14.99** *For ages 12 & up*
Also Available: **Tough Questions Jews Ask Teacher's Guide**
8½ x 11, 72 pp, PB, 978-1-58023-187-9 **$8.95**

Bible Study/Midrash

The Modern Men's Torah Commentary: New Insights from Jewish Men on the 54 Weekly Torah Portions *Edited by Rabbi Jeffrey K. Salkin*
A major contribution to modern biblical commentary. Addresses the most important concerns of *modern* men by opening them up to the life of Torah.
6 x 9, 368 pp, HC, 978-1-58023-395-8 **$24.99**

The Genesis of Leadership: What the Bible Teaches Us about Vision, Values and Leading Change *By Rabbi Nathan Laufer; Foreword by Senator Joseph I. Lieberman*
Unlike other books on leadership, this one is rooted in the stories of the Bible.
6 x 9, 288 pp, Quality PB, 978-1-58023-352-1 **$18.99**; HC, 978-1-58023-241-8 **$24.99**

Hineini in Our Lives: Learning How to Respond to Others through 14 Biblical Texts and Personal Stories *By Norman J. Cohen* 6 x 9, 240 pp, Quality PB, 978-1-58023-274-6 **$16.99**

Moses and the Journey to Leadership: Timeless Lessons of Effective Management from the Bible and Today's Leaders *By Dr. Norman J. Cohen*
6 x 9, 240 pp, Quality PB, 978-1-58023-351-4 **$18.99**; HC, 978-1-58023-227-2 **$21.99**

Self, Struggle & Change: Family Conflict Stories in Genesis and Their Healing Insights for Our Lives *By Norman J. Cohen* 6 x 9, 224 pp, Quality PB, 978-1-879045-66-8 **$18.99**

The Triumph of Eve & Other Subversive Bible Tales *By Matt Biers-Ariel*
5½ x 8½, 192 pp, Quality PB, 978-1-59473-176-1 **$14.99**; HC, 978-1-59473-040-5 **$19.99**
(A book from SkyLight Paths, Jewish Lights' sister imprint)

The Wisdom of Judaism: An Introduction to the Values of the Talmud
By Rabbi Dov Peretz Elkins
Explores the essence of Judaism. 6 x 9, 192 pp, Quality PB, 978-1-58023-327-9 **$16.99**
Also Available: **The Wisdom of Judaism Teacher's Guide**
8½ x 11, 18 pp, PB, 978-1-58023-350-7 **$8.99**

Or phone, mail or e-mail to: **JEWISH LIGHTS Publishing**
An imprint of Turner Publishing Company
4507 Charlotte Avenue • Suite 100 • Nashville, Tennessee 37209
Tel: (615) 255-2665 • www.jewishlights.com
Prices subject to change.

Congregation Resources

Empowered Judaism: What Independent Minyanim Can Teach Us about Building Vibrant Jewish Communities
By Rabbi Elie Kaunfer; Foreword by Prof. Jonathan D. Sarna
Examines the independent minyan movement and what lessons these grassroots communities can provide. 6 x 9, 224 pp, Quality PB, 978-1-58023-412-2 **$18.99**

Spiritual Boredom: Rediscovering the Wonder of Judaism *By Dr. Erica Brown*
Breaks through the surface of spiritual boredom to find the reservoir of meaning within. 6 x 9, 208 pp, HC, 978-1-58023-405-4 **$21.99**

Building a Successful Volunteer Culture
Finding Meaning in Service in the Jewish Community
By Rabbi Charles Simon; Foreword by Shelley Lindauer; Preface by Dr. Ron Wolfson
Shows you how to develop and maintain the volunteers who are essential to the vitality of your organization and community. 6 x 9, 192 pp, Quality PB, 978-1-58023-408-5 **$16.99**

The Case for Jewish Peoplehood: Can We Be One?
By Dr. Erica Brown and Dr. Misha Galperin; Foreword by Rabbi Joseph Telushkin
6 x 9, 224 pp, HC, 978-1-58023-401-6 **$21.99**

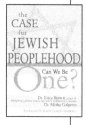

Inspired Jewish Leadership: Practical Approaches to Building Strong Communities
By Dr. Erica Brown 6 x 9, 256 pp, HC, 978-1-58023-361-3 **$24.99**

Jewish Pastoral Care, 2nd Edition: A Practical Handbook from Traditional & Contemporary Sources *Edited by Rabbi Dayle A. Friedman, MSW, MAJCS, BCC*
6 x 9, 528 pp, Quality PB, 978-1-58023-427-6 **$30.00**

Rethinking Synagogues: A New Vocabulary for Congregational Life
By Rabbi Lawrence A. Hoffman 6 x 9, 240 pp, Quality PB, 978-1-58023-248-7 **$19.99**

The Spirituality of Welcoming: How to Transform Your Congregation into a Sacred Community *By Dr. Ron Wolfson* 6 x 9, 224 pp, Quality PB, 978-1-58023-244-9 **$19.99**

Children's Books

What You Will See Inside a Synagogue
By Rabbi Lawrence A. Hoffman, PhD, and Dr. Ron Wolfson; Full-color photos by Bill Aron
A colorful, fun-to-read introduction that explains the ways and whys of Jewish worship and religious life. 8¼ x 10½, 32 pp, Full-color photos, Quality PB, 978-1-59473-256-0 **$8.99**
For ages 6 & up (A book from SkyLight Paths, Jewish Lights' sister imprint)

Because Nothing Looks Like God
By Lawrence Kushner and Karen Kushner Introduces children to the possibilities of spiritual life. 11 x 8½, 32 pp, Full-color illus., HC, 978-1-58023-092-6 **$17.99** *For ages 4 & up*

Board Book Companions to *Because Nothing Looks Like God*
5 x 5, 24 pp, Full-color illus., SkyLight Paths Board Books *For ages 0–4*

What Does God Look Like? 978-1-893361-23-2 **$7.99**

How Does God Make Things Happen? 978-1-893361-24-9 **$7.95**

Where Is God? 978-1-893361-17-1 **$7.99**

The Book of Miracles: A Young Person's Guide to Jewish Spiritual Awareness
Written and illus. by Lawrence Kushner
6 x 9, 96 pp, 2-color illus., HC, 978-1-879045-78-1 **$16.95** *For ages 9 & up*

In God's Hands
By Lawrence Kushner and Gary Schmidt 9 x 12, 32 pp, HC, 978-1-58023-224-1 **$16.99**

In Our Image: God's First Creatures *By Nancy Sohn Swartz*
9 x 12, 32 pp, Full-color illus., HC, 978-1-879045-99-6 **$16.95** *For ages 4 & up*

Also Available as a Board Book: **How Did the Animals Help God?**
5 x 5, 24 pp, Full-color illus., Board Book, 978-1-59473-044-3 **$7.99** *For ages 0–4*
(A book from SkyLight Paths, Jewish Lights' sister imprint)

The Kids' Fun Book of Jewish Time
By Emily Sper 9 x 7½, 24 pp, Full-color illus., HC, 978-1-58023-311-8 **$16.99**

What Makes Someone a Jew? *By Lauren Seidman*
Reflects the changing face of American Judaism.
10 x 8½, 32 pp, Full-color photos, Quality PB, 978-1-58023-321-7 **$8.99** *For ages 3–6*

Current Events/History

A Dream of Zion: American Jews Reflect on Why Israel Matters to Them
Edited by Rabbi Jeffrey K. Salkin Explores what Jewish people in America have to say about Israel. 6 x 9, 304 pp, Quality PB, 978-1-58023-415-3 **$18.99**; HC, 978-1-58023-340-8 **$24.99**
Also Available: **A Dream of Zion Teacher's Guide** 8½ x 11, 32 pp, PB, 978-1-58023-356-9 **$8.99**

The Ethiopian Jews of Israel: Personal Stories of Life in the Promised Land *By Len Lyons, PhD; Foreword by Alan Dershowitz; Photographs by Ilan Ossendryver* Recounts, through photographs and words, stories of Ethiopian Jews.
10½ x 10, 240 pp, 100 full-color photos, HC, 978-1-58023-323-1 **$34.99**

Foundations of Sephardic Spirituality: The Inner Life of Jews of the Ottoman Empire *By Rabbi Marc D. Angel, PhD* 6 x 9, 224 pp, Quality PB, 978-1-58023-341-5 **$18.99**

Hannah Senesh: Her Life and Diary, the First Complete Edition
By Hannah Senesh; Foreword by Marge Piercy; Preface by Eitan Senesh; Afterword by Roberta Grossman 6 x 9, 368 pp, b/w photos, Quality PB, 978-1-58023-342-2 **$19.99**

The Jewish Connection to Israel, the Promised Land: A Brief Introduction for Christians *By Rabbi Eugene Korn, PhD* 5½ x 8½, 192 pp, Quality PB, 978-1-58023-318-7 **$14.99**

Judaism and Justice: The Jewish Passion to Repair the World
By Rabbi Sidney Schwarz 6 x 9, 352 pp, Quality PB, 978-1-58023-353-8 **$19.99**

The Story of the Jews: A 4,000-Year Adventure—A Graphic History Book
Written & illustrated by Stan Mack 6 x 9, 288 pp, illus., Quality PB, 978-1-58023-155-8 **$16.99**

Ecology/Environment

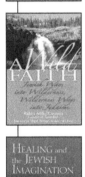

A Wild Faith: Jewish Ways into Wilderness, Wilderness Ways into Judaism
By Rabbi Mike Comins; Foreword by Nigel Savage
Offers ways to enliven and deepen your spiritual life through wilderness experience.
6 x 9, 240 pp, Quality PB, 978-1-58023-316-3 **$16.99**

Ecology & the Jewish Spirit: Where Nature & the Sacred Meet
Edited by Ellen Bernstein 6 x 9, 288 pp, Quality PB, 978-1-58023-082-7 **$18.99**

Torah of the Earth: Exploring 4,000 Years of Ecology in Jewish Thought
Vol. 1: Biblical Israel: One Land, One People; Rabbinic Judaism: One People, Many Lands
Vol. 2: Zionism: One Land, Two Peoples; Eco-Judaism: One Earth, Many Peoples
Edited by Arthur Waskow Vol. 1: 6 x 9, 272 pp, Quality PB, 978-1-58023-086-5 **$19.95**
Vol. 2: 6 x 9, 336 pp, Quality PB, 978-1-58023-087-2 **$19.95**

The Way Into Judaism and the Environment *By Jeremy Benstein, PhD*
6 x 9, 288 pp, Quality PB, 978-1-58023-368-2 **$18.99**; HC, 978-1-58023-268-5 **$24.99**

Grief/Healing

Healing and the Jewish Imagination: Spiritual and Practical Perspectives on Judaism and Health *Edited by Rabbi William Cutter, PhD* Explores Judaism for comfort in times of illness and perspectives on suffering.
6 x 9, 240 pp, Quality PB, 978-1-58023-373-6 **$19.99**; HC, 978-1-58023-314-9 **$24.99**

Grief in Our Seasons: A Mourner's Kaddish Companion *By Rabbi Kerry M. Olitzky*
4½ x 6½, 448 pp, Quality PB, 978-1-879045-55-2 **$15.95**

Healing of Soul, Healing of Body: Spiritual Leaders Unfold the Strength & Solace in Psalms *Edited by Rabbi Simkha Y. Weintraub, CSW*
6 x 9, 128 pp, 2-color illus. text, Quality PB, 978-1-879045-31-6 **$14.99**

Mourning & Mitzvah, 2nd Edition: A Guided Journal for Walking the Mourner's Path through Grief to Healing *By Anne Brener, LCSW*
7½ x 9, 304 pp, Quality PB, 978-1-58023-113-8 **$19.99**

Tears of Sorrow, Seeds of Hope, 2nd Edition: A Jewish Spiritual Companion for Infertility and Pregnancy Loss *By Rabbi Nina Beth Cardin*
6 x 9, 208 pp, Quality PB, 978-1-58023-233-3 **$18.99**

A Time to Mourn, a Time to Comfort, 2nd Edition: A Guide to Jewish Bereavement *By Dr. Ron Wolfson*
7 x 9, 384 pp, Quality PB, 978-1-58023-253-1 **$19.99**

When a Grandparent Dies: A Kid's Own Remembering Workbook for Dealing with Shiva and the Year Beyond *By Nechama Liss-Levinson, PhD*
8 x 10, 48 pp, 2-color text, HC, 978-1-879045-44-6 **$15.95** *For ages 7–13*

Social Justice

There Shall Be No Needy
Pursuing Social Justice through Jewish Law and Tradition
By Rabbi Jill Jacobs; Foreword by Rabbi Elliot N. Dorff, PhD; Preface by Simon Greer
Confronts the most pressing issues of twenty-first-century America from a deeply
Jewish perspective.
6 x 9, 288 pp, Quality PB, 978-1-58023-425-2 **$16.99**; HC, 978-1-58023-394-1 **$21.99**
  Also Available: **There Shall Be No Needy Teacher's Guide**
  8½ x 11, 48 pp, PB, 978-1-58023-429-0 **$8.99**

Conscience: The Duty to Obey and the Duty to Disobey
By Rabbi Harold M. Schulweis
This clarion call to rethink our moral and political behavior examines the idea of
conscience and the role conscience plays in our relationships to governments, law,
ethics, religion, human nature, God—and to each other.
6 x 9, 160 pp, Quality PB, 978-1-58023-419-1 **$16.99**; HC, 978-1-58023-375-0 **$19.99**

Judaism and Justice: The Jewish Passion to Repair the World
By Rabbi Sidney Schwarz; Foreword by Ruth Messinger
Explores the relationship between Judaism, social justice and the Jewish identity
of American Jews.
6 x 9, 352 pp, Quality PB, 978-1-58023-353-8 **$19.99**; HC, 978-1-58023-312-5 **$24.99**

Spiritual Activism: A Jewish Guide to Leadership and Repairing the World
  By Rabbi Avraham Weiss; Foreword by Alan M. Dershowitz
  6 x 9, 224 pp, Quality PB, 978-1-58023-418-4 **$16.99**; HC, 978-1-58023-355-2 **$24.99**

Righteous Indignation: A Jewish Call for Justice
Edited by Rabbi Or N. Rose, Jo Ellen Green Kaiser and Margie Klein; Foreword by Rabbi David Ellenson
Leading progressive Jewish activists explore meaningful intellectual and spiritual
foundations for their social justice work.
6 x 9, 384 pp, Quality PB, 978-1-58023-414-6 **$19.99**; HC, 978-1-58023-336-1 **$24.99**

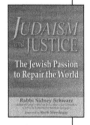

Spirituality/Women's Interest

New Jewish Feminism: Probing the Past, Forging the Future
Edited by Rabbi Elyse Goldstein; Foreword by Anita Diamant
Looks at the growth and accomplishments of Jewish feminism and what they
mean for Jewish women today and tomorrow.
6 x 9, 480 pp, HC, 978-1-58023-359-0 **$24.99**

The Quotable Jewish Woman: Wisdom, Inspiration & Humor from the Mind & Heart
  Edited by Elaine Bernstein Partnow 6 x 9, 496 pp, Quality PB, 978-1-58023-236-4 **$19.99**

The Divine Feminine in Biblical Wisdom Literature
Selections Annotated & Explained
  Translated and Annotated by Rabbi Rami Shapiro
  5½ x 8½, 240 pp, Quality PB, 978-1-59473-109-9 **$16.99**
  (A book from SkyLight Paths, Jewish Lights' sister imprint)

The Women's Haftarah Commentary: New Insights from Women
Rabbis on the 54 Weekly Haftarah Portions, the 5 Megillot & Special Shabbatot
Edited by Rabbi Elyse Goldstein   Illuminates the historical significance of female
portrayals in the Haftarah and the Five Megillot.
6 x 9, 560 pp, Quality PB, 978-1-58023-371-2 **$19.99**; HC, 978-1-58023-133-6 **$39.99**

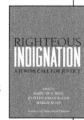

The Women's Torah Commentary: New Insights from Women
Rabbis on the 54 Weekly Torah Portions
Edited by Rabbi Elyse Goldstein
Over fifty women rabbis offer inspiring insights on the Torah, in a week-by-week format.
6 x 9, 496 pp, Quality PB, 978-1-58023-370-5 **$19.99**; HC, 978-1-58023-076-6 **$34.95**

  See Passover for *The Women's Passover Companion: Women's Reflections on
  the Festival of Freedom* and *The Women's Seder Sourcebook: Rituals &
  Readings for Use at the Passover Seder.*

Meditation

Jewish Meditation Practices for Everyday Life
Awakening Your Heart, Connecting with God
By Rabbi Jeff Roth
Offers a fresh take on meditation that draws on life experience and living life with greater clarity as opposed to the traditional method of rigorous study. 6 x 9, 224 pp, Quality PB Original, 978-1-58023-397-2 **$18.99**

The Handbook of Jewish Meditation Practices
A Guide for Enriching the Sabbath and Other Days of Your Life
By Rabbi David A. Cooper Easy-to-learn meditation techniques.
6 x 9, 208 pp, Quality PB, 978-1-58023-102-2 **$16.95**

Discovering Jewish Meditation: Instruction & Guidance for Learning an Ancient Spiritual Practice *By Nan Fink Gefen* 6 x 9, 208 pp, Quality PB, 978-1-58023-067-4 **$16.95**

Meditation from the Heart of Judaism: Today's Teachers Share Their Practices, Techniques, and Faith *Edited by Avram Davis*
6 x 9, 256 pp, Quality PB, 978-1-58023-049-0 **$16.95**

Ritual/Sacred Practice

The Jewish Dream Book: The Key to Opening the Inner Meaning of Your Dreams *By Vanessa L. Ochs with Elizabeth Ochs; Full-color illus. by Kristina Swarner* Instructions for how modern people can perform ancient Jewish dream practices and dream interpretations drawn from the Jewish wisdom tradition.
8 x 8, 128 pp, Full-color illus., Deluxe PB w/flaps, 978-1-58023-132-9 **$16.95**

God in Your Body: Kabbalah, Mindfulness and Embodied Spiritual Practice
By Jay Michaelson
The first comprehensive treatment of the body in Jewish spiritual practice and an essential guide to the sacred.
6 x 9, 288 pp, Quality PB, 978-1-58023-304-0 **$18.99**

The Book of Jewish Sacred Practices: CLAL's Guide to Everyday & Holiday Rituals & Blessings *Edited by Rabbi Irwin Kula and Vanessa L. Ochs, PhD*
6 x 9, 368 pp, Quality PB, 978-1-58023-152-7 **$18.95**

Jewish Ritual: A Brief Introduction for Christians
By Rabbi Kerry M. Olitzky and Rabbi Daniel Judson
5½ x 8½, 144 pp, Quality PB, 978-1-58023-210-4 **$14.99**

The Rituals & Practices of a Jewish Life: A Handbook for Personal Spiritual Renewal *Edited by Rabbi Kerry M. Olitzky and Rabbi Daniel Judson*
6 x 9, 272 pp, illus., Quality PB, 978-1-58023-169-5 **$18.95**

The Sacred Art of Lovingkindness: Preparing to Practice
By Rabbi Rami Shapiro 5½ x 8½, 176 pp, Quality PB, 978-1-59473-151-8 **$16.99**
(A book from SkyLight Paths, Jewish Lights' sister imprint)

Science Fiction/Mystery & Detective Fiction

Criminal Kabbalah: An Intriguing Anthology of Jewish Mystery & Detective Fiction *Edited by Lawrence W. Raphael; Foreword by Laurie R. King*
All-new stories from twelve of today's masters of mystery and detective fiction— sure to delight mystery buffs of all faith traditions.
6 x 9, 256 pp, Quality PB, 978-1-58023-109-1 **$16.95**

Mystery Midrash: An Anthology of Jewish Mystery & Detective Fiction
Edited by Lawrence W. Raphael; Preface by Joel Siegel
6 x 9, 304 pp, Quality PB, 978-1-58023-055-1 **$16.95**

Wandering Stars: An Anthology of Jewish Fantasy & Science Fiction
Edited by Jack Dann; Introduction by Isaac Asimov
6 x 9, 272 pp, Quality PB, 978-1-58023-005-6 **$18.99**

More Wandering Stars: An Anthology of Outstanding Stories of Jewish Fantasy and Science Fiction *Edited by Jack Dann; Introduction by Isaac Asimov*
6 x 9, 192 pp, Quality PB, 978-1-58023-063-6 **$16.95**

Inspiration

The Seven Questions You're Asked in Heaven: Reviewing and Renewing Your Life on Earth *By Dr. Ron Wolfson*
An intriguing and entertaining resource for living a life that matters.
6 x 9, 176 pp, Quality PB, 978-1-58023-407-8 **$16.99**

Happiness and the Human Spirit: The Spirituality of Becoming the Best You Can Be *By Abraham J. Twerski, MD*
Shows you that true happiness is attainable once you stop looking outside yourself for the source. 6 x 9, 176 pp, Quality PB, 978-1-58023-404-7 **$16.99**; HC, 978-1-58023-343-9 **$19.99**

Life's Daily Blessings: Inspiring Reflections on Gratitude and Joy for Every Day, Based on Jewish Wisdom *By Rabbi Kerry M. Olitzky* 4½ x 6½, 368 pp, Quality PB, 978-1-58023-396-5 **$16.99**

The Bridge to Forgiveness: Stories and Prayers for Finding God and Restoring Wholeness *By Rabbi Karyn D. Kedar*
Examines how forgiveness can be the bridge that connects us to wholeness and peace.
6 x 9, 176 pp, HC, 978-1-58023-324-8 **$19.99**

God's To-Do List: 103 Ways to Be an Angel and Do God's Work on Earth
By Dr. Ron Wolfson 6 x 9, 150 pp, Quality PB, 978-1-58023-301-9 **$16.99**

Our Dance with God: Finding Prayer, Perspective and Meaning in the Stories of Our Lives *By Karyn D. Kedar* 6 x 9, 176 pp, Quality PB, 978-1-58023-202-9 **$16.99**
Also Available: **The Dance of the Dolphin** (HC edition of Our Dance with God)
6 x 9, 176 pp, HC, 978-1-58023-202-9 **$19.95**

The Empty Chair: Finding Hope and Joy—Timeless Wisdom from a Hasidic Master, Rebbe Nachman of Breslov *Adapted by Moshe Mykoff and the Breslov Research Institute*
4 x 6, 128 pp, Deluxe PB w/flaps, 978-1-879045-67-5 **$9.99**

The Gentle Weapon: Prayers for Everyday and Not-So-Everyday Moments— Timeless Wisdom from the Teachings of the Hasidic Master, Rebbe Nachman of Breslov *Adapted by Moshe Mykoff and S. C. Mizrahi, together with the Breslov Research Institute*
4 x 6, 144 pp, Deluxe PB w/flaps, 978-1-58023-022-3 **$9.99**

God Whispers: Stories of the Soul, Lessons of the Heart *By Karyn D. Kedar*
6 x 9, 176 pp, Quality PB, 978-1-58023-088-9 **$15.95**

Restful Reflections: Nighttime Inspiration to Calm the Soul, Based on Jewish Wisdom
By Rabbi Kerry M. Olitzky & Rabbi Lori Forman 4½ x 6½, 448 pp, Quality PB, 978-1-58023-091-9 **$15.95**

Sacred Intentions: Daily Inspiration to Strengthen the Spirit, Based on Jewish Wisdom
By Rabbi Kerry M. Olitzky and Rabbi Lori Forman 4½ x 6¼, 448 pp, Quality PB, 978-1-58023-061-2 **$15.95**

Kabbalah/Mysticism

Seek My Face: A Jewish Mystical Theology *By Arthur Green*
6 x 9, 304 pp, Quality PB, 978-1-58023-130-5 **$19.95**

Zohar: Annotated & Explained *Translation and annotation by Daniel C. Matt; Foreword by Andrew Harvey* 5½ x 8½, 176 pp, Quality PB, 978-1-893361-51-5 **$15.99**
(A book from SkyLight Paths, Jewish Lights' sister imprint)

Ehyeh: A Kabbalah for Tomorrow
By Arthur Green 6 x 9, 224 pp, Quality PB, 978-1-58023-213-5 **$16.99**

The Flame of the Heart: Prayers of a Chasidic Mystic *By Reb Noson of Breslov. Translated by David Sears with the Breslov Research Institute* 5 x 7¼, 160 pp, Quality PB, 978-1-58023-246-3 **$15.99**

The Gift of Kabbalah: Discovering the Secrets of Heaven, Renewing Your Life on Earth
By Tamar Frankiel, PhD 6 x 9, 256 pp, Quality PB, 978-1-58023-141-1 **$16.95**
HC, 978-1-58023-108-4 **$21.95**

Kabbalah: A Brief Introduction for Christians
By Tamar Frankiel, PhD 5½ x 8½, 208 pp, Quality PB, 978-1-58023-303-3 **$16.99**

The Lost Princess and Other Kabbalistic Tales of Rebbe Nachman of Breslov
The Seven Beggars and Other Kabbalistic Tales of Rebbe Nachman of Breslov
Translated by Rabbi Aryeh Kaplan; Preface by Rabbi Chaim Kramer
Lost Princess: 6 x 9, 400 pp, Quality PB, 978-1-58023-217-3 **$18.99**
Seven Beggars: 6 x 9, 192 pp, Quality PB, 978-1-58023-250-0 **$16.99**

See also *The Way Into Jewish Mystical Tradition* in Spirituality / The Way Into... Series

Life Cycle
Marriage / Parenting / Family / Aging

The New Jewish Baby Album: Creating and Celebrating the Beginning of a Spiritual Life—A Jewish Lights Companion
By the Editors at Jewish Lights. Foreword by Anita Diamant. Preface by Rabbi Sandy Eisenberg Sasso.
A spiritual keepsake that will be treasured for generations. More than just a memory book, *shows you how—and why it's important—*to create a Jewish home and a Jewish life. 8 x 10, 64 pp, Deluxe Padded HC, Full-color illus., 978-1-58023-138-1 **$19.95**

The Jewish Pregnancy Book: A Resource for the Soul, Body & Mind during Pregnancy, Birth & the First Three Months
By Sandy Falk, MD, and Rabbi Daniel Judson, with Steven A. Rapp
Includes medical information, prayers and rituals for each stage of pregnancy, from a liberal Jewish perspective. 7 x 10, 208 pp, Quality PB, b/w photos, 978-1-58023-178-7 **$16.95**

Celebrating Your New Jewish Daughter: Creating Jewish Ways to Welcome Baby Girls into the Covenant—New and Traditional Ceremonies *By Debra Nussbaum Cohen; Foreword by Rabbi Sandy Eisenberg Sasso* 6 x 9, 272 pp, Quality PB, 978-1-58023-090-2 **$18.95**

The New Jewish Baby Book, 2nd Edition: Names, Ceremonies & Customs—A Guide for Today's Families *By Anita Diamant* 6 x 9, 336 pp, Quality PB, 978-1-58023-251-7 **$19.99**

Parenting as a Spiritual Journey: Deepening Ordinary and Extraordinary Events into Sacred Occasions *By Rabbi Nancy Fuchs-Kreimer* 6 x 9, 224 pp, Quality PB, 978-1-58023-016-2 **$16.95**

Parenting Jewish Teens: A Guide for the Perplexed
By Joanne Doades
Explores the questions and issues that shape the world in which today's Jewish teenagers live.
6 x 9, 200 pp, Quality PB, 978-1-58023-305-7 **$16.99**

Judaism for Two: A Spiritual Guide for Strengthening and Celebrating Your Loving Relationship
By Rabbi Nancy Fuchs-Kreimer and Rabbi Nancy H. Wiener; Foreword by Rabbi Elliot N. Dorff
Addresses the ways Jewish teachings can enhance and strengthen committed relationships. 6 x 9, 224 pp, Quality PB, 978-1-58023-254-8 **$16.99**

The Creative Jewish Wedding Book, 2nd Edition: A Hands-On Guide to New & Old Traditions, Ceremonies & Celebrations *By Gabrielle Kaplan-Mayer* 9 x 9, 288 pp, b/w photos, Quality PB, 978-1-58023-398-9 **$19.99**

Divorce Is a Mitzvah: A Practical Guide to Finding Wholeness and Holiness When Your Marriage Dies *By Rabbi Perry Netter; Afterword by Rabbi Laura Geller.* 6 x 9, 224 pp, Quality PB, 978-1-58023-172-5 **$16.95**

Embracing the Covenant: Converts to Judaism Talk About Why & How *By Rabbi Allan Berkowitz and Patti Moskovitz* 6 x 9, 192 pp, Quality PB, 978-1-879045-50-7 **$16.95**

The Guide to Jewish Interfaith Family Life: An InterfaithFamily.com Handbook *Edited by Ronnie Friedland and Edmund Case* 6 x 9, 384 pp, Quality PB, 978-1-58023-153-4 **$18.95**

A Heart of Wisdom: Making the Jewish Journey from Midlife through the Elder Years *Edited by Susan Berrin; Foreword by Harold Kushner* 6 x 9, 384 pp, Quality PB, 978-1-58023-051-3 **$18.95**

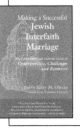

Introducing My Faith and My Community
The Jewish Outreach Institute Guide for the Christian in a Jewish Interfaith Relationship
By Rabbi Kerry M. Olitzky 6 x 9, 176 pp, Quality PB, 978-1-58023-192-3 **$16.99**

Making a Successful Jewish Interfaith Marriage: The Jewish Outreach Institute Guide to Opportunities, Challenges and Resources *By Rabbi Kerry M. Olitzky with Joan Peterson Littman* 6 x 9, 176 pp, Quality PB, 978-1-58023-170-1 **$16.95**

So That Your Values Live On: Ethical Wills and How to Prepare Them *Edited by Jack Riemer and Nathaniel Stampfer* 6 x 9, 272 pp, Quality PB, 978-1-879045-34-7 **$18.99**

Holidays/Holy Days

Who By Fire, Who By Water—Un'taneh Tokef
Edited by Rabbi Lawrence A. Hoffman, PhD
Examines the prayer's theology, authorship and poetry through a set of lively essays, all written in accessible language.
6 x 9, 272 pp, HC, 978-1-58023-424-5 **$24.99**

Rosh Hashanah Readings: Inspiration, Information and Contemplation
Yom Kippur Readings: Inspiration, Information and Contemplation
Edited by Rabbi Dov Peretz Elkins; Section Introductions from Arthur Green's These Are the Words
An extraordinary collection of readings, prayers and insights that will enable you to enter into the spirit of the High Holy Days in a personal and powerful way, permitting the meaning of the Jewish New Year to enter the heart.
Rosh Hashanah: 6 x 9, 400 pp, HC, 978-1-58023-239-5 **$24.99**
Yom Kippur: 6 x 9, 368 pp, HC, 978-1-58023-271-5 **$24.99**

Jewish Holidays: A Brief Introduction for Christians
By Rabbi Kerry M. Olitzky and Rabbi Daniel Judson
5½ x 8½, 176 pp, Quality PB, 978-1-58023-302-6 **$16.99**

Reclaiming Judaism as a Spiritual Practice: Holy Days and Shabbat
By Rabbi Goldie Milgram 7 x 9, 272 pp, Quality PB, 978-1-58023-205-0 **$19.99**

7th Heaven: Celebrating Shabbat with Rebbe Nachman of Breslov
By Moshe Mykoff with the Breslov Research Institute
5¼ x 8¼, 224 pp, Deluxe PB w/ flaps, 978-1-58023-175-6 **$18.95**

Shabbat, 2nd Edition: The Family Guide to Preparing for and Celebrating the Sabbath *By Dr. Ron Wolfson*
7 x 9, 320 pp, illus., Quality PB, 978-1-58023-164-0 **$19.99**

Hanukkah, 2nd Edition: The Family Guide to Spiritual Celebration
By Dr. Ron Wolfson 7 x 9, 240 pp, illus., Quality PB, 978-1-58023-122-0 **$18.95**

The Jewish Family Fun Book, 2nd Edition: Holiday Projects, Everyday Activities, and Travel Ideas with Jewish Themes *By Danielle Dardashti and Roni Sarig; Illus. by Avi Katz*
6 x 9, 304 pp, 70+ b/w illus. & diagrams, Quality PB, 978-1-58023-333-0 **$18.99**

The Jewish Lights Book of Fun Classroom Activities: Simple and Seasonal
Projects for Teachers and Students *By Danielle Dardashti and Roni Sarig*
6 x 9, 240 pp, Quality PB, 978-1-58023-206-7 **$19.99**

Passover

My People's Passover Haggadah
Traditional Texts, Modern Commentaries
Edited by Rabbi Lawrence A. Hoffman, PhD, and David Arnow, PhD
A diverse and exciting collection of commentaries on the traditional Passover Haggadah—in two volumes!
Vol. 1: 7 x 10, 304 pp, HC, 978-1-58023-354-5 **$24.99**
Vol. 2: 7 x 10, 320 pp, HC, 978-1-58023-346-0 **$24.99**

Leading the Passover Journey: The Seder's Meaning Revealed,
the Haggadah's Story Retold *By Rabbi Nathan Laufer*
Uncovers the hidden meaning of the Seder's rituals and customs.
6 x 9, 224 pp, Quality PB, 978-1-58023-399-6 **$18.99**; HC, 978-1-58023-211-1 **$24.99**

The Women's Passover Companion: Women's Reflections on the Festival of Freedom
Edited by Rabbi Sharon Cohen Anisfeld, Tara Mohr and Catherine Spector; Foreword by Paula E. Hyman
6 x 9, 352 pp, Quality PB, 978-1-58023-231-9 **$19.99**

The Women's Seder Sourcebook: Rituals & Readings for Use at the Passover Seder
Edited by Rabbi Sharon Cohen Anisfeld, Tara Mohr and Catherine Spector; Foreword by Paula E. Hyman
6 x 9, 384 pp, Quality PB, 978-1-58023-232-6 **$19.99**

Creating Lively Passover Seders: A Sourcebook of Engaging Tales, Texts & Activities
By David Arnow, PhD 7 x 9, 416 pp, Quality PB, 978-1-58023-184-8 **$24.99**

Passover, 2nd Edition: The Family Guide to Spiritual Celebration
By Dr. Ron Wolfson with Joel Lurie Grishaver 7 x 9, 416 pp, Quality PB, 978-1-58023-174-9 **$19.95**

Spirituality/Prayer

Making Prayer Real: Leading Jewish Spiritual Voices on Why Prayer Is Difficult and What to Do about It *By Rabbi Mike Comins*

A no-holds-barred look at why so many find synagogue at best difficult, and at worst, meaningless and boring—and how to make it more satisfying.

6 x 9, 320 pp, Quality PB, 978-1-58023-417-7 **$18.99**

Witnesses to the One: The Spiritual History of the *Sh'ma*
By Rabbi Joseph B. Meszler; Foreword by Rabbi Elyse Goldstein
6 x 9, 176 pp, Quality PB, 978-1-58023-400-9 **$16.99**; HC, 978-1-58023-309-5 **$19.99**

My People's Prayer Book Series: Traditional Prayers, Modern Commentaries *Edited by Rabbi Lawrence A. Hoffman, PhD*

Provides diverse and exciting commentary to the traditional liturgy. Will help you find new wisdom in Jewish prayer, and bring liturgy into your life. Each book includes Hebrew text, modern translation and commentaries from all perspectives of the Jewish world.

Vol. 1—The *Sh'ma* and Its Blessings
    7 x 10, 168 pp, HC, 978-1-879045-79-8 **$24.99**
Vol. 2—The *Amidah* 7 x 10, 240 pp, HC, 978-1-879045-80-4 **$24.95**
Vol. 3—*P'sukei D'zimrah* (Morning Psalms)
    7 x 10, 240 pp, HC, 978-1-879045-81-1 **$24.95**
Vol. 4—*Seder K'riat Hatorah* (The Torah Service)
    7 x 10, 264 pp, HC, 978-1-879045-82-8 **$23.95**
Vol. 5—*Birkhot Hashachar* (Morning Blessings)
    7 x 10, 240 pp, HC, 978-1-879045-83-5 **$24.95**
Vol. 6—*Tachanun* and Concluding Prayers
    7 x 10, 240 pp, HC, 978-1-879045-84-2 **$24.95**
Vol. 7—Shabbat at Home 7 x 10, 240 pp, HC, 978-1-879045-85-9 **$24.95**
Vol. 8—*Kabbalat Shabbat* (Welcoming Shabbat in the Synagogue)
    7 x 10, 240 pp, HC, 978-1-58023-121-3 **$24.99**
Vol. 9—Welcoming the Night: *Minchah* and *Ma'ariv* (Afternoon and Evening Prayer) 7 x 10, 272 pp, HC, 978-1-58023-262-3 **$24.99**
Vol. 10—Shabbat Morning: *Shacharit* and *Musaf* (Morning and Additional Services) 7 x 10, 240 pp, HC, 978-1-58023-240-1 **$24.99**

Spirituality/Lawrence Kushner

The Book of Letters: A Mystical Hebrew Alphabet
Popular HC Edition, 6 x 9, 80 pp, 2-color text, 978-1-879045-00-2 **$24.95**
Collector's Limited Edition, 9 x 12, 80 pp, gold-foil-embossed pages, w/ limited-edition silkscreened print, 978-1-879045-04-0 **$349.00**

The Book of Miracles: A Young Person's Guide to Jewish Spiritual Awareness
6 x 9, 96 pp, 2-color illus., HC, 978-1-879045-78-1 **$16.95** For ages 9–13

The Book of Words: Talking Spiritual Life, Living Spiritual Talk
6 x 9, 160 pp, Quality PB, 978-1-58023-020-9 **$16.95**

Eyes Remade for Wonder: A Lawrence Kushner Reader *Introduction by Thomas Moore*
6 x 9, 240 pp, Quality PB, 978-1-58023-042-1 **$18.95**

Filling Words with Light: Hasidic and Mystical Reflections on Jewish Prayer
By Rabbi Lawrence Kushner and Rabbi Nehemia Polen
5½ x 8½, 176 pp, Quality PB, 978-1-58023-238-8 **$16.99**; HC, 978-1-58023-216-6 **$21.99**

God Was in This Place & I, i Did Not Know: Finding Self, Spirituality and Ultimate Meaning 6 x 9, 192 pp, Quality PB, 978-1-879045-33-0 **$16.95**

Honey from the Rock: An Introduction to Jewish Mysticism
6 x 9, 176 pp, Quality PB, 978-1-58023-073-5 **$16.95**

Invisible Lines of Connection: Sacred Stories of the Ordinary
5½ x 8½, 160 pp, Quality PB, 978-1-879045-98-9 **$15.95**

Jewish Spirituality: A Brief Introduction for Christians
5½ x 8½, 112 pp, Quality PB, 978-1-58023-150-3 **$12.95**

The River of Light: Jewish Mystical Awareness
6 x 9, 192 pp, Quality PB, 978-1-58023-096-4 **$16.95**

The Way Into Jewish Mystical Tradition
6 x 9, 224 pp, Quality PB, 978-1-58023-200-5 **$18.99**; HC, 978-1-58023-029-2 **$21.95**

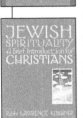

Spirituality

Repentance: The Meaning and Practice of *Teshuvah*
By Dr. Louis E. Newman; Foreword by Rabbi Harold M. Schulweis; Preface by Rabbi Karyn D. Kedar
Examines both the practical and philosophical dimensions of *teshuvah*, Judaism's
core religious-moral teaching on repentance, and its value for us—Jews and non-
Jews alike—today. 6 x 9, 256 pp, HC, 978-1-58023-426-9 **$24.99**

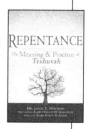

Tanya, the Masterpiece of Hasidic Wisdom
Selections Annotated & Explained
Translation & Annotation by Rabbi Rami Shapiro; Foreword by Rabbi Zalman M. Schachter-Shalomi
Brings the genius of the *Tanya* to anyone seeking to deepen their understanding of
the soul and how it relates to and manifests the Divine Source.
5½ x 8½, 240 pp, Quality PB, 978-1-59473-275-1 **$16.99**
(A book from SkyLight Paths, Jewish Lights' sister imprint)

A Book of Life: Embracing Judaism as a Spiritual Practice
By Rabbi Michael Strassfeld 6 x 9, 544 pp, Quality PB, 978-1-58023-247-0 **$19.99**

Meaning and Mitzvah: Daily Practices for Reclaiming Judaism through Prayer, God,
Torah, Hebrew, Mitzvot and Peoplehood *By Rabbi Goldie Milgram*
7 x 9, 336 pp, Quality PB, 978-1-58023-256-2 **$19.99**

The Soul of the Story: Meetings with Remarkable People ●
By Rabbi David Zeller 6 x 9, 288 pp, HC, 978-1-58023-272-2 **$21.99**

Aleph-Bet Yoga: Embodying the Hebrew Letters for Physical and Spiritual Well-Being
By Steven A. Rapp; Foreword by Tamar Frankiel, PhD, and Judy Greenfeld; Preface by Hart Lazer
7 x 10, 128 pp, b/w photos, Quality PB, Layflat binding, 978-1-58023-162-6 **$16.95**

Does the Soul Survive? A Jewish Journey to Belief in Afterlife, Past Lives &
Living with Purpose *By Rabbi Elie Kaplan Spitz; Foreword by Brian L. Weiss, MD*
6 x 9, 288 pp, Quality PB, 978-1-58023-165-7 **$16.99**

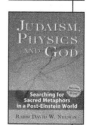

First Steps to a New Jewish Spirit: Reb Zalman's Guide to Recapturing the
Intimacy & Ecstasy in Your Relationship with God *By Rabbi Zalman M. Schachter-Shalomi*
with Donald Gropman 6 x 9, 144 pp, Quality PB, 978-1-58023-182-4 **$16.95**

Foundations of Sephardic Spirituality: The Inner Life of Jews of the Ottoman Empire
By Rabbi Marc D. Angel, PhD 6 x 9, 224 pp, Quality PB, 978-1-58023-341-5 **$18.99**

God in Our Relationships: Spirituality between People from the Teachings of
Martin Buber *By Rabbi Dennis S. Ross* 5½ x 8½, 160 pp, Quality PB, 978-1-58023-147-3 **$16.95**

Judaism, Physics and God: Searching for Sacred Metaphors in a Post-Einstein World
By Rabbi David W. Nelson 6 x 9, 352 pp, Quality PB, inc. reader's discussion guide,
978-1-58023-306-4 **$18.99**; HC, 352 pp, 978-1-58023-252-4 **$24.99**

The Jewish Lights Spirituality Handbook: A Guide to Understanding,
Exploring & Living a Spiritual Life *Edited by Stuart M. Matlins*
What exactly is "Jewish" about spirituality? How do I make it a part of my life?
Fifty of today's foremost spiritual leaders share their ideas and experience with us.
6 x 9, 456 pp, Quality PB, 978-1-58023-093-3 **$19.99**

Bringing the Psalms to Life: How to Understand and Use the Book of Psalms
By Rabbi Daniel F. Polish, PhD 6 x 9, 208 pp, Quality PB, 978-1-58023-157-2 **$16.95**

God & the Big Bang: Discovering Harmony between Science & Spirituality
By Dr. Daniel C. Matt 6 x 9, 216 pp, Quality PB, 978-1-879045-89-7 **$16.99**

Minding the Temple of the Soul: Balancing Body, Mind, and Spirit through Traditional
Jewish Prayer, Movement, and Meditation *By Tamar Frankiel, PhD, and Judy Greenfeld*
7 x 10, 184 pp, illus., Quality PB, 978-1-879045-64-4 **$16.95**

One God Clapping: The Spiritual Path of a Zen Rabbi *By Alan Lew with Sherril Jaffe*
5½ x 8½, 336 pp, Quality PB, 978-1-58023-115-2 **$16.95**

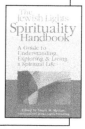

There Is No Messiah … and You're It: The Stunning Transformation of Judaism's
Most Provocative Idea *By Rabbi Robert N. Levine, DD*
6 x 9, 192 pp, Quality PB, 978-1-58023-255-5 **$16.99**

These Are the Words: A Vocabulary of Jewish Spiritual Life
By Rabbi Arthur Green, PhD 6 x 9, 304 pp, Quality PB, 978-1-58023-107-7 **$18.95**

Theology/Philosophy/The Way Into... Series

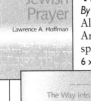

The Way Into... series offers an accessible and highly usable "guided tour" of the Jewish faith, people, history and beliefs—in total, an introduction to Judaism that will enable you to understand and interact with the sacred texts of the Jewish tradition. Each volume is written by a leading contemporary scholar and teacher, and explores one key aspect of Judaism. *The Way Into...* series enables all readers to achieve a real sense of Jewish cultural literacy through guided study.

The Way Into Encountering God in Judaism
By Rabbi Neil Gillman, PhD
For everyone who wants to understand how Jews have encountered God throughout history and today.
6 x 9, 240 pp, Quality PB, 978-1-58023-199-2 **$18.99**; HC, 978-1-58023-025-4 **$21.95**
Also Available: **The Jewish Approach to God:** A Brief Introduction for Christians
By Rabbi Neil Gillman, PhD
5½ x 8½, 192 pp, Quality PB, 978-1-58023-190-9 **$16.95**

The Way Into Jewish Mystical Tradition
By Rabbi Lawrence Kushner
Allows readers to interact directly with the sacred mystical text of the Jewish tradition. An accessible introduction to the concepts of Jewish mysticism, their religious and spiritual significance and how they relate to life today.
6 x 9, 224 pp, Quality PB, 978-1-58023-200-5 **$18.99**; HC, 978-1-58023-029-2 **$21.95**

The Way Into Jewish Prayer
By Rabbi Lawrence A. Hoffman, PhD
Opens the door to 3,000 years of Jewish prayer, making available all anyone needs to feel at home in the Jewish way of communicating with God.
6 x 9, 208 pp, Quality PB, 978-1-58023-201-2 **$18.99**

Also Available: **The Way Into Jewish Prayer Teacher's Guide**
By Rabbi Jennifer Ossakow Goldsmith
8½ x 11, 42 pp, Quality PB, 978-1-58023-345-3 **$8.99**
Visit our website to download a free copy.

The Way Into Judaism and the Environment
By Jeremy Benstein, PhD
Explores the ways in which Judaism contributes to contemporary social-environmental issues, the extent to which Judaism is part of the problem and how it can be part of the solution.
6 x 9, 288 pp, Quality PB, 978-1-58023-368-2 **$18.99**; HC, 978-1-58023-268-5 **$24.99**

The Way Into *Tikkun Olam* (Repairing the World)
By Rabbi Elliot N. Dorff, PhD
An accessible introduction to the Jewish concept of the individual's responsibility to care for others and repair the world.
6 x 9, 304 pp, Quality PB, 978-1-58023-328-6 **$18.99**; 320 pp, HC, 978-1-58023-269-2 **$24.99**

The Way Into Torah
By Rabbi Norman J. Cohen, PhD
Helps guide in the exploration of the origins and development of Torah, explains why it should be studied and how to do it.
6 x 9, 176 pp, Quality PB, 978-1-58023-198-5 **$16.99**

The Way Into the Varieties of Jewishness
By Sylvia Barack Fishman, PhD
Explores the religious and historical understanding of what it has meant to be Jewish from ancient times to the present controversy over "Who is a Jew?"
6 x 9, 288 pp, Quality PB, 978-1-58023-367-5 **$18.99**; HC, 978-1-58023-030-8 **$24.99**

Theology/Philosophy

Jewish Theology in Our Time: A New Generation Explores the Foundations and Future of Jewish Belief *Edited by Rabbi Elliot J. Cosgrove, PhD* A powerful and challenging examination of what Jews can believe—by a new generation's most dynamic and innovative thinkers.
6 x 9, 350 pp (est), HC, 978-1-58023-413-9 **$24.99**

Maimonides, Spinoza and Us: Toward an Intellectually Vibrant Judaism
By Rabbi Marc D. Angel, PhD A challenging look at two great Jewish philosophers, and what their thinking means to our understanding of God, truth, revelation and reason. 6 x 9, 224 pp, HC, 978-1-58023-411-5 **$24.99**

A Touch of the Sacred: A Theologian's Informal Guide to Jewish Belief
By Dr. Eugene B. Borowitz and Frances W. Schwartz
Explores the musings from the leading theologian of liberal Judaism.
6 x 9, 256 pp, Quality PB, 978-1-58023-416-0 **$16.99**; HC, 978-1-58023-337-8 **$21.99**

Jews and Judaism in the 21st Century: Human Responsibility, the Presence of God and the Future of the Covenant *Edited by Rabbi Edward Feinstein; Foreword by Paula E. Hyman* Five celebrated leaders in Judaism examine contemporary Jewish life. 6 x 9, 192 pp, Quality PB, 978-1-58023-374-3 **$19.99**; HC, 978-1-58023-315-6 **$24.99**

The Death of Death: Resurrection and Immortality in Jewish Thought
By Rabbi Neil Gillman, PhD 6 x 9, 336 pp, Quality PB, 978-1-58023-081-0 **$18.95**

Ethics of the Sages: *Pirke Avot*—Annotated & Explained
Translation & Annotation by Rabbi Rami Shapiro
5½ x 8½, 192 pp, Quality PB, 978-1-59473-207-2 **$16.99** *(A book from SkyLight Paths, Jewish Lights' sister imprint)*

Hasidic Tales: Annotated & Explained *Translation & Annotation by Rabbi Rami Shapiro*
5½ x 8½, 240 pp, Quality PB, 978-1-893361-86-7 **$16.95** *(A book from SkyLight Paths, Jewish Lights' sister imprint)*

A Heart of Many Rooms: Celebrating the Many Voices within Judaism
By Dr. David Hartman 6 x 9, 352 pp, Quality PB, 978-1-58023-156-5 **$19.95**

The Hebrew Prophets: Selections Annotated & Explained
Translation & Annotation by Rabbi Rami Shapiro; Foreword by Rabbi Zalman M. Schachter-Shalomi
5½ x 8½, 224 pp, Quality PB, 978-1-59473-037-5 **$16.99** *(A book from SkyLight Paths, Jewish Lights' sister imprint)*

A Jewish Understanding of the New Testament
By Rabbi Samuel Sandmel; Preface by Rabbi David Sandmel
5½ x 8½, 368 pp, Quality PB, 978-1-59473-048-1 **$19.99** *(A book from SkyLight Paths, Jewish Lights' sister imprint)*

Keeping Faith with the Psalms: Deepen Your Relationship with God Using the Book of Psalms *By Rabbi Daniel F. Polish, PhD* 6 x 9, 320 pp, Quality PB, 978-1-58023-300-2 **$18.99**

A Living Covenant: The Innovative Spirit in Traditional Judaism
By Dr. David Hartman 6 x 9, 368 pp, Quality PB, 978-1-58023-011-7 **$20.00**

Love and Terror in the God Encounter: The Theological Legacy of Rabbi Joseph B. Soloveitchik *By Dr. David Hartman* 6 x 9, 240 pp, Quality PB, 978-1-58023-176-3 **$19.95**

The Personhood of God: Biblical Theology, Human Faith and the Divine Image
By Dr. Yochanan Muffs; Foreword by Dr. David Hartman
6 x 9, 240 pp, Quality PB, 978-1-58023-338-5 **$18.99**; HC, 978-1-58023-265-4 **$24.99**

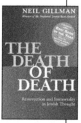

Traces of God: Seeing God in Torah, History and Everyday Life *By Rabbi Neil Gillman, PhD*
6 x 9, 240 pp, Quality PB, 978-1-58023-369-9 **$16.99**; HC, 978-1-58023-249-4 **$21.99**

We Jews and Jesus: Exploring Theological Differences for Mutual Understanding
By Rabbi Samuel Sandmel; Preface by Rabbi David Sandmel
6 x 9, 192 pp, Quality PB, 978-1-59473-208-9 **$16.99** *(A book from SkyLight Paths, Jewish Lights' sister imprint)*

Your Word Is Fire: The Hasidic Masters on Contemplative Prayer
Edited and translated by Rabbi Arthur Green, PhD, and Barry W. Holtz
6 x 9, 160 pp, Quality PB, 978-1-879045-25-5 **$15.95**

I Am Jewish
Personal Reflections Inspired by the Last Words of Daniel Pearl
Almost 150 Jews—both famous and not—from all walks of life, from all around the world, write about many aspects of their Judaism.
Edited by Judea and Ruth Pearl 6 x 9, 304 pp, Deluxe PB w/ flaps, 978-1-58023-259-3 **$18.99**
Download a free copy of the *I Am Jewish Teacher's Guide* at www.jewishlights.com.

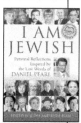

About Jewish Lights

People of all faiths and backgrounds yearn for books that attract, engage, educate, and spiritually inspire.

Our principal goal is to stimulate thought and help all people learn about who the Jewish People are, where they come from, and what the future can be made to hold. While people of our diverse Jewish heritage are the primary audience, our books speak to people in the Christian world as well and will broaden their understanding of Judaism and the roots of their own faith.

We bring to you authors who are at the forefront of spiritual thought and experience. While each has something different to say, they all say it in a voice that you can hear.

Our books are designed to welcome you and then to engage, stimulate, and inspire. We judge our success not only by whether or not our books are beautiful and commercially successful, but by whether or not they make a difference in your life.

For your information and convenience, at the back of this book we have provided a list of other Jewish Lights books you might find interesting and useful. They cover all the categories of your life:

Bar/Bat Mitzvah	Life Cycle
Bible Study / Midrash	Meditation
Children's Books	Men's Interest
Congregation Resources	Parenting
Current Events / History	Prayer / Ritual / Sacred Practice
Ecology / Environment	Social Justice
Fiction: Mystery, Science Fiction	Spirituality
Grief / Healing	Theology / Philosophy
Holidays / Holy Days	Travel
Inspiration	12-Step
Kabbalah / Mysticism / Enneagram	Women's Interest

Stuart M. Matlins, Publisher

Or phone, mail or e-mail to: **JEWISH LIGHTS Publishing**
An imprint of Turner Publishing Company
4507 Charlotte Avenue • Suite 100 • Nashville, Tennessee 37209
Tel: (615) 255-2665 • www.jewishlights.com
Prices subject to change.

For more information about each book,
visit our website at www.jewishlights.com

Printed in the USA
CPSIA information can be obtained
at www.ICGtesting.com
JSHW022329140824
68134JS00019B/1375